UNIV   GHAM
WITHDRAWN
FROM THE LIBRARY

Human Dignity and Human Cloning

Human Dignity and
Human Cloning

Edited by
Silja Vöneky and Rüdiger Wolfrum

University of Nottingham
Hallward Library

MARTINUS NIJHOFF PUBLISHERS
LEIDEN / BOSTON

A C.I.P. Catalogue record for this book is available from the Library of Congress.

Printed on acid-free paper.

100512471X

ISBN 90-04-14233-9
© 2004 *Koninklijke Brill NV, Leiden, The Netherlands*

Brill Academic Publishers incorporates the imprint Martinus Nijhoff Publishers.
http://www.brill.nl

All rights reserved. No part of this publication may be reproduced, stored in a retrieval system, or transmitted in any form or by any means, electronic, mechanical, photocopying, microfilming, recording or otherwise, without written permission from the Publisher.

Authorization to photocopy items for internal or personal use is granted by Brill Academic Publishers provided that the appropriate fees are paid directly to The Copyright Clearance Center, 222 Rosewood Drive, Suite 910, Danvers MA 01923, USA. Fees are subject to change.

Printed and bound in The Netherlands.

Table of Contents

II. Other International Resolutions and Declarations

III. Council of Europe

IV. European Union

V. German Law

Preface

The controversial questions of human cloning have been frequently discussed during the last couple of years. At the latest, since the birth of the sheep Dolly in 1996 some have considered it a realistic vision that cloning may become a technique used on human beings in the future. News about the realisation of this vision has stirred the emotions of the public. The ethical and legal discussions have been complicated by the argument that the cloning technique may be used for different reasons, namely for reproductive or therapeutic/research purposes such as the development of embryonic stem cells. Both ways of cloning thus serve different ends that may, in the view of some, lead to their different ethical evaluation.

With this collection of articles we try to find an intercultural and interdisciplinary approach to the problems of human cloning and the understanding of the concept of human dignity. We hope that the different views expressed, to some extent advance our understanding of the different ethical and legal solutions and that they bring us closer to "a new best solution" under the given circumstances. The articles published are mainly contributions of the participants of the Conference "*Towards an International Ban on Human Cloning – Religious and Ethical Perspectives, the International Community, and the Protection of Embryos*" held at the Max Planck Institute for Comparative Public Law and International Law in Heidelberg in October 2003. We are grateful to the authors for updating their versions in May 2004. As most of the texts closely follow the Conference lectures, footnotes are in general reduced to a minimum.

In accordance with the interdisciplinary approach the book is divided into four parts. The *first part* aims at fostering the understanding of how and why different religious traditions have different approaches to human cloning. It focuses on the Islamic, Buddhist, Jewish and Christian views and their ethical or philosophical backgrounds with articles written by *Ali-Reza Sheikholeslami, Andrew Huxley, Jens*

Schlieter, *Manfred Oeming* and *Robert Spaemann*. This is necessary in order to understand the deeper reasons for cultures arguing differently with regard to cloning and to better understand why they come to different solutions. Moreover, it will open our eyes for the common ground and the shared principles concerning human creation and the concept of human dignity. The understanding of different religious and ethical concepts is not only a useful background for understanding the problems of cloning from different points of view, it also sheds new light on the legal discussions on the international level in the last part of the book.

In order to create a discussion based on facts and in addition to the ethical and religious overview, the scientific perspective of human cloning has to be taken into account. This is achieved in the *second part* with an article submitted by *Ernst-Ludwig Winnacker*. The progress of the natural sciences raises new questions that religion, ethics and law must deal with. The natural sciences' perception of cloning has to influence not only our general understanding of the problems related to cloning but also our ethical judgements. Furthermore, if we understand "what human life is and what can be done with it" by cloning techniques, the essence of some ethical and legal discussions becomes more obvious.

The *third part* of the book deals with the legal limits to human cloning on the German (national) level. It is shown that whether and to what extent the German Basic Law protects against human cloning are much disputed issues. The German debate focuses on the principle of human dignity laid down in the German Basic Law; however, this principle is at the same time too ambiguous to give us clear guidance. The articles of *Christian Starck*, *Jörn Ipsen*, *Horst Dreier* and *Wolfgang Graf Vitzthum* bring clarity to the debate and the different legal arguments. The text of *Brigitte Zypries*, which is based on a lecture held at Humboldt University in October 2003, covers – from a German point of view – the questions of cloning, of so-called pre-implantation diagnosis, of research with embryonic stem cells and of heterologous insemination.

The *last part* brings us to the international plane. It shows whether and to which extent certain instruments of international law – especially the 1998 Additional Protocol to the Convention on Human Rights and Biomedicine – cover the cloning of human beings (see the article of *Hans Lilie*) and which lacunae have to be filled by general human rights treaties (see *our* article). The principle of human dignity also seems to be a cornerstone of the international legal order.

Having brought to light the existing rules of international law, the next article concentrates on the debates at the United Nations since 2001 concerning an international convention against (reproductive) cloning. There is no general consensus, whether there shall be a convention prohibiting *all forms* of human cloning or merely a convention prohibiting *reproductive* cloning of human beings. The article of *Mahnoush H. Arsanjani* gives a deep insight into the reasons underlying the different approaches. However, *Arsanjani* and *Spiros Simits*, in his concluding article, are sceptical as to whether a future international convention would be an adequate instrument to tackle the main problems of biotechnology. *Simits* demonstrates other methods, e.g. legally non-binding recommendations and codes of practice, and other fora, such as the European Community, to solve the problems in this field step-by-step.

Alongside the interdisciplinary articles, this publication includes in its annex the most relevant official documents. The annex contains the relevant draft conventions, soft-law and legally binding instruments on the international, European Union and German national levels. These are included to facilitate the reader in following more closely the arguments expressed in the articles.

The book could not have been published without the assistance and efforts of the following members of the Max Planck Institute for Comparative Public Law and International Law in Heidelberg, and we are very grateful for their efforts: *Niels Petersen*, who spotted mistakes and brought all the texts into shape; *Joseph Windsor*, and *Andreas Magnusson*, who did the translations of many articles and the final native speaker check; *Markus Benzing* and *Ebrahim Afsah*, who helped to organise the conference. Moreover, we thank the other members of the interdisciplinary research project "The Status of the extracorporeal Embryo", financed by the German Federal Ministry of Research, for fruitful discussions during the last years.

Heidelberg, July 2004

Silja Vöneky
Rüdiger Wolfrum

List of Contributors

Arsanjani, Mahnoush H.

Deputy Director of the Codification Division of the Office of Legal Affairs (OLA) of the United Nations. She served as the Secretary of the Committee of the Whole of the Rome Conference on the establishment of the International Criminal Court and as Deputy Secretary of the Assembly of States Parties to the Rome Statute.

Within the Ad Hoc Committee on an International Convention against the Reproductive Cloning of Human Beings, set up by the UN General Assembly in 2001, she acted as Deputy Secretary of the Ad Hoc Committee and Secretary to its Working Group of the Whole. As such, she has closely followed the various initiatives and negotiations which have led to discussion on an international convention in the General Assembly's Sixth Committee. She has published widely on various subjects in public international law.

Dreier, Horst, Dr.

Professor for Legal Philosophy, Constitutional and Administrative law at the University of Würzburg since 1995. Prior to this, Professor Dreier was Professor at the University of Hamburg from 1991. He is a member of the German National Ethics Council and the Bavarian Academy of Sciences.

Huxley, Andrew, M.A., B.C.L. (Oxon)

Senior Lecturer in the Laws of Southeast Asia at the School of Oriental and African Studies, University of London, and a barrister of 2 Garden Court, Temple. He specialises in Burmese law, Buddhist law, Tort, Equity and Comparative Legal Theory. He edited Religion, Law and Tradition: comparative studies in Religious Law (London: Routledge Curzon, 2002). He appeared as an expert witness in John Doe & others v. Unocal & others (July 2003, Los Angeles Supreme Court).

Ipsen, Jörn, Dr.

Professor of Public Law and Director of the Institute of Local Government Law at the University of Osnabrück. Deputy Member of the Constitutional Court of Lower Saxony. His publications include: Richterrecht und Verfassung, 1974; Rechtsfolgen der Verfassungswidrigkeit von Norm und Einzelakt, 1980; Staatsrecht I (Staatsorganisationsrecht), 1986 (15th ed., 2003); Staatsrecht II (Grundrechte), 1997 (6th ed. 2003).

Lilie, Hans, Dr.

Professor of Penal Law and director of the Interdisciplinary Center on Medicine, Ethics and Law at the University of Halle. Professor Lilie was legal advisor of the German Foreign Ministry during the negotations of the Convention against (Reproductive) Cloning. Furthermore, Professor Lilie is chair of the student union in Halle and vice president of the German Korean Legal Society.

Oeming, Manfred, Dr.

Professor of Theology at the University of Heidelberg. He is also vice chancellor of the College of Jewish Studies in Heidelberg. In his research, he focuses inter alia on the historiography in Israel and the dialogue between the Jewish and Christian religions.

Schlieter, Jens, Dr.

Assistent at the Indology Department, University of Bonn and a member of the Research-Group "Culture-Transcending Bioethics" of the German Research Foundation. Dr. Schlieter studied philosophy in Vienna and Bonn, specialising in Tibetan and Buddhist studies. He holds a Ph.D. in philosophy. In his research, he presently focuses on the bioethical positions in modern South East Asian and Tibetan Buddhism, in particular with a view to their possible contribution to a universal bioethical approach.

Sheikholeslami, Reza

Professor and Soudavar Chair of Persian Studies at the Oriental Institute, Oxford University, and a Professorial Fellow at Wadham College, Oxford. Among his publications are The Structure of Central Authority in Qajar Iran, 1871-1896 and The Political Economy of Saudi Arabia. At present, he is preparing a manuscript on the emergence of political community in Iran in the early twentieth century.

Simitis, Spiros, Dr. Dres. h.c.

Former Professor of Labour and Civil Law, Computer Science and Law at the University of Frankfurt; Director of the Research Centre for Data Protection; visiting professor at the Universities of Berkeley, Yale and Paris; Data Protection Commissioner of the State of Hesse (1975-1991); Consultant of the EC-Commission in matters of Data Protection; Chairman of The High Level Experts Group on Social Rights of the EC-Commission (1998-1999); Chairman of the German National Ethics Council, since 2001.

Spaemann, Robert, Dr.

Professor of Philosophy at the Universities of Stuttgart, Heidelberg and Munich from 1962 to 1992. During this time, he was also visiting professor at the Sorbonne University in Paris and at the University of Rio de Janeiro. Since 1992, he is honorary professor at the University of Salzburg. One of his pivotal publications is Happiness and Benevolence (Glück und Wohlwollen - Versuch über die Ethik).

Starck, Christian, Dr.

Professor of Public Law at the University of Göttingen since 1971; habilitation for Public Law and Theory of Law at Würzburg 1969; justice of the Constitutional Court of Lower Saxony since 1991; member of the Academy of Sciences at Göttingen since 1982. International Association of Constitutional Law, member of executive committee since 1981.

Graf Vitzthum, Wolfgang, Dr. Dr. h.c., LL.M. (Columbia)

Professor of Public and Public International Law at the Eberhard Karls University of Tübingen, Editor of Völkerrecht, de Gruyter Verlag Berlin, New York, 3rd edition 2004. Graf Vitzthum has written extensively on questions of fundamental rights and human dignity in the context of modern medical and ethical problems during the last 20 years.

Vöneky, Silja, Dr.

Senior Researcher at the Max Planck Institute for Comparative Public Law and International Law. Publications include, inter alia, the Laws of

War and International Environmental Law. Moreover, Dr. Vöneky's focus of research is the use and function of Ethic Commissions and questions of EC Law and Public International Law in regard to research and cloning of human embryos and stem cell research. She represents the Institute at the interdisciplinary Research Project "The Status of the extracorporeal Embryo" which is financed by the German Federal Ministry of Research.

Winnacker, Ernst-Ludwig, Dr.

Professor of Biochemistry at the University of Munich since 1980, and since 1984 also Director of the Laboratory for Molecular Biology - Gene Centre of the University of Munich. Since 1990, he has held a Visiting Professorship at Harvard Medical School. Prof. Winnacker is President of the German Research Foundation (DFG).

Wolfrum, Rüdiger, Dr. Dr. h.c.

Professor of Law at the Universities of Heidelberg and Hamburg and Director of the Max Planck Institute for Comparative Public Law and International Law in Heidelberg since 1993. From 1996 to 2001, Professor Wolfrum was vice-president of the German Research Foundation (DFG). Since 2002, he has been vice-president of the Max Planck Society and since 1996 judge at the International Tribunal for the Law of the Sea. Furthermore, he is member of the working group "biodiversity" of the European Academy for the Research into Consequences of Scientific-Technological Developments.

Zypries, Brigitte

Federal Minister of Justice since 2002. Previously, Ms Zypries was Secretary of State in the Federal Ministry of the Interior since 1998 and worked as research assistant at the Federal Constitutional Court from 1988 to 1990. Her main projects as Minister of Justice have been and are the reform of the penal law concerning sexual crimes and the reform of the German federal system.

List of Abbreviations

AJIL	American Journal of International Law
al.	alii
approx.	approximately
AöR	Archiv des öffentlichen Rechts
AVR	Archiv des Völkerrechts
Art.	Article
BT	Deutscher Bundestag (German Parliament)
BVerfGE	Bundesverfassungsgerichtsentscheidungen (Report on the Decisions of the German Constitutional Court)
cf.	confer
Ca.	California
CBDI	Steering Committee on Bioethics
DFG	German Research Foundation (Deutsche Forschungsgemeinschaft)
Doc.	Document(s)
doi	Digital Object Identifier
DÖV	Die öffentliche Verwaltung
DRiZ	Deutsche Richterzeitung
ECJ	European Court of Justice
ECR	European Court Reports
ed.	editor/edition
eds.	editors
e.g.	for example (*exempli gratia*)
et seq.	and the following (*et sequentes*)
ETS	European Treaties Series

EU	European Union
Eur. Ct. H.R.	Reports of Judgements and Decisions of the European Court of Human Rights
F.A.Z.	Frankfurter Allgemeine Zeitung
Gen	Genesis
Harvard J. L. & Tech.	Harvard Journal of Law and Technology
HdbStR	Handbuch des Staatsrechts (ed. by J. Isensee and P. Kirchhof)
Hum. Rts. L.J.	Human Rights Law Journal
Hum. Rts. Quarterly	Human Rights Quarterly
IAP	InterAcademy Panel on International Affairs
ibid.	in the same place (*ibidem*)
id.	the same (*idem*)
ILM	International Legal Materials
ILO	International Labour Organisation
ISIM Newsletter	Newsletter of the International Institute for the Study of Islam in the Modern World
JZ	Juristenzeitung
KritV	Kritische Vierteljahresschrift
loc. cit.	in the place cited (*loco citato*)
l.r.	leading record
MIT	Massachusetts Institute of Technology
Nature AOP	Nature Advance Online Publication
Nature Med.	Nature Medicine
N. Engl. J. Med.	New England Journal of Medicine
NJW	Neue Juristische Wochenschrift
No.	number
O.A.S.	Organisation of American States
OAU	Organisation of African Unity
OJ	Official Journal
p./pp.	page/pages
para.	paragraph
PID	pre-implantation diagnosis
Res.	Resolution

S. Cal. L. Rev.	Southern California Law Review
S. Ct.	Supreme Court Reporter
sect.	section
sess.	session
supp.	supplements
UN	United Nations
UNESCO	United Nations Educational, Scientific and Cultural Organization
U.N.T.S.	United Nations Treaty Series
Vol.	Volume
WHO	World Health Organisation
WissR	Wissenschaftsrecht
ZaeFQ	Zeitschrift für ärztliche Fortbildung und Qualitätssicherung
ZRP	Zeitschrift für Rechtspolitik

Part 1

Human Creation and Human Dignity in
Religious and Ethical Perspectives

The Creation and the Dignity of Man in Islam

Reza Sheikholeslami, Oxford

I. The Koran: The Central Pillar

It is fallacious to discuss the position of man in Islam. Islam, as a way of life, has developed in the course of history and in interaction with major historical events in a vast geographic expanse. Many primordial associations and different existing patterns of social control, at times, have gained the sanctity of religion, while others have become irrelevant, as the objective bases on which they once rested gave way. In this continuous flux, in which Islam is continuously in the state of becoming, and where different Muslims uphold different ideas, it is of necessity inappropriate to make pronouncements on what Islam is. Islam, like other global and historical belief systems, is what Muslims consider it to be and at that time alone.

In order to study a belief system, even within a very limited context, one needs to analyse it sociologically, as well as theologically. If the research is successfully carried out, one may be able to discuss the attitude of a well-defined community within a time framework. One cannot, however, generalise this finding to the many divergent communities, which exist now or have existed longitudinally.

In the case of Islam, however, in contrast to most other global belief systems, there exists a specific body of writings, *revelations*, which constitute the very pillar of what a Muslim *should* believe in, i.e. the Koran. The Koran by definition is the pillar of the faith. While Muslims can and do disagree on matters of practice, they cannot differ as to the truth of the message of God. It is, therefore, essential to go back to the fundamentals, where Muslims are in unison.

This is not the place to discuss the sciences which have developed vis-à-vis the Koran. However, to justify the methodology of limiting the discussion to the Koran, it is necessary to point out that the place of the Koran in Islam is much more focal than the Bible is in Christianity. The Koran, of which one version exists only, is believed by Muslims to be literally the words of God, and Mohammad's significance, one may say, his only significance, separating him from every other man, was to bring God's message to mankind. The Koran is believed to have co-existed with God since eternity. Nothing in Islam, the Prophet included, is sacred other than the Book. Everything else is a matter of rites, communal obligations, and matters that can be, in certain cases, discarded or altered.

Therefore, to discuss creation and man's dignity according to the Book is the most essential way one can look at the question in Islam.[1] The choice is not capricious. Islam is the Book. What is often discussed as the unalterable face of Islam, i.e., the *Shari'ah*, the religious path, Islamic jurisprudence, has developed in the course of history and under specific social conditions. It may change in the course of history as well, and it often does. The Koran does not change. One's understanding of it, of course, may.

II. Man, God's Divine Masterpiece

It is important that one should deal with the question of creation as narrated in the Koran first. God created the original man and woman through divine intervention, but once Adam and Eve were created, the continuation of the human race is a consequence of the natural process of interaction of man and woman, somehow overseen by God. The original act, therefore, as a divine act of creation, cannot be replicated. There is an implicit assumption that there is only one method for procreation and that one method is divinely sanctioned, namely life as a consequence of a pair's interaction. Chapter 5, Verses 1-3 read:

Mankind, fear your Lord, who created you of a single soul
And from it created its mate.
And from the pair of them scattered abroad many men and women.

---

[1]   For citations from the Koran, I have relied on *A.J. Arberry*, The Koran Interpreted (1955).

The Koran becomes more affirmative as to the creation of man as an act of divinity in Chapter 15, Verse 24:

We who give life and make to die.

All life, therefore, not just the original act of creation, is of divine origin. It is God who is the source of life, and it is only God who can take life away. The assumption that God recognises no partners in breathing life unto mankind is clearly there. The furious condemnation of anyone assuming that others can give life appears in other Koranic chapters, as we shall see.

Significantly, God elevates man to a position so high that the Lord becomes the recipient of man's legacy. Thus in verse 25, God reminds man that,

It is We who are the inheritor.

The transformation of man from dust to a noble creature is the manifestation of a divine act of love. God has created man from the lowest ingredients and has given him the highest status:

Surely, We created man of clay, of mud moulded.[2]

The discussion of the creation of man is at the core of the Koran, as we shall see. Chapter 22, Verses 5 and onwards become much more explicit and detailed about the creation of mankind.

O men, if you are in doubt as to the Uprising (The Day of Resurrection), surely We created you out of dust.
Then of a sperm drop.
Then of a blood clot.
Then of a lump of flesh, formed and unformed.

The importance of this, the creation of man by God, is seemingly so significant to God as an achievement that He feels the need to make it very clear to man. He tells him all this in order,

That We make clear to you.

In the subsequent verses, the Lord emphasises His role as the creator even when the process is apparently taking a natural course. What is seemingly only natural has the divine will behind it.

And We establish in the wombs, what we will, till a stated term.
Then We deliver you as infants.
Then you may come of age.

---

[2]   Verse 26.

In Chapter 23, God gives an even fuller account of the creation of man. God is indeed, if I may be allowed to use the word, very proud of His own creation, almost boastful.

Verses 10-15 are very explicit:

> *We created man of an extraction of clay.*
> *Then We set him up, a drop, a receptacle secure.*
> *Then We created of the drop a clot (blood clot).*
> *Then We created of the clot a tissue.*
> *Then We created of the tissue bones.*
> *Then we garmented the bones in flesh.*
> *Thereafter, We produced him another creature.*

God, in fact marvels at His own creation. He is so deeply impressed by what He has done that He turns to praise of Himself.

> *So, blessed be God, the fairest of all creators.*

In praising Himself, God is indeed marvelling at man, admiring him: the fair phenomenon He has created.

The creation of man, as God's masterpiece, naturally places man on an elevated plain. In detail, the Lord tells us the long arduous process He went through in order to create such a fair being. However, in Chapter 32, Verses 5-7, He once again assures man that surely the Lord is his creator. But this verse takes a giant jump. After reiterating the tale of the creation of man and the continuity of the genre, apparently through succeeding demeaning starts for each man and progress towards nobility in each case:

> *And He originated the creation of man out of clay.*
> *Then He fashioned his progeny of an extraction of mean water.*

God goes much further. He imbues man with the divine spirit: His own Spirit. So that man, who was born from the lowest of the low, "the mean water", now becomes, in fact, divine. Because,

> *Then He shaped him, and breathed His spirit in him.*

The shape of man is, therefore, divinely ordained and his spirit is godly. One can deduce that what God has so carefully fashioned, no man, in fact nothing and no one, can emulate nor alter. The vessel of the divine spirit cannot be broken by man. Man's nobility is, in fact, a sacred gift from God.

So frequently God returns to the theme of the creation of man, that it seems that man is the external indicator of God's existence.[3]

In Chapter 35, Verse 12, the Lord reassures man that,

> *God created you of dust.*
> *Then a sperm drop.*
> *Then He made you pairs.*
> *No female bears or brings forth, save with His knowledge.*

There are major chapters in the Koran on Man and Woman. The many examples that one can produce do not add to the story of man's creation substantially, yet their sheer number indicate the importance of the creation of man, and, in fact, the importance of man in the Koran. So much of the Koran is devoted to the subject of creation, that it is almost as though the most significant aspect of God's divine authority is manifested and almost legitimised by the creation of man: God's masterpiece. And He made everything else to comfort man. Thus,

> *It is God who made for you the earth a fixed place*
> *And heaven an edifice.*
> *And He shaped you, and He shaped you well.*
> *And provided you with good things.*

At this point, based on all the Lord has done for man, He concludes that,

> *That, then, is your God, your Lord, so blessed be God.*[4]

The subsequent verses repeat the story of the creation and all God has done for man.

God's anger is most manifest when He observes that man, whom He has created, and for whom He has created so much, shows ingratitude by his recognition of false gods. No sin in Islam is worse than *shirk*, which in Arabic is etymologically derived from the verb *to share,* and in ordinary vernacular means *polytheism.* Islam is very adamant that God alone is the Creator; that He alone has established a course of life for His creatures within which they can make some choices. Man's doubts as to the Creator are damned.

Chapter 36, Verses 75-78, if one is allowed to say, expresses God's deep disappointment.

---

[3] Incidentally, the title ayatollah means in Arabic an indicator/proof of God. In the Koran, God refers to all humanity as indicators/proofs of His existence.

[4] Chapter 40, Verse 66.

Has not man regarded how that We created him? Of a sperm drop?
Then lo, he is a manifest adversary.
And he has struck for us a similitude. And forgotten his creation.

At this point, God, hurt, but still very loving towards what He has created, makes an encouraging offer.

He (the man) says, "Who shall quicken the bones when they are decayed?"
Say, "He shall quicken them who originated them the first time."

III. Free Will and the Dignity of Man

The dignity of man in Islam has already been addressed, albeit in a peripheral manner. The point, however, is so forcefully forwarded in the Koran that it requires more detailed analysis. Man, as he is represented in the Koran, is a divine creation. God not only created him, but also thought that He created him well. As a creation of God, one can deduce that man is untouchable. His destruction is manifestly the destruction of the divine order, the work of God, an attack on the Deity himself. As man is the carrier of God's spirit, those who change or destroy him, change or destroy the spirit of God. God assures the Prophet that He has created heaven and earth to serve man. The destruction of man is tantamount to making the universe that God created futile. What has been discussed above may have serious implications as far as the conception of human rights is concerned. The focus in this volume is, however, on the legitimacy of cloning and what religion may say about it. It is therefore, significant to see what specifically the Koran says on the topic of human dignity.

The portrait that emerges of God's relationship with man can best be represented by a love affair. When God sounds hurt in the Koran, when He feels rejected by man, it is the pain and agony and vengefulness of a spurned lover. He has indeed created what He has fallen in love with. He has bestowed on the beloved the heaven and earth. The pain that the beautiful creature, after all this, may take another lover is too much to bear. The least He can expect is recognition and gratitude. *For, indeed We created man in the fairest stature.*[5]

---

[5] Chapter 97, Verse 1.

In this regard, Chapter 15 is even more telling:[6]

> And the earth, We stretched it forth.
> And cast on it firm mountains
> And We caused to grow therein of everything, justly weighed.
> And there appointed for your livelihood, and for those you provide not for.
> [...]
> And We loose the winds, fertilising.
> And We send down, out of heaven water.
> Then We give it to you to drink.

The lover raises the beloved and gives her material things, but these are insufficient. He wants to guarantee her respect, dignity and authority. All should recognise the status of the beloved and kneel before her, including those who have the most prominent status positions. Even the angels have to recognise their humble positions regarding the creature of God.

> And when the Lord said to the angels,
> See I am creating a being out of a clay, mud moulded.
> When I have shaped him and breathed my spirit in him, fall you down, bowing before him.
> Then angels bowed themselves, all together.
> Save Satan. He refused to be among those bowing.
> Said He (God), "What ails thee, Satan, that you are not among those bowing?"

The argument between God and Satan continues. As an archangel, Satan, finds it below him to bow before a creature made of mud. God, angered by the disrespect for His love, expels Satan from heaven, sending him down to the lowest of the low.

> Said He (God) "Then go thou forth hence. Thou art accursed.
> Upon thee shall rest the curse, till the Day of Doom.

It was pointed out earlier that the worst sin in Islam is to consider that God has a partner. Of all His creatures, it is only man that He angrily admonishes for this offence. Of all His creatures, it is man that He deeply loves and has done so much for.

In Chapter 2, Verses 152-155 God repeats the theme of all He has done for man and that man has shown love for others.

---

6   Selections from Verses 15-34.

Surely the creation of the heavens and the earth, and the alteration of the night and day, and the ship that runs in the sea, with profit to men, and the water that God sends down with heaven therewith, reviving the earth after it is dead [...]

And the list of divine endeavours and gifts continues. Then God, hurt, after all the love He has shown towards man, says:

Yet there be men who take to themselves compeers (a person of equal standing to God) apart from God, loving them as God is loved. But those who believe love God more ardently.

The dignity of man is derived from the belief that man is God's creation, and the creation that God loves most. At his disposal, God has placed all He has created. When he errs, God is still loving and forgiving. With one exception only, every chapter in the Koran begins with *In the Name of God who is Kind and Forgiving.* As the Koran is addressed only to man, it is towards man that the Lord is kind and forgiving. Of all His creatures God promises eternal life, in the form of resurrection, only to man. In Chapter 17, Verse 72, God tells his messenger Mohammad that,

We have honoured the Children of Adam, and carried them on land and sea, and provided them with good things, and preferred them greatly
Over many of those We created.

In the earlier verses in the same chapter, the Lord assures man again of His love for mankind. And yet again, the command to all archangels to bow before man is repeated. Again Satan, Iblis, refuses to humble himself. Again he loses his elevated honoured position and becomes a downcast — the worst. The fact that God allows Satan to operate on earth as a personification of evil, influencing man to go astray, is an indication of the degree of freedom God allows His creation. He has imbued man with reasoning. He has shown him the way. Satan has his chance to affect man's actions. It depends all on man to decide. For, in Chapter 55, Verse 1, God lists the attributes He has given to man:

The All-merciful has taught the Koran. He created man. And He has taught him the explanation.

The conclusion one can reach is that there is a Day of Judgement for man alone, because it is only to man that God has given the power of reason, i.e., intellect. As a being who can judge and has the freedom to choose between evil and good, only he can be judged. Only he can be punished. Only he can be held responsible. Man alone has knowledge, a

gift from God, the most generous gift, and one that man can incremen-
tally add upon. Chapter 96, Verse 1 reads:

> *Recite: Thy Lord is the most generous, who taught you with the pen.*
> *Taught man that he knew not*

Man's nobility as God's creation is paradoxical. As God has created
him and has created everything for him, he is noble. His centrality is
guaranteed. And, yet he is created from a speck of dust. He exists in the
final analysis between grandeur and wretchedness. His special place is
not unproblematic.

IV. The Limits of Human Reason

The story of the creation of man, as it is recited in the Koran, is a very
personal story of giving, love, pride and betrayal. A sad story. Man is
created by the Lord to perfection. The world is put at his disposal. The
winds blow for him. The rain falls because of him. The Creator loves
His creation. He orders all around him to love him and respect him.
The one who does not is damned. God can make man to love Him and
to choose no one but Him. However, He is a loving lover. He wants the
beloved to love Him freely. After all, the beloved, with his ability to
reason, must know what God has done for him. He errs repeatedly. The
lover is still compassionate, kind, giving and forgiving.

Man is not made in the image of God, as the Christian motto would
have us believe. Man, the Koran tells us, is, however, proof of God's
existence. Thus, the relationship provides dimensions of similarity.
Imagining God is condoned, but imagery of God is condemned. In this
sense, there is absolutely no place in Islam for the dogma of incarnation. God does not take any shape and form and is conceptualised as an
abstraction. Any claim that He may take a human's shape, (incarnation)
or the shape of humanity, (man as image of God) will necessarily negate
His divinity. It is only in the mystical Islamic schools that human and
divine natures overlap. Such proclamation has no place in the Koran.
Similarly, the metaphor of the "children of God" cannot have a place in
the Koran, where man is forcefully reminded that God is "not begotten,
and has not been begotten". (Chapter CXII, Verse 2) It may be natural
to deify one's origins, and it has been a common cultural phenomenon
to worship one's ancestors. But the Koran, in spite of putting man at
the centre of the universe, is intolerant of granting him divine attributes.

Natural forms are not placed, in the Koran, in a continuum of overlapping properties. The "Great Chain of Being" will imply that man as the highest natural form would need to take only a short leap to climb up the ladder that leads to the highest form. While some schools of mysticism hold that some men may bear resemblance to God, this is clearly in contradiction to the Koranic injunctions. Men have dignity, not because they are God's children or resemble him at all, but because men are created by God. Again the Koran returns to the theme of creation. If creation is set aside, man enjoys no other dignity.

On the other hand, it is necessary to consider that men have certain qualities that God possesses, as well. Men can bring about changes in their environment, have understanding, knowledge, passion, and kindness. God, also, can bring about changes, be benevolent or wrathful. Such parallelism, that one observes in the Koran, may imply that the similarity thesis may have some roots in the Koran. However, it should be pointed out that while there may be similarity between the qualities that God and man both possess, there is no similarity quantitatively between the attributes of God and man. God's attributes are held with no sense of limit. Man's knowledge is limited in contrast to God's infinite wisdom. The quantitative difference separates man from God. It also explains an enigma, namely: If God has given man reason, why does man err and rebel against God's will? The answer may rest in that God's gift of reason is not without limits. It is this limitation that forbids man from the act of procreation, unsupervised by the divine light.

The Pali Buddhist Approach to Human Cloning

Andrew Huxley, London

Pali Buddhism would approach this ethical issue from three directions:

1. *questioning the motives of the cloners*

Human cloning involves intentional human action: do we classify this action as 'skilful' or 'unskilful' (in Pali, kusala / akusala kamma; in English, good or bad karma)?

2. *protecting the interests of the cloned*

Buddhists are committed to treat all sentient beings with metta (loving-kindness). From this derives an analysis that overlaps with the European rights / interests / expectations approach.[1] Will a cloned human, qua cloned, get less metta than a standard-issue human?

3. *Is the cloning process itself ethically flawed?*

Would human cloning weaken institutions – such as the family – on which human flourishing depends? Or would it interfere with natural processes – such as karma – on which the flourishing of all sentient beings depends?

I shall discuss these three issues in turn, before venturing a conclusion.

1. Questioning the Motives of the Cloners

Nothing ever repeats itself exactly: it is never the same river into which we step. So we cannot accurately predict *all* the motives of *all* future

---

[1]   See *D.V. Keown/C.S. Prebish/W.R. Husted*, Buddhism and Human Rights (1998).

cloners. Our predictions will always be inaccurate, but we must predict consequences as best we can in order to reach an informed moral judgement. It seems to me that motives will typically vary according to whose DNA I am cloning. I would clone myself for motives other than those which might persuade me to clone a great politician, or to clone some great artist or thinker who is an inspiration to the world, or to clone Brigitte Bardot. I shall consider the motivation behind these categories (self-cloning, political cloning, sex-industry-cloning and great-mind-cloning) separately.

a) Cloning Myself

The Buddhist vices of grasping, need, desire, and attachment to a false-image of the self[2] are pithily exemplified by the act of self-cloning. Anyone who wants to clone themselves must, according to the Buddha dharma, be deeply mistaken about the true nature of the world.

b) Cloning King Pasenadi

King Pasenadi of Kosola was a contemporary of Gautama Buddha who was converted to the new doctrine shortly after the Buddha's enlightenment [S i 68].[3] They met frequently [M ii 120], and cooperated in matters of monastic discipline [V iv 112]. In the *Aggana sutta* (the classic canonical statement of Buddhist political philosophy) the Buddha described Pasenadi as an exemplary king [D iii 83]. If Pali Buddhists could justify cloning any one political figure, it would be Pasenadi.[4] I believe that some Buddhists would condone such political cloning, since attitudes have changed through time. We may explore this by means of a speculative example.

---

[2]   See *P. Harvey*, The Selfless Mind: personality, consciousness and nirvana in early Buddhism (1995).

[3]   References in this form are to the Pali Canon and the commentaries thereto. Save for punctuation, I follow the standard abbreviation system outlined in *V. Trenckner* (ed.), Critical Pali Dictionary 1 (1936), 37-69, and updated by *O. v. Hinüber*, A Handbook of Pali Literature (1996).

[4]   King Ashoka of Pataliputta is also admired by the Buddhist tradition, but he has two disadvantages: he never met the Buddha, and he spent some years as a cruel king before his repentance and conversion.

In five year's time, let us say, a member of the Kennedy dynasty marries a member of the Nehru / Gandhi dynasty and has twelve children. Forty years on, the toughest of these children rules the United States of Amerindia as King Gandhi-Kennedy I, having shown the optimum blend of charisma and skill-in-ruling. We can well imagine what would lead his staff to create twenty clones of their king to act as his pro-consuls over the unruly provinces of Mesopotamia, Guatemala and Java. Would these motives be condemned by Buddhist political philosophy? The Pali canon only offers scattered thoughts on political science, but its underlying logic would, I think, condemn such a scheme. A change of attitude comes in the Pali literature of the 5th century CE, which offers a more detailed treatment of Buddhist politics and, at the same time, promotes a fantasy about the 'wheel-turning emperor' (the king who, ruling by dharma, gets to rule the entire known world). Buddhist politics as it was actually practised in Southeast Asia over the last millennium, might well endorse the cloning of King Gandhi-Kennedy I so as to enrich the stock of 'wheel-turning kings'. In my personal opinion, this rests on a misunderstanding of the Buddha's message, but the Pali Buddhist tradition would, I think, take the opposite view.

c) Cloning Queen Nanda

The Pali canon contains several descriptions of gorgeous women. From among these I select Queen Nanda, whom the Buddha in his antepenultimate incarnation described thus:

> This woman beauteous in every limb, her lips like plates of gold ... with eyes like a pigeon ... and slender waist ... her hair long, black and a little curled ... with breasts like the *tindook* fruit – not too long, not too short, not hairless and not too hairy.[5]

To clone Queen Nanda, or her modern equivalent, might finally reveal the degree to which sex appeal is a corporeal or a mental phenomenon:

> Lord Buddha explained almost 2600 years ago ... how the ... fertilised egg is still only matter. For a new life to begin mentality must join with this special matter.... Scientists are still using ... biological

---

[5]   The Great Tunnel Jataka (#546); *E. Cowell/W. Rouse*, The Jataka translated from the Pali by Various Hands (1907).

matter.... They can never manufacture mentality, or the matter that is produced by *kamma* or *citta*.[6]

Ms. Nanda-clone would share Ms. Nanda's DNA, but would have someone else's mind. If we could quantify the degree to which Nanda-clone's breasts are less attractive than Nanda's, we would have quantified the extent to which sex is in the head. Leaving such research opportunities aside, the motivation for sex-industry-cloning will almost certainly involve pimping, which is unethical on two counts: it exploits others and it is driven by greed for money. If, without reserving 25% of their future earnings, someone were to clone Britney Spears and Brad Pitt with the sole intention of increasing human happiness, their action would be ethically neutral. The Britney-cloner would be like the chef who invents a delicious new way to cook cabbage, or the musician who composes *Fidelio*. Utilitarians would commend those who invent new opportunities for sentient beings to derive pleasure, but Buddhists would neither commend nor condemn.

d) Cloning the Buddha (or Nelson Mandela or Pablo Picasso or Jimi Hendrix)

If sex-industry-cloning is ethically neutral as long as it is carried out for the right reasons, perhaps great-mind-cloning might be ethically positive? The paradigm case for Buddhists would be to clone Gautama Buddha. For more than 2000 years the tradition has been preserving samples of Gautaman DNA:[7] Perhaps all along, the hidden purpose of the relic-cult has been to facilitate the cloning of a Buddha. Buddhicide (the killing of an enlightened being) is one of the 'instant karma' offences: it is so heinous that its karmic effects will be felt in this lifetime. If killing a Buddha is terribly bad karma, maybe cloning a Buddha is amazing good karma?

Such speculations woefully miss the point. What makes a Buddha is not the body, but the mind. A Buddha clone's body would decode Gautama's DNA, not Gautama's mentality. The Buddha-clone's mentality would decode the karmic balance of whomever or whatever

---

[6]   *R. Kirkpatrick*,   Cloning   and   Buddhism   (2000), http://www.humancloning. 150m.com/article8.html.

[7]   His teeth, hair and bones are enshrined as relics in most of Asia's major Buddhist locations.

he happened to reincarnate.[8] It might be that of a good earthworm, or of a bad God.

2. Protecting the Interests of the Cloned

William LaFleur, a bioethicist at the University of Pennsylvania, locates the fundamental Buddhist approach to cloning in *metta* (loving-kindness, compassion):

> More important for Buddhists would be the sense that we avoid research likely to result in cruelty to individuals or in more general misery than already exists in our world. It's the compassion matter again.[9]

Does compassion for the cloned justify a ban? The case is far from obvious. Cloned children will certainly face difficulties we cannot yet imagine, but will they be any more severe than the difficulties facing orphans, step-children and adopted children through the ages? A more immediate threat to children is posed by the international trade in rockets, cluster-bombs and machine guns. On *metta* grounds, banning the arms trade is a far more urgent moral task than banning human cloning.

Joel Feinberg has identified a particular right of which the cloned are deprived: he calls it *the right to an open future*:

> The parents might actually limit the child's opportunities for growth and development: a child cloned from a basketball player, for instance, might be denied any educational opportunities that were not in line with a career in basketball.[10]

Tibetan Buddhism would have some difficulty meeting this objection. The Dalai Lama (and the other Tibetan incarnate Lamas) receive no wider an education than the basketball star's clone. Pali Buddhism, though it does not have incarnate Lamas, is also one of the virtue traditions. Therefore education is a matter of training the child in virtue, rather than facilitating the child's free choice among her infinite

---

[8] Gautama himself, by reason of his parinibbana, can no longer be reincarnated.

[9] W. *LaFleur*, quoted in Glenn McGee (ed.), The Human Cloning Debate (2nd ed., 2001), 285-288.

[10] See http://www.wikipedia.org/wiki/Human_cloning#Ethics.

possibilities. The Buddhist education system in Southeast Asia (which by 1800 had produced a higher rate of literacy than any in Europe) aims to mould the child in the image of the good, rather than draw out (*e-ducare*) the child's potential. Therefore Pali Buddhists would dispute the existence of Feinberg's right to an open future.

3. The Cloning Process Itself

Certainly human society would change in unpredictable ways if human cloning became common. But, as my teacher David Daube pointed out, there is no reason for the standard assumption that such change must be for the worse. In 1971 he spoke at a conference in Washington D.C. about the ethical implications of a world in which most births were test-tube births. He proposed the following thought-experiment: *Imagine we live in a world where all births are test-tube births. What would our reaction be if somebody suggested the introduction of sex-procreation?* It is easy to envisage the arguments for the status quo: 'In our test-tube society there is more equality, more genuine mutual care. We avoid possessiveness and the dangers of out-of-kilter dynamics in the hothouse of a small family.' So Daube counselled that 'We should keep an open mind on the absence of father and mother in the traditional sense, rather than rush into unconditional condemnation.' With an open mind, then, how might cloning *per se* diminish human flourishing?

a) Confusing Kinship Terminology: 'My Mother Is My Twin"

Each culture inherits its own kinship vocabulary, which reinforces its own cultural norms: Antigone is expected to bury her brother, a New Guinean highlander is expected to marry her sororal cross-cousin, and a German Catholic must not marry his deceased wife's sister. The more that cultures sacralise these vocabularies and norms, the more threatening cloning will be to them. The Canon Law offers Catholics a sacred family law. A Vatican committee recently objected that:

In the cloning process the basic relationships of the human person are perverted: filiation, consanguinity, kinship, parenthood.[11]

The *fiqh* likewise preserves a family law and inheritance law that is God-given. Thomas Eich summarises some Sunni debates:

What would be the status of a female baby whose DNA is identical to her 'mother's'? She could neither be termed 'daughter', nor 'sister' nor 'mother'. This confusion would have decisive repercussions in other fields of *shari`a* law.[12]

The Buddhist cultures of mainland Southeast Asia are linguistically far more varied than those of Europe. The Khmer, Tai and Burmese languages are as different from each other as German is from Arabic, and each of these languages has its own kinship vocabulary. Nonetheless Robert Lingat has argued for an underlying similarity in the family structures which these languages represent.[13] Whether or not Lingat is correct, Southeast Asian family law and kinship terminology is not (unlike its Muslim and Catholic equivalents) sacred. It is contained in the local genres of *dhammathat* and *rajathat*, which books contain law for the Buddhist laity of Southeast Asia. Since these genres are admittedly post-canonical, their rules and principles may be altered or ignored whenever Buddhist ethics calls for it. Buddhists would not, therefore, accept this argument against human cloning.

b) Confusing Karma: 'All His Clones Share His Karma'

Each clone is born to this world bearing a particular karmic load which determines whether she starts this life as rich or poor, lucky or unlucky, loved or neglected. Since Buddhism does not recognise any uncaused effect, everyone 'inherits' someone else's karmic balance. Hence Buddhist moral identity differs sharply from European notions of self and person. The European self lasts for three-score-years-and-ten, while the Buddhist moral agent lasts for several lifetimes. As Michael Barnhart puts it:

---

[11] The Pontifical Academy for Life, Reflections on Cloning (1997), www.vatican.va/roman-curia/pontifical_academies/acdlife/documents.

[12] *T. Eich*, Muslim voices on Cloning, ISIM Newsletter 12:38-9, June 2003, 39.

[13] *R. Lingat*, Les Régimes Matrimoniaux du Sud-Est de l'Asie, Tome 1: Les Régimes Traditionnels (1952).

> [Buddhist] moral identity ... is disconnected from our sense of self....
> By contrast, in traditional Hinduism, the spectator self is the seat of
> such moral or karmic identity so that there is an experiencing self at
> the core of one's moral identity, and consequently comparisons with
> a soul or self make much more sense.[14]

Might cloning interfere with the natural processes by which karma
links various lives into a single moral identity? If so, there would be
convincing Buddhist reason to ban it. The argument might go like this:

> If the DNA-donor's karmic balance is inherited by all his clones, the
> DNA-donor can cheat the system by creating enough clones to di-
> lute the unfavourable balance: If he is 100 units of karma overdrawn
> (which merits rebirth in the 6th circle of hell), he might share his
> overdraft between ten clones, who each inherits 10 units (which
> merits rebirth as a butterfly).

This false argument mistakes the metaphor of 'inheritance' for reality.
Children and clones inherit DNA from their parents and DNA-donors.
But they do not 'inherit' their parent's karma. Reincarnation is not
(*pace* the Egyptian pharaohs) a family affair. I cannot be reincarnated as
my own child since I cannot have been dead at the moment my child
was conceived. For the family-reincarnation-fallacy to work, karma
would have to operate solely through the DNA. But karma plainly
operates in other ways as well: it arranges for people to adopt children,
to die of infectious diseases and to slip on banana skins. The Abbot of
the Zen Centre at Berkeley, Ca. asks rhetorically (expecting the answer
'no'):

> Is my clone's experience the same as mine? When my clone drinks
> wine, do I get drunk?[15]

Since everyone, clones included, inherits the karmic load of the sentient
being whom they reincarnate, the clone is in no better or worse
position than a natural child.

The chances are against the clone reincarnating a human being (as
opposed to a god, a ghost or an animal). If humans clone millions of
extra children, will karma run out of sentient beings to reincarnate?
That seems unlikely. The more humans we create, the more other life-
forms we destroy. Karma should always have enough earth-worms and

---

[14]   M. *Barnhart*, Nature, Nurture, and No-Self: Bioengineering and Buddhist Values, Journal of Buddhist Ethics 7 (2000), 35-53.

[15]   M. *Weitsman*, quoted in Glenn McGee, supra note 9, 285-288.

mosquitos at its disposal to promote to the ranks of cloned humanity. This does not constitute a valid argument against human cloning.

4. Conclusions

Only a fully enlightened being can trace all the effects of a single act into the future. The rest of us have to make decisions on the basis of inadequate data. Buddhist epistemology therefore offers various defeasible principles as aids to decision making under imperfect conditions. What Europeans call 'the precautionary principle' is built into the most basic Buddhist list of those acts which entail bad karma. The five bad acts are killing, theft, bad sex and lies (all of which necessarily hurt others) and self-intoxication by drink or drugs (which may sometimes not hurt others). Getting drunk is banned on the precautionary principle: it *increases the risk* of killing, theft, bad sex and lies. Balancing the best forecasts we can make, will the technology of human cloning increase the risk of bad acts, bad words and bad thoughts?

Pali Buddhists would reject the arguments against cloning discussed in sections 2 and 3. But they would find the arguments under section 1 extremely persuasive: in the great majority of circumstances, the motives of the cloner will make the act of cloning an *akusala kamma*. This is enough to attract the precautionary principle. I have reached this conclusion informed by my exposure to Burmese Buddhism. I am reassured to find agreement in someone writing from within the Thai Buddhist tradition:

> Before proceeding with human cloning there are some questions Buddhism wants us to consider. For example, could we embark on a course of action that will have unforeseeable but unalterable consequences in the future? ... At this stage we cannot be certain about the social and psychological ramification that such experiment may bring on the already fragile fabric of familial and social relationships in our world.... Should we act, then, on the basis of ignorance of future consequences in matter that affect men, women, children and families? The unforeseeable and unalterable consequences of human cloning can be the first step eventually down a slipping slope. Ac-

cordingly the possible negative consequences will outweigh the benign ones.[16]

If cloning is to be banned, Buddhists would prefer it to happen at the international level. In matters of karma, Buddhist ethics claims global validity. If human cloning does more harm than good, cloners will suffer the same karmic consequences in Vienna as in Vientiane, in Manchester as in Mandalay.

---

[16] *P. Ratanakul*, Buddhism, prenatal diagnosis and human cloning, in N. Fujiki/D.R.J. Macer (eds.), Bioethics in Asia (2000), 405-407, www.biol.tsukuba. ac.jp/~macer/asiae/biae405.html.

Some Aspects of the Buddhist Assessment of Human Cloning

Jens Schlieter, Bonn

> When medical technology offers reincarnation,
> Buddhist Bioethics will certainly flourish.
> *Damien Keown/James J. Hughes*

I. Introduction

I would like to start with some general observations concerning the role of contemporary Buddhism in the worldwide discussion about the ban on human cloning.

Some Asian Buddhists seem to hold no massive objection against the idea of cloned human beings, that is, against so-called 'reproductive cloning'. The biomedical procedure of an artificial, asexual reproduction does not offend religious feelings or basic value sets of Buddhists, if certain preconditions of the procedure of cloning are fulfilled.[1]

Things look different though regarding the so called 'therapeutic cloning', or cloning for research purposes. In this case Buddhists mostly express their concern about a technique that implies the death of human beings in the embryonic phase of their existence. Uncomfortable as it may seem, many Asian Buddhists express – compared with Western ap-

---

[1] This 'neutral' attitude, although it can be observed, does not lead automatically to a more permissive cloning legislation in countries with a considerable number of Buddhists. Reasons for this – mainly grounded in the structure of Buddhist ethics, and the minor attention paid by monastic Buddhists to legal procedures of lay communities – will be discussed below.

proaches – exactly opposite opinions concerning reproductive cloning on the one, and therapeutic cloning on the other hand.

Certainly, there is a large variety of Buddhist approaches to human cloning. They differ not only with respect to the major traditions of *Theravāda*, currently prevalent in Southeast Asian countries, and *Mahāyāna* traditions of Central and East Asia. Since there is no central institution in Buddhism that could single out heterodox opinions, nearly every attitude can call itself 'Buddhist'. Another important distinction should be noticed, namely that monks and nuns follow stricter rules of conduct than lay Buddhists. But most probably lay Buddhists are those who are really engaged in biomedical research.

This gets even more complicated if ethical assessments of Western Buddhists are taken into consideration. They are much more in line with positions based on Christian and Humanistic grounds, for example the ideas of human rights and dignity.

The internal diversity of opinions is enhanced by the fact that the larger number of Asian Buddhists seem to be rather calm and undisturbed by ethical discussions about cloning or the status of unborn human beings.[2] Many of them think that cloning will cause no new problems to society or mankind that could not be dealt with easily.

II. Buddhist Evaluation of Deeds and Actions

If Buddhists want to know if an action such as cloning poses ethical problems, they try to find out if it is a skilful or an unskilful action for those involved.

If the intention behind an action is to kill or harm a living being, the action is thereby rendered unwholesome. Greed, fanaticism and delusion as motives all have the same unwholesome effect. Buddhist ethics could thus be called 'intentionalist' ethics. But they also consider the outcome of actions for the doer of deeds. Unwholesome actions will lead to bad *karma* and will therefore imply an increase of personal suffering in the next rebirth. Every ethically relevant action is believed to have an effect on the perpetrator's next life. So Buddhist ethics can be characterised as

---

2   An overview of Buddhist discussions of biomedical medicine can be found in *J. Schlieter*, Die aktuelle Biomedizin aus der Sicht des Buddhismus, in Schicktanz/Tannert/Wiedemann (eds.), Kulturelle Aspekte der Biomedizin (2003), 132.

'consequentionalist in private matters' too. Furthermore, Buddhist ethics focus on the consequences for the offender. They are 'offender-centred', as I would like to call it, and not 'victim-centred'. Last but not least Buddhist ethics can be characterised as "contextual" ("situation ethics"), due to the fact that instructions differ in relation to the spiritual status of the people involved.

Obviously these previously specified characteristics ('intentionalism', 'consequentionalism', 'offender-centrism' and 'contextualism') will have a considerable effect on the Buddhist assessment of human cloning. Before discussing some of the arguments, I would like to point out some other important strands of Buddhist anthropology—arguments that are not often mentioned in Buddhist statements on cloning but are nevertheless influential. They are grounded in a different view of human nature, of nature in general, and in a different cosmology.

III. Cloning, and the Buddhist Concepts of (Human) Nature

1. Theory of 'No-self'

An important Buddhist background feature of the ethics of cloning may be referred to as the non-substantialist Buddhist anthropology. A key Buddhist concept, the theory of "No-self" advises Buddhists not to identify themselves with their empirical existence. One should not assume or believe that body, feelings, volition, mind or consciousness point to the existence of a "substantial self". Actually Buddhists train themselves to overcome suffering by gaining insight into the unstable illusory nature of the 'person' and thus their own 'ego'.

What happens to a clone, then, is – from the point of view of ultimate existence – just part of the conventional existence of a 'person'.[3] Certainly, very few Buddhists argue ethically with the conventional existence of a human being. Most of them are eager to separate soteriology (or, 'metaphysics') and ethics of worldly existence. In any case, seen from ultimate reality a clone will neither be a deficient copy, because there is no original 'person', nor a helpless victim, because 'he' as every other human being shall not cling to his worldly existence but shall

---

[3]   Cf. *E. Falls et al.*, The Koan of Cloning: A Buddhist Perspective on the Ethics of Human Cloning Technology, Second Opinion 1 (1999), 44.

proceed on the Buddhist way to liberation. It is therefore not astonishing that very few Asian Buddhists are concerned with possible mental problems of cloned humans.

2. Nature and Creation

In most Buddhist traditions there is no difference made between a good (or at least neutral) and a deficient, man-made nature. Artificiality does not mean that those products are against the course of nature. If they were 'unnatural', they would not be able to exist at all. The 'naturalness of nature' is no guiding principle. Instead, emphasis is put on the following criterion: Do changes of the natural course imply suffering for sentient beings? Or do changes lead to a better position for beings to overcome suffering, the highest goal in Buddhism? Some Buddhists hold it to be true that elimination of diseases or prolonging human life could count as progress in the right direction.

3. *Karma* and Embryology

It is widely believed in Buddhism that a human being comes into existence by a consciousness-spirit (Sanskrit: *gandharva/vijñāna*) that enters at the time of conception (the 'coming-together', i.e., intercourse). In contrast to other religious traditions, Buddhists regard three conditions as necessary preconditions for conception: Semen, an ovum (called 'blood' in pre-modern Buddhist embryology), and a consciousness awaiting rebirth. It is worth mentioning, "that Buddhism believes that however premature and small this fetus is compared to an adult, in this fetus all physical and psychic attributes are already present".[4]

Although an embryo is seen as a human being, it is not seen as something *created*. Buddhists do not believe in God as the creator of the world and mankind. Coming into existence functions according to the

---

[4] *S. Taniguchi*, Biomedical Ethics from a Buddhist Perspective, Pacific World New Series 3 (1987), 75, 76. Cf. *idem*, A Study of Biomedical Ethics from a Buddhist Perspective (MA Thesis, 1987); *idem*, Methodology of Buddhist Biomedical Ethics, in Camenisch (ed.), Religious Methods and Resources in Bioethics (1994), 31.

laws of *karma* – as rebirth in relation to a former life.[5] Generating a clone thus would not violate the laws of creation.[6]

Buddhists do not think they owe their life to God or that they are bound to remain in the role of a 'creature'. It is open for anyone to try to reach Buddhahood, which is exactly to overcome the boundaries of human existence. To accept the limits of human nature goes against the grain of Buddhist 'soteriological' expectations; Buddhists do not hope for a saviour ('soter') to help them in transcending their human condition.

Buddhists emphasise instead that they actually do rely on the law of *karma*: "Each resulting being from cloning procedures would be a different individual with his or her own Karmic heritage from past lives"[7]. In a way one might say that Buddhists have a neutral attitude toward man-made artefacts. Whatever can be done technically must be within the scope of nature and is therefore – by its *status* alone – beyond good or evil. This is not to say that there are no Buddhist arguments against cloning. It is only to demonstrate that these arguments have other foundations than their Western counterparts.

Most Buddhist monks and scholars of various schools I spoke to recently (Tibetan *Mahāyāna*, Sinhalese and Thai *Theravāda* Traditions) told me that they fail to see in which respect a clone would differ in status from any ordinary human being. Interestingly, they are more concerned that a human clone might not be treated *as* a human, expecting thereby a lot of suffering for the clone.

4. Dignity and Sanctity of Life

As one of the last of the important differences, I would like to take a look at the Western concept of "dignity". Many Buddhists do indeed argue against the concept of dignity in the Kantian formulation, that the use of fellow human beings merely as means and not an end, the viola-

---

[5] Cf. *D. Keown*, Buddhism and Bioethics (1995), 89.

[6] It will be shown elsewhere that the topos of a soulless monster created by taboo-breaking humans seems to be a peculiar grand récit (hybris, Golem etc.) of the 'Western' culture.

[7] *A.W.P. Guruge*, Bioethics: How Can Humanistic Buddhism Contribute?, Hsi Lai Journal of Humanistic Buddhism 3 (2002), 86, 114.

tion of bearers of an incomparable value, is an unethical act called "instrumentalisation". But as Damien Keown pointed out, one looks in vain in Buddhist scriptures "for any explicit reference to human dignity".[8] The preciousness of human life results from the rare possibility to attain Buddhahood. In the words of the Burmese leader of the democracy movement, Aung San Suu Kyi: "Buddhism ... places the greatest value on man, who alone of all beings can achieve the supreme state of Buddhahood.... Human life therefore is indefinitely precious".[9] But this 'spiritual functionality' is in my personal understanding not equivalent to Western notions of human dignity and human rights. Buddhists ethics might therefore come closer to the general notion of 'sanctity of life', because almost *all sentient beings* are included within the scope of ethics.

I would like to move the focus now from the fundamental aspects that seem to offer a rather liberal background of the overall idea of cloning to the more specific arguments presented in favour or against the concrete action of cloning.

IV. Buddhist Evaluations of the Cloning Procedure

1. Reproductive Cloning for Infertile Couples

If Buddhists speak in favour of cloning, they mostly think about the intention to help infertile couples. The Buddhist bioethicist Pinit Ratanakul said that, if human cloning "could satisfy the parenting desire of childless couples and if it does not cause pain and suffering to all parties concerned nor destruction of life, Buddhism will have no difficulty in accepting it".[10]

For Buddhists the most intricate questions arise when the *motives* of cloning are guided by loving-kindness and compassion, but the *action* itself implies harm. The currently used cloning-techniques of mammals

---

[8]   *D. Keown*, Are there 'Human Rights' in Buddhism?, Journal of Buddhist Ethics 2 (1995), 3, 13.

[9]   *Aung San Suu Kyi*, Freedom From Fear (1991), 174.

[10]   *P. Ratanakul*, Buddhism, Prenatal Diagnosis and Human Cloning, in N. Fujiki/D.R.J. Macer (eds.), Bioethics in Asia (1997), 405, 407. Cf. *idem*, Human Cloning: Thai Buddhist Perspectives, in Roetz (ed.), Cross-Cultural Issues in Bioethics: The Example of Human Cloning (forthcoming).

seem to imply a lot of harm. In the most common procedure the cell-nucleus of an oocyte is taken out and replaced by a somatic cell nucleus of a donor. This procedure is not problematic for Buddhists since the transfer does not take place after a 'conception' ('descent of consciousness'). On the other hand, up to now currently the procedure still causes a great number of miscarriages[11] that Buddhists describe as deaths of human beings. But will the cloning procedure, if generally accompanied by loss of embryo or foetus be itself called a 'killing'? To find an answer Buddhists examine the *intentions* of the cloning parties. Should the intentions of couples and physicians using cloning as a method of artificial procreation be judged as 'intentions to kill'? Somparn Promta, member of the Bioethics Advisory Board of the Thai National Health Foundation, puts emphasis on the fact that the intention is directed towards creating a new being. The whole act is therefore governed by the motive of bringing something to life,[12] which could be interpreted as something positive. However, Huimin Bhikkhu, fully ordained Buddhist monk and Professor at the Taipei National University, argues that it is a serious misdeed to allow any action to be accompanied by the death of an embryo.[13]

But visionaries say the technique itself might change in the future. If humans could be cloned by so-called "embryo splitting", and if this technique could be perfected to a method without additional losses, it could be theoretically used as another argument in favour of a more permissive position.

2. Cloning for Research Purposes

The case of so-called 'therapeutic cloning' seems to be for many Buddhists much clearer. Since there is not the direct advantage of bringing

---

[11]   Not to speak of the recent disappointment triggered by the poor health of cloned animals.

[12]   See *S. Promta*, A Buddhist View of Cloning, The Nation, December 14, 2001, 5. Cf. *idem*, Moral Issues in Human Cloning. A Buddhist Perspective (2002), online: http://www.thainhf.org/Bioethics/Document/aoy.pdf (Thai); English translation: Moral Issues in Human Cloning. A Buddhist Perspective (2002, typoscript, via mail: 05.08.03).

[13]   Huimin (Bhikkhu), Buddhist Bioethics: The Case of Human Cloning and Embryo Stem Cell Research, Chung-Hwa Buddhist Journal 15 (2002), 457.

to life a new being, but merely an instance of taking life with rather uncertain effect for others, they tend to apply here the precept of abstaining from killing.

That one being will be deprived of his chances, namely, to live a happy life and to reach the spiritual goal, only for the sake of the welfare of others, will be an unbearable situation especially for many *Mahāyāna* Buddhists who strive for "all beings to be happy and free from suffering".[14]

An 'embryonic sacrifice' for the sake of better treatment for severe diseases is something that many Buddhists do not support. At first glance there might be a possible comparison of the idea of sacrifice for the sake of others in the Mah y na Ideal of the compassionate Bodhisattva. Spiritually developed Mah y na Buddhists might understand themselves as acting in the role of a Bodhisattva, helping the sick by offering themselves in self-sacrifice.[15] But in crucial aspects the two situations are not comparable. The Bodhisattva is able to *choose* to sacrifice himself. He knows the recipient of his donation, which makes this intentional action a noble one. But if a human clone is made only for the purpose to be sacrificed, he is *not intentionally choosing* to be a donor for the sake of others. And without a good intention on his part there is, for Buddhists, no good deed here to be found.

Even more so, if a clone is merely used to provide spare organs or tissues for an existent individual: A Buddhist will certainly express his or her rejection of such a use of a human being.

V. Conclusion

Biomedical research in countries like Thailand, Vietnam, China, Taiwan, Korea, and Japan, is at present in many aspects neck-and-neck with the research done in the Western world. The situation occurs that some Buddhists in these countries no longer seek ethical or legal solu-

---

[14] *R.Y. Nakasone*, What can Buddhism Offer Biomedical Ethics? Bukky gaku Kenky 47 (1991) 1, 14. Cf. *idem*, The Opportunity of Cloning, in M.C. Brannigan (ed.), Ethical Issues in Human Cloning: Cross-disciplinary Perspectives (2001), 95.

[15] See e.g. *H. Durt*, Two Interpretations of Human-flesh Offering: Misdeed or Supreme Sacrifice, Journal of the International College for Advanced Buddhist Studies 1 (1998), 236.

tions based solely on Western ethical or anthropological assumptions. Moreover, the rise of post-colonial self-consciousness in combination with high admiration for scientific achievements, sometimes encouraged by substantial interest in profit, might lead some Buddhists in these countries to postpone further ethical discussions in order to progress with cloning.

Nevertheless it seems to be difficult to find out whether Asian policy makers or biomedical researchers refer to their Buddhist cultural or anthropological presuppositions in a sincere, authentic manner or not. One has to count with the possibility that a reference to a certain "cultural attitude" shall merely serve the purpose to legitimise permissive action-guides. In this case it would be an "instrumentalisation" of cultural facts.

A recent example may illustrate this difficulty. The Korean cloning specialist Woo Suk Hwang published in the Science magazine (February 2004) the revolutionary outcome of his cloning experimentation resulting in the extraction or establishment of a stem cell line gained from a cloned human blastocyst.[16] Hwang stated in various interviews, his experimentation ought to be ethically in line with (his) Buddhist faith: „I am a Buddhist, and I have no philosophical problem with cloning. And as you know, the basis of Buddhism is that life is recycled through reincarnation. In some ways, I think, therapeutic cloning restarts the circle of life".[17] In this statement as well as in other comments Hwang tries to define "therapeutic cloning" as "reproductive cloning," which is admissible only as a mere *description* of the *first phase* of cloning procedures. Nevertheless, the ethical question arises with the interruption of the development of an embryo (for research purposes etc.), a fact that is concealed when both cloning concepts are lumped together. Indeed, it is difficult to ascertain if Hwang's convictions are based on principal Buddhist beliefs. But it is highly questionable that Hwang's comments can be brought in line with common Buddhist ethical reflections, if by him the 'factum brutum,' the intentional killing of an embryo, is not acknowledged. At least, it would be necessary for a 'Buddhist' argumentation, to give either evidence that this killing shall serve a higher purpose, or that it is

---

[16] *W.S. Hwang et al.*, Evidence of a Human Embryonic Stem Cell Line Derived from A Cloned Blastocyst, www.sciencexpress.org [10.1126/science.1094515]; February 12, 2004.

[17] *W.S. Hwang* in C. Dreifus, 2 Friends, 242 Eggs and a Breakthrough: A Conversation with Woo Suk Hwang and Shin Yong Moon, New York Times (February 17, 2004), www.nytimes.com/2004/02/17/science/17CONV.html

purpose, or that it is not an instance of killing at all, for example, because the 'consciousness-principle' is descending at the moment of nidation.

A quick look at the first legal regulation on human cloning in an Asian
country where Buddhism plays an important role, namely, Japan,
shows that the law is far from a clear ban. The 'Human Cloning Regulation Act', enabled in November 2000, is widely seen as allowing some
possible applications. It neither prohibits all cloning techniques, nor
does it regulate all possible ways of implanting cloned embryos into the
uterus (compare Jiro Nudeshima's as well as Tade Mathias Spranger's
interpretations[18,19]). But most interestingly, as Masahiro Morioka
pointed out recently, Article 2 of the Supplementary Provisions uses the
wording "sprout (or bud) of human life" (Jap.: *hito no seimei no hoga*)[20]
for the (possible) human somatic clone embryo, thereby evoking a
somewhat religious connotation. It may show a vitalist understanding
of the clone embryo as a *potential* human being.

Anyhow, the role of Japanese Buddhists in the legal procedures seems
to be rather small so far. But that may not be taken as a sign of a permissive attitude. It may demonstrate only a certain reserve toward legal
regulations.

In Thailand, various Buddhists in relevant positions (Bioethics-
Committee-members, physicians, Government Officials, and Buddhist
scholar-monks) expressed that it will not be easy to implement a formal

---

[18] *J. Nudeshima*, Human Cloning Legislation in Japan, Eubios Journal of
Asian and International Bioethics 11 (2001), 2.

[19] For example, the transfer of human split embryo, i.e., an embryo produced by a split of a human fertilized embryo or a human embryonic clone embryo outside a human uterus into an uterus of a human is not prohibited (*T.M.
Spranger*, The Japanese Approach to the Regulation of Human Cloning, Biotechnology Law Report 5 (2001) 700, 701), referring to Art. 4-5 of the The Law
Concerning Regulation Relating to Human Cloning Techniques and Other Similar Techniques (No 146/2000; a provisional English translation can be found
at: http://www.mext.go.jp/a_menu/ shinkou/seimei/eclone.pdf).

[20] Compare the provisional translation of the law No 146/2000 (see previous note), 13. The Japanese bioethicist *Masahiro Morioka* (Osaka University)
said in a lecture at the DFG-Conference Cross-Cultural Issues in Bioethics:
The Example of Human Cloning, Bochum, December 5, 2003, that in his eyes
the English translation of the law, which uses "the beginning of a human life"
instead of "bud of a human life" fails to take account of the religious connota-
tions that the latter may have for Japanese.

ban on cloning into Thai law. On the international scale, however, the Thai delegate to the UN-Legal-Committee for the possible convention draft against human cloning, Manasvi Srisodapol, voted simultaneously for a ban of reproductive cloning and, on the other hand, in favour of formulating 'appropriate guidelines' for therapeutic cloning. This position, he commented, would be in line with the Bioethics Committee in his home country.[21]

A 'premature' ban on cloning[22] by the West and transnational organisations could possibly have an unwanted counter-effect. If Asian ethical and anthropological presuppositions are not taken into account, the implementation of a law against cloning might lead to just a temporarily tenable solution.

---

[21] "The Thai National Centre for Genetic Engineering and Biotechnology had appointed a bio-ethics team to develop appropriate guidelines for therapeutic cloning, which it was believed could provide important answers in the treatment of diseases," said *Srisodapol* according to a press release of the Fifty-seventh General Assembly (http://www.unhchr.ch/huricane/huricane.nsf/0/BCD26DF64D647DE4C1256C5A004F55FF?opendocument), 6th Committee's 17th Meeting on 18 October 2002.

[22] E.g. a ban that is without further 'incultured' explanations based on the idea of dignity, as, for example, is the case in para. 11 of the UNESCO's Universal Declaration on the Human Genome and Human Rights (declared 11/1997, reprinted in the annex of this volume, under II 13).

The Jewish Perspective on Cloning

Manfred Oeming, Heidelberg[*]

I. Ancient Jewish Principles of Ethics and Medical Ethics

In order to understand the modern Jewish perspective on the cloning of human beings[1] – this perspective is quite homogenous despite the many and great differences and discussions within Judaism – we must comprehend the basics of Old Testament and Jewish ethics. Ten basic ethical assumptions, which will be listed below, inform the ethical evaluation of cloning from a Jewish point of view.

1. Jewish ethics rests on two main pillars: the Hebrew Bible, or Tenach, and the rabbinic Tradition, especially the Talmud but also the so-called Responses, i.e. the answers given by valued rabbinic teachers throughout the ages – answers to questions of Halacha, of ethical actions in everyday life. Because they predate modern science, genetics does not fall within the scope of the majority of these texts, and they thus do not speak directly to the ethical implications of cloning by genetic engineering. Whether cloning should be allowed, and to what degree, cannot be

---

[*]   I write this article as a Christian theologian and an Old Testament scholar but with a lot of sympathy for the Jewish position.

[1]   See *R. Cole-Turner*, Human Cloning. Religious Responses (1997); *Y. Nordmann*, Zwischen Leben und Tod – Aspekte der jüdischen Medizinethik (2nd ed., 2000); *B. Freedman*, Duty and Healing, Foundations of a Jewish Bioethic (1999); *J.R. Cohen*, In God's Garden, Creation and Cloning in Jewish Thought, Hastings Center Report 4 (1999), 7-12; National Bioethics Advisory Commission (ed.), Ethical Issues in Human Stem Cell Research, Vol. III, Religious Perspectives (2000); *F. Rosner*, Biomedical Ethics and Jewish Law (2001); *J.H. Evans*, Playing God? Human Genetic Engineering and the Rationalization of Public Bioethics (2002).

decided on the basis of these texts alone. All answers to current issues must be drawn by contemporary rabbinic leaders as continuation and logical explication of these two ancient main pillars. As experts in this tradition, the rabbinical authorities are responsible for ensuring that current ethical decisions are made in the spirit of Moses as the original recipient of revelation. The argumentative flow within Jewish medical ethics is often hard to understand for those on the outside; it is full of detours and many references, incomprehensible to non-rabbis. These, however, are a direct result of the intimate connection to a tradition that has its ultimate starting point at Mount Sinai.

2. All medical issues must be based on the principle of *piku'ach nefesch* (hebr. = "rescue of a soul, saving a life"). This principle states that all other commandments are void in the face of a life-threatening situation: whether Sabbath, purity, or ritual – all religious taboos are unimportant when a human life faces immediate danger.[2] This reveals a central principle of the Jewish religion, the belief that human life possesses holiness as well as absolute, inviolable and infinite value.[3] Lord Immanuel Jakobovits (1921-1999), former Chief rabbi of Great Britain and expert in the area of the Jewish medical ethics, formulated an appropriate description of this old principle: "… the value of human life is infinite and beyond measure, then that any part of life – if only a hour or even one second – is of precisely the same worth as seventy years of it, just as any fraction of infinity, being indivisible, remains infinite. Accordingly, to kill a decrepit patient approaching death constitutes exactly the same crime of murder as to kill a young, healthy person who may quietly have many decades to live".[4] But the question is: When does life begin?[5]

---

[2]   There are three exceptions: idolatry, fornication, and murder: Babylonian Talmud Joma 82b; Pessachim 25a-b; Sanherdrin 74a.

[3]   See e.g. *M.D. Tendler*, Medical Ethics, A compendium of Jewish Moral (1975).

[4]   *I. Jakobovits*, Medical Experimentation on Humans in Jewish Law, in F. Rosner/J.D. Bleich (eds.), Jewish Bioethics (1979), 379; see *id.*, Jewish Medical Ethics. A Comparative And Historical Study Of The Jewish Religious Attitude To Medicine And Its Practice (1975).

[5]   For the Old Testament traditions see *H. Utzschneider*, Der Beginn des Lebens – Die gegenwärtige Diskussion um die Bioethik und das Alte Testament, Zeitschrift für Evangelische Ethik 46 (2002), 135-143; *M. and H. Köckert*, Ungeborenes Leben in Exodus 21, 22-25, Wandlungen im Verständnis eines Rechtssatzes, in: Hübner/ Laudien/Zachhuber (eds.), Lebenstechnologie und Selbstverständnis. Hintergründe einer aktuellen Debatte, Religion – Staat –

3. The point of the beginning of life is disputed among the rabbis. The usual answer is: Life begins with the first breath the newborn takes. Others argue that life starts when the main part of an embryo comes out of the mother's body:

> Our Rabbis taught: How far does one search? Until [one reaches] his nose. Some say: Up to his heart. If one searches and finds those above to be dead, one must not assume those below are surely dead. Once it happened that those above were dead and those below were found to be alive. Are we to say that these Tannaim dispute the same as the following Tannaim? For it was taught: From where does the formation of the embryo commence? From its head, as it is said: Thou art he that took me out of my mother's womb, and it is also said: Cut off thy hair and cast it away. (Babylonian Talmud, Tractate Joma, 85a)

A third position declares that the newborn child has a special status: it is not really capable of surviving until the thirtieth day after the birth.

> It was taught, R. Simeon b. Gamaliel said: Any human being who lives thirty days is not a nefel (= miscarriage), because it is said, and those that are to be redeemed of them from a month old shalt thou redeem. An animal [which lives] eight days is not a nefel, for it is said, and from the eighth day and henceforth it shall be accepted for an oblation, etc. This implies that if it [an infant] does not last [so long], it is doubtful. (Babylonian Talmud, Tractate Sabbath 135b)

In the end there is a discussion between the roman emperor Marcus Antonius and rabbi Jehuda ha Nassi:

> Antoninus also said to Rabbi, 'When is the soul placed in man; as soon as it is decreed [that the sperm shall be male or female, etc.], or when [the embryo] is actually formed?' He replied, 'From the moment of formation.' He objected: 'Can a piece of meat be unsalted for three days without becoming putrid? But it must be from the moment that [God] decrees [its destiny].' Rabbi said: This thing Antoninus taught me, and Scripture supports him, for it is written, and thy decree hath preserved my spirit [i.e., my soul].

> Antoninus also enquired of Rabbi, 'From what time does the Evil Tempter hold sway over man; from the formation [of the embryo], or from [its] issuing forth [into the light of the world]?! — 'From the formation,' he replied. 'If so,' he objected, 'it would rebel in its

Kultur, Interdisziplinäre Studien aus der Humboldt-Universität zu Berlin 3 (2004), 43-73.

mother's womb and go forth. But it is from when it issues.' Rabbi said: This thing Antoninus taught me, and Scripture supports him, for it is said, at the door [i.e., where the babe emerges] sin lieth in wait. (Babylonian Talmud, Tractate Sanhedrin 91b)

This indicates that in a small group of rabbis (partly influenced by Greek conceptions of prenatal existence of the soul) taught that in the moment of the divine decree to create the world the existence of each person was "created" by the thought of God. This is the fundamental talmudic reference for later reflections on the status of prenatal beings.

4. But in every case it is clear that the status of the unborn foetus is not that of a person. Before the birth it belongs to the mother, is part of her property. In case of violation it is necessary to pay her compensation. The lucid biblical basis for this point of view is Ex 21:22-25:

> If men struggle with each other and strike a woman with child so that she has a miscarriage, yet there is no *further* injury, he shall surely be fined as the woman's husband may demand of him, and he shall pay as the judges *decide*. But if there is *any further* injury, then you shall appoint life for life, eye for eye, tooth for tooth, hand for hand, foot for foot, burn for burn, wound for wound, bruise for bruise.

The person who caused the spontaneous abortion of the foetus is in no respect a murderer; it is a case of physical injury of the mother.

5. Conception is understood to have occurred only after the fertilised egg has securely found a place in the uterus. Outside this environment the embryo is considered to be practically nothing. The ethical principle probably most important for our discussion is contained in the statement that a fertilised egg must have nested in the uterus for at least 40 days (for a male) or 80 days (for a female), before it can be considered a developing human being. In the Babylonian Talmud, Berachot 47b one finds the clearest reference:

> Which is a first born both [in respect] of inheritance and of redemption from a priest? If [a woman] discharges a sac full of water or full of blood or an abortion consisting of a bag full of many-coloured substance; if [a woman] discharges something like fish or locusts or reptiles, or creeping things, or if she discharges on the fortieth day [of conception][6], [the infant] which follows after [these discharges] is

---

[6] To the expression "fortieth day" the Soncino-Edition of the Babylonian Talmud notes: "Because until the morrow of the fortieth day of conception the

a firstborn both [in respect] of inheritance and redemption from a priest. Neither a foetus extracted by means of the caesarian section nor the infant which follows is either a first born for inheritance or a firstborn to be redeemed from a priest.

In the tractate Nidah 30a/b we can read another text supporting the position:

> R. Ishmael ruled [if she miscarried on] the first forty-eight days she continues [her periods of uncleanness and cleanness] for male as for menstruant etc. It was taught: R. Ishmael stated, scripture prescribed uncleanness and cleanness in respect of a male and it also prescribed uncleanness and cleanness in respect of a female, as in the case of the former his fashioning period corresponds to his unclean and clean periods so also in the case of the latter her fashioning period corresponds to her unclean and clean periods. They replied: The duration of the fashioning period cannot be derived from that of uncleanness. Furthermore, they said to R. Ishmael, a story is told of Cleopatra the queen of Alexandria that when her handmaids were sentenced to death by royal decree they were subjected to a test and it was found that both [a male and a female embryo] were fully fashioned on the forty-first day. He replied: I bring you proof from the Torah and you bring proof from some fools! But what was his 'proof from the Torah'? If it was the argument, 'Scripture prescribed uncleanness and cleanness in respect of a male and it also prescribed uncleanness and cleanness in respect of a female etc.', have they not already replied, 'The duration of the fashioning period cannot be derived from that of uncleanness'? — The Scriptural text says, she bear, scripture thus doubles the ante-natal period in the case of a female. But why [should the test spoken of by the Rabbis be described as] 'proof from some fools'? — It might be suggested that the conception of the female preceded that of the male by forty days. And the Rabbis? — They were made to drink a scattering drug and R. Ishmael? — Some constitution is insusceptible to a drug. Then said R. Ishmael to them: A story is told of Cleopatra the Grecian queen that when her handmaids were sentenced to death under a government order they were subjected to a test and it was found that a male embryo was fully fashioned on the forty-first day and a female embryo on the eighty-first day. They replied: No one adduces proof from fools. What is the reason? — It is possible that the handmaid with the fe-

---

foetus is considered as mere water, an embryo taking more than forty days to form."

male delayed [intercourse] for forty days and that it was only then that conception occurred. And R. Ishmael? — They were placed in the charge of a warden. And the Rabbis? — There is no guardian against unchastity; and the warden himself might have intercourse with them. But is it not possible that if a surgical operation had been performed on the forty-first day the female embryo also might have been found in a fully fashioned condition like the male? — Abaye replied: They were equal as far as these distinguishing marks were concerned.

Should a woman lose the embryo by miscarriage before day 40, then this embryo is considered to be "mere water" ([Aramaic]: *maja be'ama*)![7] The woman is not considered ritual impure and the miscarried embryo must not be buried. The requirement of 40 days is arbitrary; there are no recognisable reasons for this demarcation line, only the general symbolism of forty days (and nights) in the bible: it is the period before the beginning of something very important (e.g. the duration of the flood according to [Gen 7:4], the waiting of Moses for the revelation of the tora [Ex 24;18]; the wanderings of Elija to the mount of God [1 Ki 19:8]).

The problem of abortion is sometimes connected with this "deadline".[8] But usually the decision for or against abortion is separated from this period of 40 days and must be decided by a completely different argumentation, e.g. the protection of the mother or the survivability of the severely handicapped newborn. In the orthodox halachic tradition abortion is especially forbidden because of the principle *sh'chatat zerah*[9] *(hebr.* = "spill , destruction of the seed"; cf. Gen 38:4-10).

---

[7]   Jevamot 69b; Nidda 30b; Keritot 1: 3.

[8]   Cf. *A. Wiedner*, Abortion in the first forty Days, in Roodyn (ed.), Pathways in Medicine (1995), 136-138; *Nordmann*, supra note 1, 46.

[9]   See *J.D. Bleich*, Abortion in Halakhic Literature, in Contemporary Halakhic Problems, Vol. I (1977), 325-371; *B. Herring*, Abortion, in Jewish Ethics and Halacha for Our Times — Sources and Commentary, Vol. I (1984), 25-45; *F. Rosner*, The Jewish Attitude Toward Abortion, The Morality of Abortion, in Studies in Torah Judaism: Modern Medicine and Jewish Law (1972), 53-88; *I. Jakobovits*, Jewish views on abortion, Human Life Review 22 (1996), 55 – 64.

6. For all religious, ritual and ethical discussion there is an important boundary, the capacity of the human eye. There can be no (moral) responsibility for that which cannot be seen with the naked eye.[10]

7. All ethical decisions must be informed by a careful and rational deliberation of possible consequences. Jewish ethics is, without a doubt, informed by a utilitarian aspect: if I accept certain risks, then I must be sure that these risks are worth taking. On the other hand, if the expected benefits of a certain action far outweigh possible risks, then this action is ethically permissible, even necessary.

8. The world view of the Old Testament is anti-mythological and anti-magical. Already in early Judaism, the explanation of the world is noticeably rational, informed primarily by causality: everything has its reason. M. Weber spoke correctly of an "Old Testament rationalism"[11] and of an "elimination of the magic world by older Jewish prophecy."[12] We need only remember the creation account in Gen 1, where the text speaks of sun and moon.[13] These objects are not gods, not powers with a will of their own as in all religions of the surrounding Ancient Near East; they are simply luminescent bodies, giant lamps to light day and night. What an incredible degree of rationalism! Demons and gods are removed from nature. Nature is not determined by a plurality of personal powers. There is only *one* God who has dethroned all others.

9. A central concept of Old Testament anthropology is the concept of *imago dei*, i.e. the idea that human beings are made in the image of God! Everyone is an image of God. The interpretation of this concept is a matter of debate within rabbinic tradition as well as current scholarship:[14] Some understand it in a final sense: God has completed his crea-

---

[10] Of course the halachic decisions of modern rabbis integrate the discoveries of microbiology but only partly and very hesitantly.

[11] *M. Weber*, Gesammelte Aufsätze zur Religionssoziologie I, (1920), 122; Gesammelte Aufsätze zur Religionssoziologie III, 415.

[12] *Weber*, Religionssoziologie I, loc. cit., 94; cf. *W. Schluchter*, Religion u. Lebensführung II, Studien zu Max Webers Religions- und Herrschaftssoziologie (1991), 127-196.

[13] "Then God said, 'Let there be lights in the expanse of the heavens to separate the day from the night, and let them be for signs, and for seasons, and for days and years; and let them be for lights in the expanse of the heavens to give light on the earth'; and it was so."

[14] Cf. *C. Dohmen*, Die Statue von Tell Fecherije und die Gottebenbildlichkeit des Menschen, Ein Beitrag zur Bilderterminologie, Biblische Notizen 22 (1983), 91-106; *W. Groß*, Die Gottebenbildlichkeit des Menschen nach Gen 1,

tion ("In the beginning God created heaven and earth", Gen 1:1), and
one result of this completed creation is humans in the image of God. A
different understanding, promoted primarily by Rashi, interprets creation as a beginning (In the beginning of the creation of heaven and earth
...): In the process of ongoing creation God made humans his partners,
his long arm, his stewards carrying out his mandate. The special dignity
of every human being is realised in that. He has the honour of contributing to and continuing God's creation. The creation account is a basic
statement on the right, even the duty, to develop natural science and
technology. From this point of view, the Christian attitude is an uptight
view of science, continually afraid of interfering with sovereign areas of
God's rule. From a Jewish perspective, human beings do not make
themselves co-creators of God, do not play God, but God himself
makes them in his image. As images, humans must rule over nature,
study it dispassionately, and utilise their insights by developing technology. The Old Testament is a motor of scientific development.

10. God gives us the command: "Subdue the earth!" – this commandment contains a breathtaking empowerment, the so-called *Dominum
terrae*[15]. Human beings are lifted out of nature. They remain part of it
but stand over and against it and shall rule over it. As a Christian and an

---

26.27 in der Diskussion des letzten Jahrzehnts, Studien zur Priesterschrift und
zu alttestamentlichen Gottesbildern, Stuttgarter biblische Aufsatzbände 30
(1993/1999), 37-54; *M. Welker*, Person, Menschenwürde und Gottebenbildlichkeit, Jahrbuch für biblische Theologie 15 (2000), 247 - 262.

[15]   On the discussion over this (often misunderstood) term see *N. Lohfink*,
"Macht euch die Erde untertan"?, Studien zum Pentateuch, Stuttgarter bibli-
sche Aufsatzbände 4 (1988), 11, 28; *K. Koch*, Gestaltet die Erde, doch heget das
Leben! Einige Klarstellungen zum dominium terrae in Gen 1, in Spuren des
hebräischen Denkens, Beiträge zur alttestamentlichen Theologie, Gesammelte
Aufsätze, Vol. 1 (1991), 223-237; *C. Uehlinger*, Vom dominium terrae zu einem
Ethos der Selbstbeschränkung? Alttestamentliche Einsprüche gegen einen ty-
rannischen Umgang mit der Schöpfung, Bibel und Liturgie 64 (1991), 59-74; *U.
Rüterswörden*, Dominium terrae, Studien zur Genese einer alttestamentlichen
Vorstellung, Beihefte zur Zeitschrift für die alttestamentliche Wissenschaft 215
(1993); *B. Janowski*, Herrschaft über die Tiere, Gen 1, 26-28 und die Semantik
von rdh, in Die rettende Gerechtigkeit, Beiträge zur Theologie des Alten Tes-
taments 2 (1999), 33-48; *M. Weippert*, Tier und Mensch in einer menschenarmen
Welt, Zum sog. dominium terrae in Genesis 1, in Mathys (ed.), Ebenbild Gottes
- Herrscher über die Welt, Studien zu Würde und Auftrag des Menschen, Bib-
lisch-theologische Studien 33 (1998), 35-55. It was shown that with this expression is meant a respectful and protecting attitude regarding the other creatures
of God.

Old Testament scholar, I have always been proud of this honour given to us by God as his co-creators.[16] I understand the Bible to have placed us in a superior realm of freedom.

II. Modern Consequences of These Ethical Principles for the Issue of Cloning

Reproductive cloning as well as therapeutic cloning and interference into the germ course, thus the medical-technical manipulation of the hereditary property of future generations, are the "hottest iron" of biotechnology and are subject – still – to an almost world-wide ethical and religious taboo. Not so in Israel and in Judaism. The Israeli and Jewish attitude is remarkably liberal.[17] That is justified in the antique principles described above and relatively well comprehensible: The rational, pro-scientific world view of the Old Testament results in a large degree of religious openness towards research, also within the area of genetics. When human beings change the structure of genes in order to improve creation, this is not arrogance, but the consequence of our empowerment to co-develop creation (*imago dei*).[18] It is not an interference in the sphere of God, forbidden by religious taboos, but the fulfillment of a divine commandment (*dominum terrae*). Genetical screening, in vitro fertilisation as well as pre-implantation diagnostics are not an ethical problem; on the contrary, many rabbis even recommend their use.[19]

In regards to cloning, however, action must be bound by two important limitations: the *dignity of every human being* must be protected. It can

---

[16]   See *M. Welker*, What is Creation? Reading Genesis 1 and 2, Theology today 48 (1991), 56-124.

[17]   For the legal situation in Israel see *G. Ben-Or*, The Israeli Approach to Cloning and Embryonic Research, Heidelberg Journal of International Law 60 (2000), 763-770.

[18]   *M. Welker*, Schöpfung und Wirklichkeit, Neukirchener Beiträge zur Systematischen Theologie 13 (1995).

[19]   For genetic screening and cloning see *Rosner*, supra note 1, 205-218; also *M.D. Tendler*, author of the classical monograph Medical Ethics – A compendium of Jewish Moral (1975), is a proponent of genetic engineering as stem-cell research (see e.g. http://www.jewishsf.com/bk010223/sfastemcell.shtml; http://reason.com/ ml/ml051701.shtml).

never be permissible to genetically engineer a human being for use as "spare parts" and as a perfect organ donor for his genetic twin. Genetic duplication is not a problem per se – nature also produces identical twins – but rather the misuse of the genetic twin as a resource. On the other hand, it would be completely irreconcilable with the dignity of the individual, if one would reduce him or her, images of God, to a certain function. It cannot be ethical to "breed" soldiers, farmers, or intellectuals. Whether to belong to a protecting, sustaining or teaching category of society is the decision of each individual and cannot be relegated to others. In conclusion we can say: using the chances created by cloning should be permissible as long as every cloned human being is guaranteed equal status with the non-cloned individual, with the same access to autonomy, rights and freedom. "Cloning, like all other technologies, is morally neutral. Its moral valence depends on how we use it."[20] But: in the face of the high risk of deformities and handicaps that reproductive cloning can produce, this procedure is – at the moment – out of discussion in Judaism.

But it is necessary to make a principal distinction between reproductive and therapeutic cloning! Therapeutic cloning is not as dangerous as reproductive cloning. Especially research with stem-cells can be used to fight against such diseases as diabetes, Alzheimer's or cancer. The isolation and use of stem-cells can decrease suffering and save lives (*piku'ach nefesch*). Therapeutic cloning is thus not an ethical problem; on the contrary, intensive research into genetic therapy is demanded by religion. Isolating stem-cells is ethically permissible as this occurs far earlier than the boundary of day 40 stated in the Talmud. The use of fertilised eggs before their attachment to the uterus is no problem at all. Clumps of cells (zygotes) are pre-embryos and do not have the ethical status of personhood. According to the argumentation that every embryo has no special status especially during the first 40 days and is not protected per se, then – from a Jewish point of view – it is much better to perform research on him and to detect therapeutical possibilities and to save lives than to destroy him without any benefit for humankind.

---

[20]   *E. Dorff*, cited according to http://mishkantorah.org/parasha/5763/ judaism_and_cloning.pdf. Cf. *M. Broyde*, Cloning People: A Jewish Law Analysis of the Issues, Connecticut Law Review 30 (1998), 503, 532-533, arguing that, once the technical complexities of human cloning are resolved, human cloning will be another form of assisted reproduction and is likely to be permitted by Jewish law.

A Jewish point of view expects many medical blessings from genetic engineering; risks undoubtedly created by this process can be justified in light of the utilitarian balance of cost and benefit. This is even clearer than with genetically modified seeds in agriculture: human genetic engineering is clearly limited. Whereas genetically modified corn may spread its seed over an area of 20 miles, thus genetically contaminating wide ranges of land, human genetic engineering is limited to one person.

According to the Old Testament traditions and the Jewish law, the dangers of misuse and malformations do not justify a total ban on therapeutic cloning![21]

---

[21]   In spite of the fact that official proclamations of the protestant and the catholic churches declare strict opposition against any research with embryonic stem-cells, there are different voices from other theologians, see e.g. *R. Anselm/U. Körtner* (eds.), Streitfall Biomedizin, Orientierung in christlicher Verantwortung (2003).

Christianity and Western Philosophy

Robert Spaemann, Stuttgart

I am not a theologian, but the Christian perspective on moral questions is not, in itself, specifically Christian. That which *is* specifically Christian lies in one's motivation. Christianity bestows divine authority on that which everyone can understand through basic human intuition. St. Paul asserted that the commandments revealed on Mt. Sinai are written in the heart of every Gentile; each person knows fundamentally what is good and evil. Reflection on good and evil, then, is philosophical reflection – even when theologians are doing the reflecting. The Christian perspective implies creative order, an internal structure of reality which can be understood by any human who seeks in goodwill. Goodwill, however, cannot be substantiated once again because it is self-defining. Kant discussed the "fact of reason" that cannot be derived and has its pinnacle in the recognition of each human being as an end in himself. This necessitates an initial decision, by which we simultaneously decide on our own dignity.[1] Whoever would claim that certain humans could be left at the disposal of others, that they could be used as mere material, that in the *dominium terrae* they belong to the *terra* and are thus not themselves images of God – whoever would make such claims would thereby also exclude himself from the universal community of humanity. In Judeo-Christian terms, every human is an image of God. But what does this mean practically?

The term "person" has been used in more recent philosophy, particularly since Kant, to describe this status as an "end in itself." The term is

---

[1] In general to the notion of human dignity, see *R. Spaemann*, Begriff der Menschenwürde, in Böckenförde/Spaemann (eds.), Menschenrechte und Menschenwürde (1987), 295-313.

now often used in an interaction analysis, whereby personhood means that a human being, who is affected by another's action, is itself the address for justification. That is, whoever acts on another human must be able to justify this act in regard to this other human – not merely in regard to other humans, not with regards to a community, not in regard to a majority, but with regard to the very person affected. Practically, this defines "person." Yet the term "person" has also recently been used to replace "human rights" with "person rights" – as Norbert Hoerster suggested. Not every human is to be counted as a person. Rather, personhood requires certain characteristics: reason, self-awareness, a relationship to one's own biography. And all humans do not meet these criteria (for example, the severely mentally disabled, embryos, little children, as well as senile elderly and the sleeping).

Christianity, however, insists upon the extensive synonymity of the terms human and person, and there are reasons for this. It has always been present in the Judeo-Christian tradition. Cf. Psalm 22.11: "I was cast upon thee from the womb". This corresponds phenomenologically with our personal experience. The mother tells her child, "when I was pregnant with you"; one says, "I was conceived at such and such a time"; and no one says "at that time an organism was conceived, which later developed self-awareness and became me." On the contrary, the word "I" means exactly that human being, that biological organism, which can (after having come to a certain awareness) speak of itself as "I." Saying "I" does not refer to some abstract "I" but to a particular human being. It can even be that only others can tell me who I was and what happened to me. My mother tells me who I was then, or people tell me what I did as a small child. I do not remember, but it was I. Recognition as a person cannot depend on empirical criteria, because they are always debatable. One may assert, personhood begins with feeling, with perception; another might claim, it begins with the first form of self-awareness. Depending on the criterion, then, embryos would be protected from the third month or not until they are infants after birth or, according to Peter Singer, only after the second year of life. Entry into the community of persons would thus be understood as a sort of conferral of human dignity, a sort of co-optation: based on certain criteria, certain beings are co-opted into the human community. But to me it seems decisive for "person" status that it is obtained by virtue of ones own right, and that it not be conferred. It follows that the term "human" may not be defined; rather, whoever is conceived by humans must be considered a human, and thus a person. The moment a human organism begins existing, we must recognize it as a person. This is not a metaphysical postulation; instead, if follows from the person's status as a being that takes, by virtue of its own right, its rightful place in the community of persons.

The question we must answer, then, is whether or not cloning is reconcilable with the end-in-oneself quality of every individual human being. One argument against cloning suggests that the uniqueness of individuality is violated by copying. But the existence of identical twins makes this argument weak. Each monozygotic twin has a separate, own identity. A person's identity does not rest on structural uniformity of DNA. However, other reasons do render cloning irreconcilable with a human's quality as an end in her- or himself. Hans Jonas asserted an important reason. He protested that a clone is a delayed twin who will always be faced with a twin sibling, advanced in years. The clone's future is not open; it knows too much. The clone sees approximately how it will look in twenty years or which diseases it will develop, but how can he or she react? Perhaps it does not want this at all. Perhaps it will reject its own now-suspicious propensities and choose, in protest, a contrary way of life, simply to be unlike its model. Thereby, again, it is rendered indirectly – negatively – dependent on its model. Furthermore, a human's characteristics are always only what they are in a given biographical context of civilization. Someone with Beethoven's genetic structure, twenty years later, is not Beethoven. The clone of a famously generous philanthropist could, with the identical genetic constitution but in another situation and another environment, become an equally infamous criminal. The qualitative identity of genetic structure is a factor, the importance of which is only determined in relation to all other factors.

In my opinion, another reason speaks not only against cloning, but also against any genetic manipulation. We simply cannot take responsibility for the qualitative self-identity of a human being. If a human were to ask me, "how can you justify that I have this or that character trait, or that I look the way I do?" there would be no answer. Any discourse on justification presupposes humans with their own identities who already form a universal community of discourse. No one should be able to say, "you are how you are because I wanted it that way." One could, of course, respond that no human determines how she or he is. And if humans do not owe their qualitative identity to others, then they owe it to nature. Is that somehow better? The answer must be: yes, it *is* better. The organic naturalness of our qualitative identity is a requirement for fundamental equality among persons in human society. We all owe our existence to the same origin. And it would have grave consequences, if a human were the product of other humans, not only in a qualitative sense, but also with respect to basic existence. The latter pertains to *in vitro* fertilization – "forcing" a human into existence. Fundamentally, we cannot take responsibility for the existence or non-existence of a human. Regarding responsibility for non-existence, one derives the prohibition on killing. Yet the same holds true for responsibility for existence. Conception is not the purposeful production of a human. The formation of a human is the side-effect of an interaction, for which Gottfried Benn's words hold true: "Denkt doch nicht, daß ich an euch dachte als ich mit eurer Mutter ging, / ihre Augen wurden immer so schön bei der Liebe" ("do not think that I thought of you when I went with your mother, / her eyes always became so beautiful during love.") If a child were to consider its life unsuccessful and itself a failure and were to say to its father, "why did you bring me into existence?" the father could answer, "you were formed in the same way as every other human, by my interaction with your mother – that is, by nature." This answer would not be true, had the child been "produced" instead of conceived. There is a duty of justification, here, which no one can fulfill.

Modern forms of birth control have given the impression that there is now a qualification to this duty of justification for the conception or non-conception of a child. This is mistaken. Humans are still formed "by nature": one must *do* something, in order to prevent formation. Sometimes this is justifiable, sometimes not. But no justification is required in order to conceive a child. If one were required, there would not be any sufficient reason. For any justification presumes a community for discourse, but creating a member of this community cannot be sufficiently justified and need not be. The same standard for the determination of qualitative identity also applies to existence. Sloterdijk suggested that what can no longer be accomplished by upbringing should be realized through breeding – namely the propagation of certain ways of life. But ways of life are not propagated by breeding – they are passed on culturally, not genetically inherited. Certainly, one could genetically favor specific characteristics, but again one would face the above-mentioned objection to violating the equal status of persons. To replace upbringing with genetic manipulation would defeat the most important purpose of upbringing itself: the development of free self-determination.

I can reconcile myself to my own upbringing. I can say, "my parents did such and such with me." But Bertolt Brecht admonished not to ask what they made of me, but rather what I have made of that, which they made of me. With genetic manipulation, however, the person is already irreversibly (pre)determined by the very characteristics, to which he or she must reconcile him- or herself. They cannot be undone. The person could, of course, respond variously to the genetic structure but could never revise it. There can be emancipation from upbringing, but from breeding there is no emancipation. The breeder would always remain the master of the product. Moreover, these processes are only possible based on consumptive embryo-research. If these are forbidden, so too are those actions which can only be realized through consumptive embryo-research.

Part 2

Human Cloning from a Scientific Perspective

Human Cloning from a Scientific Perspective

Ernst-Ludwig Winnacker, Bonn

Clones are genetically identical individuals which arise through asexual or vegetative reproduction. The phenomenon of genetic identity is widespread in nature. Not only is vegetative reproduction the reproduction mechanism of choice most if not all single-cellular organisms, i.e. bacteria, yeasts and fungi, it is also active in higher plants when they reproduce through sprouting or budding. Even in mammals, and thus in people, clones exist naturally and are known as monozygotic twins. They arise through an accidental splitting process when the embryo tries to leave the *zona pellucida* at the 100-150 cell stage. If this slipping process is only partially completed, such that some cells remain within the *zona*, they can develop separately and independently parallel to the "main" embryo. The frequency of twin births is one in eighty-five, and one in ten twin births leads to identical twins. Thus approximately 4 - 8 million people among the existing human population represent identical twins. It is interesting to note that the natural frequency of identical individuals is constant within mammals at about 0.1 to 0.2% of all natural births, as if nature could not afford any higher values.

The process of embryo splitting can be used in farm animals to produce genetically identical offspring. The process is of little practical interest or significance since the numbers are limited and since the offspring has to be produced before knowledge about the exact properties of the developing animal can be ascertained.

These limitations changed dramatically with the successful introduction of nuclear transplantation technologies, exemplified by the birth of the sheep "Dolly" in July 1996.[1] Nuclear transplantation is defined as the introduction of a cell nucleus from an adult donor cell (a somatic cell with a full chromosomal complement) into an enucleated egg cell (oocyte). The process had been tried prior to "Dolly", in particular in the frog system, in order to prove the hypothesis that every cell of a mammalian organism carries a full chromosomal complement. These early experiments never resulted in the development of adult animals, but rather stopped at the tadpole stage.

Since "Dolly", nuclear transplantation (NT) experiments have been repeated successfully with many species, lately even with rats, but never with primates.[2] Common to all of these efforts is the observation that the process is and remains extremely inefficient and error-prone. The proportion of live offspring per NT embryo transferred can reach 50 % and more in cows, but, in general, does not exceed 1 – 2 %. In addition, those few animals that live to birth suffer from various abnormal phenotypes, i.e. placental abnormalities, fetal overgrowth and overweight, respiratory diseases, liver fibrosis, cardiac myopathies and many other defects. Even the sheep "Dolly" died prematurely after six years with symptoms of arthritis. The observed abnormalities can depend on the donor cell type used in the NT experiments. It has, for example, been shown[3] that animals derived from cumulus cell nuclei tend to be obese, or that, in the pig system, there are no placental abnormalities.

Interestingly enough, in cases where offspring could be produced from cloned animals, the observed deficiencies are not heritable, indicating that other than pure genetic mechanisms are at work in nuclear transplantation.

Such mechanisms do, in fact, exist. It is long known that the various cell types in a living organism carry the same genetic complement, yet they serve quite different functions. In order for a liver cell to work as a liver cell it has to activate a characteristic set of genes while other genes have to be turned off. In this way it is prevented that hair grows in the liver or that insulin is produced in the brain, even though these functions are potentially present in all cells. Genes can be classified as to their respective activities in different cell types. Housekeeping genes are needed for

---

[1]   *I. Wilmut/A.E. Schnieke et al.*, Viable offspring derived from fetal and adult mammalian cells, Nature 385 (1997), 810-813.

[2]   *C. Simerly et al.*, Science 300 (2003), 29, 7.

[3]   *K.L. Tamashiro et al.*, Cloned mice have an obese phenotype not transmitted to their offspring, Nature Med 8 (2002), 262-267.

activities common to all cells, for example for securing the energy supply. Tissue-specific genes are activated only in particular cell types and pluripotency genes are expressed exclusively in embryonic cells that are able to generate the wide variety of cell types which later make up the entire organism.

Genetic controls over gene function are exerted via genetic switches. These are stretches of DNA, usually situated in front of the gene itself, which signal to the genetic reading machinery whether it should read a gene into its protein equivalent or not. Silencing of genes occurs through chemical modifications along these switches. These include the transfer of methyl-groups onto CpG dinucleotides, the modification of histones and thus the overall structure of the genetic material. In order to fit into the cell nucleus the genetic material (DNA) has to be compressed, which is achieved by winding it around itself through the help of a set of proteins, called histones. In order for this highly compressed structure to become accessible for the genetic reading machinery, histones have to be chemically modified through phosphorylation.

All of these mechanisms are reversible. Otherwise it would not have been possible for the cloned sheep "Dolly" to originate. "Dolly" was produced through the transfer of a nucleus from a highly specialised udder cell into the cytoplasm of an enucleated egg cell. It thus had to be "reprogrammed" from a state compatible with that of an udder cell and its characteristic function into an embryonic state. In this state most tissue-specific genes are turned off while all the pluripotency genes are now turned on.

Apparently, this "reprogramming step" is highly inefficient and prone to errors. Presumably it occurs in a stochastic manner, such that only a small proportion of chimeric cells ever reaches a state appropriate for embryonic development to occur. In the past six years no mechanisms have been identified with which this "reprogramming" step could be influenced or improved in a directed manner. What is known however is that different cell types work better, i.e. more efficient than others. For example, cloning by nuclear transfer is 20-30 times more efficient from embryonic cells than from adult cells. This appears reasonable, since in embryonic cells most of the pluripotency genes will already be turned on and most tissue-specific genes will be turned off, thus requiring less "reprogramming" than adult cells. It has occasionally been proposed,[4] but not yet shown, that the genome of adult stem cells might

---

[4]   *K. Hochedlinger/R. Jaenisch*, Nuclear transplantation, embryonic stem cells, and the potential for cell therapy, N. Engl. J. Med 349 (2003), 275-286.

resemble that of embryonic cell types. Adult stem cells which have by now been identified for most differentiated adult cell types thus may be more amenable to reprogramming than adult cells.

A particular type or set of reversible modifications of a given cell is called its genetic imprint. In contrast to genetic changes which lead to mutations, these reversible modifications are known as epigenetic modifications.[5]

In principle, everything which has been said also applies to our species. Thus cloning of human beings through nuclear transfer technologies must be regarded as feasible. However, apart from many ethical and moral reasons which are described elsewhere in this book, the described uncertainties and inefficiencies alone speak convincingly against such applications. Intentions to try this out regardless of such concerns, up to announcements that cloned babies have actually been born, continue to gratify the emotional and sensational urges of certain people. Fortunately enough such announcements have so far turned out to be fabrications.

In addition to the use of NT technologies to produce a cloned embryo, NT technologies have been proposed for cell therapeutic applications. In this mode, cloned embryos would not be implanted into the uterus of a female organism, but instead used to generate autologous embryonic stem cell lines. These, in turn, would be outgrown into functional cells which can be used in cellular therapies. This latter procedure is called "therapeutic cloning", in contrast to the term "reproductive cloning" which describes the cloning of individual organisms.

"Therapeutic cloning" is often mentioned together with another problem of cell therapies, namely the problem of immunological rejection of allogeneic (foreign) transplants. Embryonic stem cells derived from a person other than the patient to be treated are recognised as foreign and rejected unless the patient is immunosuppressed. However, embryonic stem cells produced by nuclear transplantation from the patient's own cells are genetically identical, thus eliminating the risk of immune rejection. There is one caveat however. The cytoplasm of the enucleated recipient egg cell (oocyte) contains mitochondria which, in turn, carry a small genome of their own. The protein products of this genome are not products derived from the patients own genome but are foreign to them. Since the number of these proteins is small it is expected that they

---

5   W. Shi/V. Zakhartchenko/E. Wolf, Epigenetic reprogramming in mammalian nuclear transfer, Differentiation 71 (2003), 91-113.

will not induce immunological incompatibility. Whether this is correct or not remains to be seen.

In the mouse system, the various experimental prerequisites for "therapeutic cloning" have been developed. Thus, protocols have been established to differentiate murine embryonic stem cells into functional cells of many specificities. These protocols entail the use of growth and differentiation factors which are normally used in the genesis of functional cells and organs. In addition, it has been possible to generate nuclear transfer embryonic stem cells in the mouse through the use of nuclei from various somatic cell types and, even more importantly, to coax these chimaeric embryos into functionally differentiated cells. Moreover, the group around R. Jaenisch (MIT; reference 4) has been able to use such embryonic cell lines to treat mice with certain genetic defects. Thus, in principle, this cell therapeutic approach appears feasible.

In order for these technologies to be applied to human patients a number of technical prerequisites have to be fulfilled. First of all, the cell line populations must be defined, if they are not homogeneous, and they must be safe. The safety issue relates to the bad experiences with the nuclear transfer technology process as it affects the health and yield of cloned animals. It is often argued that since abnormal fetal development is the most important inadequacy observed in cloned laboratory or farm animals this problem should not be relevant to "therapeutic cloning" since it occurs in the absence of any fetus and therefore of fetal development. This is certainly correct. However, it is not clear whether reprogramming does not affect other parameters of cell development which are significant for the use of therapeutic applications, i.e. the question whether such cells gain oncogenic potential during their selection procedure or whether they eventually display signs of premature aging of an extent which precludes any practical use of such cells. It will be extremely difficult to exclude these concerns convincingly. Thus, although I regard nuclear transfer technologies as important and indispensable research tools for cell biology and for differentiation processes, I consider them a delusion as far as therapeutic applications are concerned.

There are additional problems with "therapeutic cloning". One of these concerns the donation of egg cells. Egg cells are not abundant in the human female and have to be obtained by superovulation. This hormone induction process carries a small but significant risk of infertility in the range of 2 to 4%. Whether such a risk can be waved by an individual decision remains to be seen and to be discussed. Schöler et al.[6] have recently shown that mouse embryonic stem cells in culture can develop into oogonia that enter meiosis, i.e. recruit adjacent cells to form follicle-like structures, and later develop into blastocysts. It is not yet clear whether such cells can be fertilised. If, eventually, the donation of egg cells could be circumvented the ethical issues surrounding egg cell donation would of course disappear.

A final difficulty regarding the use of therapeutic cloning relates to the fact that both, therapeutic as well as reproductive cloning, use the same cellular intermediate. One method is to transplant it into the uterus of a female organism, another is culture *in-vitro* to grow out into embryonic stem cell lines. Once these technologies have been optimised, the temptation to utilise a reproductive rather than a therapeutic approach must be paramount and hence difficult to control. Therefore both procedures should be banned together.

Such a decision may be simplified by the expectation that future scientific progress may provide alternatives. One potential alternative to the use of nuclear transfer embryonic stem cells may be adult stem cells. Adult stem cells have been found in most if not all organs where they have been looked for. They are not linked to the embryonic (or totipotent) state and, therefore, to its legal, ethical and moral difficulties. However, at present they are difficult to isolate and to grow. At one time it was thought that adult stem cells, especially those from bone marrow, could be easily made to differentiate into many different functional cell types. Unfortunately this was shown to be incorrect. Whether a novel cell type recently isolated from bone marrow, so-called multipotent adult progenitor cells, will turn out to be as flexible as presently thought remains to be seen.[7]

The field of stem cell biology is in an early stage. In fact, it is so volatile that I would not be surprised if novel technologies based on recent advances in genomics and proteomics did not result in the discovery of novel cell types which could be manipulated in such a way as to avoid the problematic detour through a state of totipotency.

---

[6]   K. Hübner et al., Derivation of oocytes from mouse embryonic stem cells, Science 300 (2003), 1251-1256.

[7]   Y. Jiang et al., Pluripotency of mesenchymal stem cells derived from adult marrow, Nature 418 (2002), 41-49.

Part 3

Limits to Human Cloning under the German Constitution

The Human Embryo is a Person and not an Object

Christian Starck, Göttingen

I. How Does Cloning Work?

Cloning (Greek Klón = twig, shoot) signifies the artificial production of genetically identical copies of a cell. Cloning represents a technique, which can serve various goals.

1. In the case of so-called *therapeutic cloning*, which is sometimes also described in trivialising fashion as nuclear transplantation, the somatic cell nucleus of the patient to be treated is transferred into a denuclearised, unfertilised ovum, which is in the metaphase of the second chromosomal division. In this phase the fertilisable ovum has reached a point at which asexual reproduction is possible in the following way: so long as the membranes of the donor cell and the recipient ovum are close and extensively enough together, the application of a suitable electrical pulse can bring about a local fusion of both membranes. In this way the donor cell is taken up into the cytoplasm of the recipient ovum. This is activated by the electrical pulse.[1] Out of the process comes a new totipotent cell, which can develop into a blastocyst in the same way as a fertilised ovum. In other words, embryonic development has begun.

---

[1] This description is from "Bericht zur Frage eines gesetzgeberischen Handlungsbedarfs beim Embryonenschutz auf Grund der beim Klonen von Tieren angewandten Techniken und der sich abzeichnenden weiteren Entwicklung", German Parliament, Printed Matter (*Bundestagsdrucksache*), No. 13/11263, 8 (26 June 1998).

By this means it is possible to produce embryonic stem cells with the genetic inheritance of the patient. From this one should be able to acquire tissue and organs with the characteristics of the patient without risk of immunological rejection. Apart from providing substitute organs for the cell donor, cloning also opens up the possibility of basic research into embryonic stem cells. The selection of stem cells necessary for therapeutic research amounts to an exploitation of the embryo.[2]

2. *Reproductive cloning*, which takes place in the way already described, aims to preserve the embryo, which is then implanted within a uterus and supposed to develop into a human being with the same genetic makeup as the cell nuclear donor. In other words, it makes a child with only one genetic parent. The success rate for higher living beings is 1:1000.[3]

3. *Cloning for diagnostic purposes* is the term applied to the separation of daughter cells in early divisions of a blastocyst. This amounts to the artificial production of monozygotic twins/triplets etc. The clone is used for diagnostic purposes, and in the case of an unfavourable diagnosis, the original embryo is destroyed.

II. What Does the Basic Law Have to Say about This?

Article 1 of the Basic Law begins with the phrase, "human dignity is inviolable". This is not a statement of fact; rather, it is a constitutional guarantee which is expressed at the beginning of the constitution with particular emotive force as the foundational norm for the entire legal order. Apart from this, the normativity of the human dignity provision emerges quite unmistakeably from the second sentence of Article 1, which obligates all state power to "respect and protect" human dignity.[4]

---

[2] On therapeutic cloning and the remaining scientific, technical obstacles, see *R. Müller-Terpitz*, Die Empfehlungen der DFG zur Forschung mit menschlichen Stammzellen, Wissenschaftsrecht 2001, 271, 273 et seq.; *H.-G. Dederer*, Menschenwürde des Embryos in vitro? Der Kristallisationspunkt der Bioethik-Debatte am Beispiel des therapeutischen Klonens, AöR 127 (2002), 2 et seq.

[3] Pschyrembel Dictionary of Sexuality (Wörterbuch der Sexualität) (2003), 277.

[4] Cf. also *H. v. Mangoldt/F. Klein/C. Starck*, Das Bonner Grundgesetz, Vol. I (4th ed., 1999) Art. 1, No. 16.

The full and detailed extent of the human dignity guarantee is still controversial in peripheral matters. But as far as cloning is concerned, it is sufficient to point to the guarantee's prohibition on making human beings the mere object of the ends of others. This is prohibited to both the state as well as to private individuals.

In both of its abortion decisions of 1975 and 1993 the Federal Constitutional Court decided that unborn human life also falls under the protection of the human dignity guarantee, because the different phases of pre-natal development represent indistinguishable steps in the development of an individual human being.[5] Wherever human life exists it merits human dignity.

So when does the human being, which the human dignity guarantee protects, come into existence? A fertilised ovum with its double chromosomes, or the asexually produced cloned embryo, contain the complete programme for that development as a human being which activates the dignity protection. At the point of combination of nuclei or the production of a totipotent cloned cell, a continual self-directed process of development has begun which proceeds without decisive, qualitative hiatus capable of differentiating the organism from what it is at birth.[6] Human dignity belongs to human beings simply on the basis of their membership in the species Homo sapiens. Human rights presuppose that no one has the power to determine whether anyone is the subject of these rights. Those people, who see in this a "biologistic contraction" and who require for the human dignity guarantee the social recognition of a being capable of communication, fail to recognise that the potential for a communicating person is already programmed in the embryo.

Can embryos be treated as objects? The constitutional guarantee of human dignity exists in the context of a moment in the history of ideas which should not be overlooked in interpreting the guarantee. The philosophical tradition distinguishes between persons and things. Kant writes,

> "for the offspring is a *person*, and it is impossible to form a concept of the production of a being endowed with freedom through a physical operation. So from a *practical point of view* it is a quite cor-

---

[5]   BVerfGE 39, 1, 41; BVerfGE 88, 203, 252.

[6]   For this reason, the Swiss Federal Court expressly affirmed the constitutionality of the ban on exploitative research. See BGE 119, Section I, a) Verfassungsrecht, 460, 499 et seq., 503.

rect and even necessary idea to regard the act of procreation as one by which we have brought a person into the world without his consent and on our own initiative.... [The parents] cannot destroy their child as if he were something they had *made* (since a being endowed with freedom cannot be a product of this kind) or as if he were their property, nor can they just abandon him to chance, since they have brought not merely a worldly being but a citizen of the world into a condition which cannot now be indifferent to them even just according to concepts of right".[7]

If one denies the fertilised ovum the dignity of a person and treats it merely as a thing, one has to show how a thing at some point can become a person, which seems to me philosophically and juridically impossible. At this point the argument extends beyond the sphere of validity of the Basic Law and embraces all legal orders which stand in the tradition of the Enlightenment.[8]

Since embryos possess human dignity they may only be produced in vitro for the purpose of implantation in the woman from whom the ovum derives. For this reason one cannot argue from the "homelessness" of the not-yet-implanted embryo in order to question its developmental potential and hand it over to research. In vitro fertilisation is only justified as an individual therapeutic measure. If the embryo produced in vitro is not implanted in a birth mother but is used for purposes of research or for the healing of others or destroyed after diagnosis, it has only been used as a means for the ends of others, and its character as an end in itself is denied. This has to be treated as a breach of human dignity. Similarly, a balancing test between the right to life of the embryo and the expected advantages of research exploiting embryos in order to lengthen the life of others would also violate human dignity. It is impermissible from the very outset. Only an attacker's right to life may be infringed in (self-)defense. But the embryo is not attacking anyone.[9]

New interpretations have been sought which attempt to delay the point at which constitutionally protected life begins. Constitutional protection of life and dignity does not then apply to embryos or at least not to

---

[7]   *I. Kant*, The Metaphysics of Morals, 28 (English translation by Mary Gregor, 1996); emphasis in original.

[8]   *C. Starck*, Verfassungsrechtliche Grenzen der Biowissenschaft und Fortpflanzungsmedizin, JZ 2002, 1065, 1069 et seq.

[9]   Ibid., 1072.

early embryos, which have come to be called pre-embryos, following English use. Alternatively the right to life of embryos and the goals of research are placed in principle on an equal status in a relation of balancing. By way of justification reference is made to English language literature in which supposedly differentiated and thus more accurate views as to the beginning of life dominate. Behind these arguments lies the presupposition that rights and dignity are ascribed, or in other words granted or guaranteed. The argument runs so as to question the combination of nuclei as the beginning of individual human life from the perspectives of continuity, potentiality and identity.[10]

The argument proceeds to the point whereby embryos may be produced in vitro for purposes of research. What one is dealing with is research material, or in other words things. By contrast one has to insist that the embryo is someone and not something, a who and not a what.

III. The Human Being as a Clone

A final note, as regards reproductive cloning. Here we are not concerned with the destruction of an embryo. On the contrary the embryo is supposed to develop into a human being because it is intended to live as a copy of the cell donor. At present, reproductive cloning in the case of human beings is still a matter of pure experiment. Recall: the success rate is 1:1000. This means that the embryos which are being produced are being treated as things with which to be experimented. Quite apart from this argument one has to take account of the fact that the clone, even if it were to develop into a human being, would share in the age of the cell donor on account of its genetic structure. In other words it would be born as a temporally stunted human being. This fact, and asexual reproduction in general, are breaches of taboo which represent an infringement of the human dignity guarantee.

---

[10] See especially *W. Heun*, Embryonenforschung und Verfassung – Lebensrecht und Menschenwürde des Embryos, JZ 2002, 571 et seq.

Does the German Basic Law Protect against Human Cloning?

Jörn Ipsen, Osnabrück

If the question were raised, whether the German Basic Law "prohibits" cloning, my answer could be rather short. But this is not the case. The constitution as the basic law of a state does not normally prohibit acts of individual citizens. However, the assertion that the German Basic Law does not prohibit cloning has to be qualified: Human Cloning is prohibited by an ordinary law – § 6 of the Act for Protection of Embryos[1] – and can be punished by imprisonment up to 5 years.

In contrast to my first statement the subject of this part is: "Does the German Basic Law protect against Human Cloning?". Therefore, the obviously more complex question is raised: whether and to what extent embryos are protected by the constitution. This question cannot be answered in one sentence but rather leads us into the dogmatic intricacies of fundamental rights.

I would like to begin with the premise that various legal and moral values find their expression in the Basic Law – especially with respect to fundamental rights.[2] But the pertinent constitutional provisions do not contain any ideological principles or philosophical doctrines, nor can they be derived from these provisions. This is particularly the case with regard to the term "Human Dignity", which we will consider soon. Historically, this term was used by philosophical authors in connection

---

[1]   Reprinted in the annex of this volume, under V 20.

[2]   The Constitutional Court postulates an "order of values" (Wertordnung): BVerfGE 5, 85, 204 et seq.; 6, 55, 72; 7, 198, 204 et seq.; 21, 362, 371 et seq.; 49, 89, 141. See *H. Goerlich*, Wertordnung und Grundgesetz (1973).

with a specific meaning.[3] However, this does not justify the conclusion
that Art. 1 Basic Law codifies their concept of Human Dignity.

Another premise of fundamental rights dogmatics is the difference between the *right* and the *object the right protects*.[4] "Human life" is the
object which is protected by Art. 2 (2) Basic Law as well as various
norms of ordinary law. Art. 2 (2) guarantees the "right to live" and is
therefore also an individual right. The bearer of this right can object to
any state intervention. Therefore intervention must be justified with regard to this individual's right. Even if there is no apparent bearer of this
right it does not mean that the object is not protected. In so far that legal protection is recognized as a fundamental right the state is obliged
to protect these objects even if there is no apparent bearer of the individual right.[5]

Although this appears abstract it will soon become concrete. A human
embryo is not a *bearer of fundamental rights* and therefore is also not
the *bearer of the right of Human Dignity*.[6] The question which was
raised at the beginning – does the Basic Law *protect against Human*

---

[3]   Cf. *H. Dreier*, in idem (ed.), Grundgesetz-Kommentar, Vol. I (1996), Art.
1 I, No. 7-12; *M. Herdegen*, in Maunz/Dürig, Grundgesetz, Vol. I, Art. 1, No.
7-12; *C. Starck*, in v. Mangoldt/Klein/Starck, Bonner Grundgesetz-Kommentar,
Vol. I (4th ed., 1999), Art. 1, No. 3-8.

[4]   Cf. *J. Ipsen*, Staatsrecht II: Grundrechte (7th ed., 2004), No. 45 et seq.; *id.*,
Gesetzliche Einwirkungen auf grundrechtlich geschützte Rechtsgüter, JZ 1997,
473 et seq.

[5]   *Ipsen*, Staatsrecht II, supra note 4, No. 89 et seq.

[6]   See *Dreier*, supra note 3, No. 47 et seq.; *W. Heun*, Embryonenforschung
und Verfassung – Lebensrecht und Menschenwürde der Embryos, JZ 2002, 523;
E. Hilgendorf, Klonverbot und Menschenwürde – Vom Homo sapiens zum
Homo xerox? Überlegungen zu § 6 Embryonenschutzgesetz, Festschrift H.
Maurer (2001), 1157; *H. Hofmann*, Die versprochene Menschenwürde, AöR
118 (1993), 376; *Ipsen*, Staatsrecht II, supra note 4, No. 213; *id.*, Der "verfassungsrechtliche Status" des Embryos in vitro, JZ 2001, 989 et seq.; *R. Merkel*,
Forschungsobjekt Embryo (2002), 110; *E. Schmidt-Jortzig*, Systematische Be-
dingungen der Garantie unbedingten Schutzes der Menschenwürde in Art. 1
GG, DÖV 2001, 931 et seq.; *H. Sendler*, Menschenwürde, PID und Schwanger-
schaftsabbruch, NJW 2001, 2148, 2150; the "dominant opinion" postulates also
the embryo as a bearer of Human Dignity: see BVerfGE 39, 1, 41; 88, 203, 251;
W. Höfling, in Sachs (ed.), Grundgesetz-Kommentar (3rd ed., 2002), Art. 1, No.
51; *H.D. Jarass/B. Pieroth*, Grundgesetz-Kommentar (6th ed., 2002), Art. 1,
No. 6; *P. Kunig*, in v. Münch/Kunig (eds.), Grundgesetz-Kommentar, Vol. 1
(5th ed., 2000), Art. 1, No. 14.

Cloning – cannot be answered only by taking Art. 1 (1) Basic Law into consideration. This article declares that Human Dignity is inviolable and obliges the state to respect and to protect it. If an embryo were a bearer – and therefore subject – of the right of Human Dignity, the state would be obliged to use all means at its disposal to prevent any manipulation of an embryo's genotype or its elimination – since this would be in direct violation of the embryo's Human Dignity.[7]

Since embryos are not the bearers of individual rights they do not possess the right of being spared genetic manipulation. Before protest arises I would like to point out that the assumption that an embryo is the *bearer of fundamental rights* would not only exclude genetic manipulation but also abortion. The entire medical-ethical discussion suffers from this obvious contradiction: The frequently postulated protection of the embryo *in vitro* – on the basis of Human Dignity – does not appear to exclude the possibility of aborting the embryo after implantation without sanction.[8]

I am unable at this time to detail the entire legal discussion about when fundamental rights can be assigned to the unborn. I would, however, like to point out that the repeated invocation of Human Dignity as a fundamental right, which is supposedly entitled to all – even prenatal – life, stands in sharp contrast to the legal provisions and the social reality of abortion. I respect the ten-year struggle for the protection of prenatal life by the Constitutional Court. But it cannot be overlooked that an embryo:

- is only protected by an obligatory consultation within the first twelve weeks after implantation;

- is not protected at all in cases where abortion is tolerated based on medical or social grounds; and

- is also only protected in cases with criminological grounds, such as rape or incest, after certain established deadlines have expired.

---

[7] This is an inconsistency of the "dominant opinion", especially of the Constitutional Court: Human Dignity is also claimed for prenatal life during the first three months of pregnancy when its development is at its mothers discretion.

[8] Cf. *Heun*, supra note 6, 523 ("pre-embryo"); *Ipsen*, supra note 6, 990 et seq.; *Merkel*, Forschungsobjekt Embryo, supra note 6, 110 et passim.

The Second Senate of the Constitutional Court declared abortion to be "illegal" even after an obligatory consultation.[9] This attempt at a compromise cannot hide the fact that the Constitutional Court tolerates abortion within the first 12 weeks. Statistics which are occasionally published about abortion – in this sense "legal" abortion – show a widespread social acceptance.[10] I say this with a resigned undertone, because I am myself a determined opponent of this solution. On the other hand, after witnessing decades of discussion about abortion I must admit that the *legal situation* is indeed quite different.

From a legal standpoint, logic dictates that if the termination of prenatal life is left to the mother's discretion for the first three months, it is not recognised as either a bearer of Human Dignity nor as an entity with the individual right "to live". If this holds true, the act of abortion becomes not *state intervention* but rather an intervention tolerated by the state. If an embryo were indeed the bearer of this fundamental right its Human Dignity would be "infringed" upon since it can be eliminated by the mother without criminal sanction. At this stage I would like to point out an intolerable contradiction within the medical-ethical discussion: On the one hand, the idea of Human Dignity is claimed for the embryo; on the other hand, abortion is regarded as a kind of human right.[11]

In my mind it is irrefutable that embryos are not bearers of fundamental rights and therefore are not bearers of the Human Dignity. Nevertheless, as the highest value of the Basic Law, Human Dignity is certainly not without medical-ethical significance. I want to verify this with a short digression about the *dignity of the dead*. The legal status of a human being – and therefore the capacity to be the subject of fundamental rights – is terminated upon death.[12] This does not exclude Human Dignity's being assigned to the dead. This "Dignity" must be respected by the living and ensures that the dead are not just regarded as disposable material by law.[13]

The after-effects of Human Dignity as an individual's post-mortem right after death do not establish a binding program for the legislator. Rather they oblige the legislator to create a minimum of legal protec-

---

[9] BVerfGE 88, 203, 255.

[10] See *Merkel*, Forschungsobjekt Embryo, supra note 6, 75 et seq.

[11] *Heun*, supra note 6, 523, No. 100 qualifies this position as "ridiculous".

[12] See *Ipsen*, Staatsrecht II, supra note 4, No. 214.

[13] Cf. *Dreier*, supra note 3, No. 52 et seq.

tion – in accordance with the *Untermaßverbot*.[14] This is a consequence of the retroactive effect that results from the after-effects of Human Dignity. This has direct legal consequences for Human Dignity. Assuming for one moment that contrary to the cultural traditions the legal system does not contain any special provisions to protect the dead, it would inevitably affect the respect for Human Dignity of the living. These social-psychological processes are well-known and are found in all cultures and cultural epochs. This can be summed up to the effect that the reputation of a human beginning during his or her lifetime – and therefore the individual's Human Dignity – is mirrored in the burial process and how the dead are memorialized. Neglect of the cultural aspects of the burial process could be seen as a result of the decline of our common values – with Human Dignity at the forefront of that value system.[15]

Human Dignity has similar "pre-effects". It affects all stages of prenatal life and imposes corresponding obligations on the legislator to protect the unborn. In the perspective of the Constitutional Court such obligations to protect individual fundamental rights must take into consideration the limits of the *Unter-* and *Übermaßverbot*.[16] However, it is the very duty of the legislator to transform these obligations into concrete legal norms. That such obligations can be derived from the fundamental right of Human Dignity is irrefutable in my opinion. If embryos *in vitro* or *in utero* were without any legal protection and could be produced or destroyed at will, prenatal life would literally become worthless. Consequently, Human Dignity as an individual's right would be seriously affected. In my opinion, legislation and the practice of abortion have almost taken us to this point.

According to this logic, the obligation of the legislator to protect prenatal life at every stage can be derived from the objective value of Human Dignity. Just to mention it in passing, this has also been affirmed by Constitutional Court decisions and is the prevailing opinion found in constitutional law literature. The concrete question is therefore: whether the legislator is obliged to protect Human Dignity by prohibiting Human Cloning. With respect to the hierarchy of norms the ques-

---

[14]   This dogmatic figure was created by the Constitutional Court in the second abortion-decision. See BVerfGE 88, 203, 254.

[15]   Cf. *Ipsen*, supra note 6, 993.

[16]   See BVerfGE 88, 203, 254; *Ipsen*, Staatsrecht II, supra note 4, No. 93 et seq.

tion is: if § 6 EmbSchG did *not* exist, would the legislator be obliged to enact a similar provision?

It should come as no surprise that I will make a principal distinction between *therapeutic* and *reproductive* Cloning. It is obvious that using gene technology to ease illness cannot be placed in question – either ethically or constitutionally.[17] Research on embryos *in vitro* and the development of stem cell therapy clearly become necessities to advance Human Dignity. To provide the relief and cure from the illnesses to which mankind is subjected represents an incomparably more important value of constitutional protection.

The situation is categorically the opposite with respect to "reproductive Cloning". By the way, I do not believe in a real danger of dictators setting up a living terracotta-army. Mental programming as a tool to create rabid followers is a much used technique. This technique is certainly more effective than what can be achieved by genetic engineering. Furthermore, history clearly documents that dictators do not normally have the patience to wait 20 years until their cloned warriors are able to carry their own weapons. However, reproductive Cloning infringes upon the fundamental right of Human Dignity at its very core, and the discussion of an – also international – ban on Cloning is therefore extremely productive.[18]

Every person is genetically unique – leaving the rare case of identical twins out of the equation. The universal fact that each individual is biologically unique represents the very core of Human Dignity. This fact is continually reaffirmed by current genetic research - as well as by everyday experience. It is not my intent at this time to deal with the subjective and the objective formulas to interpret the fundamental right of Human Dignity. These formulas are doubtful especially when they are put in opposition to each other.[19] It is important at this juncture to consider – hypothetically – the consequences of using potential genetic technology to produce human beings with identical hereditary factors in reserve or at any time in the future.

If the average – mainstream – person would even begin to take notice of the mere possibility of multiplying individuals by using genetic material, it would radically alter not only his or her perception of self and

---

[17]   See *Merkel*, Forschungsobjekt Embryo, supra note 6, 264 et seq.; *Dreier*, supra note 3, No. 59.

[18]   See the contribution of *R. Wolfrum/S. Vöneky* in this volume.

[19]   Cf. *Dreier*, supra note 3, No. 37 et seq.

perception of others, but even his or her perception of personal identity. This could potentially cause a Copernican revolution directly affecting the concept of Human Dignity. The most profound reason for respect of humans for each other, and therefore of Human Dignity, is man's inherent individuality.

In brief summation, the Basic Law does protect against Human Cloning. Art 1 (1) Basic Law imposes the obligation on the legislator to prohibit reproductive Cloning and the obligation to ensure by appropriate measures that these prohibitive rules are enforced. However, these obligations are not valid in the case of therapeutic Cloning.

Does Cloning Violate the Basic Law's Guarantee of Human Dignity?

Horst Dreier, Würzburg

I. Introduction

When considering whether cloning *generally* violates the guarantee of human dignity in Art. 1 (1) Basic Law, one must fundamentally differentiate between reproductive cloning – vividly referred to as "cloning to produce children" – and therapeutic cloning, also called "research cloning". The goal of reproductive cloning is to bring about pregnancy and the subsequent birth of a human, who is genetically identical with the "original" (that is, the donor of the somatic cell). It is thus a matter of procreation through asexual means by producing a genetic copy of another human being. The goal of therapeutic cloning, in turn, is not the birth of a human, but the extraction of replacement tissue or replacement organs in order to heal serious, degenerative diseases (for example, brain and nerve disorders such as Alzheimer's or Parkinson's). The designation "research cloning" thus appropriately indicates that medical application is still a long-term goal and that the immediate goal is to research the fundamentals. Due to the identical genetic structure, breeding tissue or organs by using cloning methods eliminates the otherwise notorious problem of immunological rejection.

Firstly, we will deal with the question of whether reproductive cloning is forbidden in Germany (section I). Thereafter therapeutic cloning will be examined more closely (section II). Questions concerning the interpretation of existing *statutory* rights are left aside, and the attention is instead given to a single question of *constitutional* law: whether the two forms of cloning constitute a violation of the guarantee of human dignity in Art. 1 (1) Basic Law.[1]

II. Reproductive Cloning

Due to its contradictory structure, the reality of reproductive cloning is distinct from almost all other currently debated issues of bioethics. The problem with embryo research, PID, and therapeutic cloning is that human life is destroyed in an early stage of its development; thus, these processes are highly controversial and require careful justification. Reproductive cloning, in contrast, is intended to bring about a new human life; new humans are meant to be born. Why, then, must precisely this be denounced and banned? This is the decisive and fundamental question.

The answer to be found in almost all relevant national and international documents and according to many scientific opinions, is that (reproductive) cloning violates human dignity. Of course, most analyses neglect to specify exactly *whose* human dignity would be violated. For a more precise debate, the argumentation must be more rational and comprehensible. Whose human dignity does (reproductive) cloning actually violate? Three objects of violation are possible: firstly, the clone, that is, the "copy"; secondly, the cloned, that is, the "original"; and, lastly, a more collective object of violation, which could roughly be paraphrased as the "society" or the "legal community." In my opinion, it is the third potential object of violation that offers the decisive argument for a ban on reproductive cloning. There are no convincing arguments that demonstrate a violation of the dignity of either the clone or the cloned. This assertion can be concluded from the following reflections.

---

[1]   This article closely follows the Symposium speech and uses few footnotes. For a more thorough analysis of all significant aspects with extensive reference to the complex literature, cf. *H. Dreier*, in idem (ed.), Grundgesetz-Kommentar, Vol. I (2nd ed., 2004), Art. 1, para. 1, No. 1 et seq. ("verfassungs- und ideengeschichtliche Herkunft"), No. 50 et seq. ("Menschenwürdetheo-rien"), No. 81 et seq. ("Status pränidativen Lebens"), No. 108 et seq. ("reproduktives Klonen und therapeutisches Klonen"), No. 116 et seq. ("Gattungs-würde"), No. 168 et seq. ("Menschenbild").

1. Violation of the Dignity of the Clone (the "Copy")?

Despite the multi-layered complexity of the arguments, absolute unity prevails on one point: in the case of birth of a clone, this cloned human would have an undiminished right to life, human rights and human dignity. A cloned individual would not be a second-class human or in any other way an inferior living being.

Hence, the attempt is made to identify a violation of human dignity in that the very act of creating the clone is said to violate the clone's dignity, which then would require that such acts be forbidden. However, this argument leads to a practically insurmountable counterargument, which was used and debated already in the bioethics discussions of the 1980s and 1990s (mostly in the contexts of surrogate motherhood and genetic therapy). The question is, namely, whether one's dignity can be violated by a procedure to which one owes one's very life. Such a construction encounters drastic objections in philosophy, constitutional law and criminal law. Thus, it is a categorical mistake to find a violation of the *child's* self-determination in the partial or complete determination of that child's genetic structure: before creation (here, the birth of a clone), no personal identity exists, whose dignity or self-determination could be violated. Otherwise, the absurd consequence would follow that one would have to condemn cases of normal procreation as acts violating both the right to self-determination and human dignity (P. Lerche). Therefore, self-determination as an expression of human dignity cannot be extended to those processes that compose the human's genetic constitution and shape her or him after birth. Moreover, with artificial production of genetically identical individuals, one can hardly assert that the human dignity of the respective person – who otherwise would not even exist – has been violated solely by the procreation. When the procreative act takes place, no being exists, whose human dignity *could* be violated; following birth, he possesses the right to life and human dignity as every other human being does. As every other born human, he lacks every possibility to influence his own genetic constitution. From this point of view, procreation itself is the basic case of heteronomy. In other words, one has no right to a specific genetic makeup and also, thus, no right not to be born and no right to not have been born in the way one was born.

2. Violation of the Human Dignity of the Cloned (the Original)?

At times, it is assumed that reproductive cloning violates the human dignity of the cloned original, that is, the donor of the somatic cell. This may well be assumed in case of involuntariness, that is, in a case of cloning without consent of the donor, since this would disrespect his genetic uniqueness. The act of cloning would demonstrate reproducibility of the cloned person against his will and would therefore challenge the status of his uniqueness. Cloning of a deceased person would have important ramifications for general personal rights, constitutionally protected by Art. 1 (1) Basic Law, in conjunction with Art. 2 (1).

Less certain is whether the voluntary reproduction of a living cell-donor can be regarded as a violation of his individual human dignity. Constitutional and criminal legal scholarship (predominantly) denies this. The reason is that such a protection of human dignity against its individual bearer is difficult to postulate and to construct without contradiction. The argument that one cannot renounce one's human dignity, occasionally cited to demonstrate a violation of dignity, fails to recognise that the protection of dignity in this situation turns against its bearer and deprives him of the individual autonomy which Art. 1 Basic Law seeks to guarantee.

That the fabrication of new human life through reproductive cloning nevertheless constitutes a violation of human dignity, can be more easily understood if it is detached from its individual bearer and placed on higher level of society as a legal community.

3. Violation of Human Dignity on the Legal Community Level?

The act of reproductive cloning completes the fabrication of new human life with a predetermined, deliberate and systematically chosen gene configuration. Here one must separate human dignity from individual capacity and establish it in its reciprocal constitution on a higher structural level, that of the legal community. The legal community cannot allow the artificial reproduction of individuality and its quasi factory-like production, since this would endanger the objective requirements of the uniqueness and individuality of every person. It is probable that the broad consensus – not encountered in other issues of biotechnology – concerning the prohibition of reproductive cloning is based hereupon; it may have its roots in feelings of shame and indignation, deeply set basic notions of parenthood, or of anxiety from regarding what is considered to be a monstrous act, which violates a taboo. Such a prohibition of reproductive cloning on the quasi supra-individual level, normatively underpinned by Art. 1 (1) Basic Law, neither attempts to incorporate genetic coincidence into the protection of human dignity nor does it attempt to invoke a distinct idea of man (*Menschenbild*) allegedly underlying the Basic Law. The sanctioning of reproductive cloning would not violate the human race in a biological sense, but rather the concrete society and the continually renewable context of interaction within society, in which and through which dignity is constituted according to the theory of communication (H. Hofmann). Reproductive cloning would undermine the conditions for the possibility of human interaction in a concrete legal community. The notion of the legitimacy of the systematic fabrication of human beings though artificial reproduction of genetic individuality would bring with it the risk of "security of orientation" (K. Seelmann) concerning the supporting normative fundaments of the political community. The collective self-conception of a society based on the dignity of individuals would be endangered. Following this line of argument, reproductive cloning would not directly affect the dignity of the clone and that of the cloned only marginally. Yet, the prohibition preserves and contains prerequisites for successful societal interaction as it recognises the uniqueness of every individual. Art. 1 (1) becomes quasi self-reflexive.

4. The Dignity of Species?

The previous argumentation should not be understood as a pleading for a concept of a dignity of species (*Gattungswürde*). It is not to be seen as relating to biology, but rather to society. It merely accepts that in certain extreme cases, with redress to the evidence and the consensus of an intolerable approach to this matter, dignity is to be established on a quasi-interactive level, namely, the communication and action structure of a concrete legal community. Also in this case, the concrete human being, or more precisely the human being incorporated into the legal community, remains the reference and the starting point.

The current discussion of the dignity of species particularly in the bio-ethical debate, on the other hand, is concerned with the dignity of mankind, which is considered to be protected. Statements about a distinct idea of man (*Menschenbild*) in the Basic Law or of the "essentiality" of human beings tend in the same direction. The concern is no longer for the dignity of the individual human being in his concrete existence but for an advanced entity, at the end of humankind. Such an account can clearly invoke neither the wording nor the history of the norm nor the philosophy of Kant. The German Federal Constitutional Court does not support this position either, though its reference to human beings as "species beings" (*Gattungswesen*) is often cited. This reference, in the relevant decision, aims to strengthen the protection of the individual: every (born) human being should benefit from the protection of Art. 1 (1) Basic Law solely because he belongs to the human race. A depersonalised protection of the species was not intended.

In addition, the dignity of humanity is not easily inferred from the character of Art. 1 (1) Basic Law as a norm of objective law or from the category of the objective legal contents of the Basic Law. The commitment of the State to the dignity of humans as an objective legal norm requires, like the objective legal contents of the Basic law, a personal object of protection. These may i.e. be human beings endowed with dignity, whose protection is then – regardless of its enforceability through the concrete subject – surrendered to the State authority, as expressly formulated by Art. 1 (1) Basic Law. The objective side is of no use when such a subject does not exist. There are misgivings about trying to compensate this absence by splitting up human dignity into a subject of protection and a legal subject.

The reason why such a species-oriented concept of dignity nonetheless is represented is the inability, when answering difficult bioethical questions – in the field of PID or cloning –, to recognise the violation of any individual human dignity. It is in any case believed that these developments must be governed by recurrence to Art. 1 (1) Basic Law. It is from time to time postulated that the "inviolability of the human genome is an integral part of human dignity" and the "prevention of the accidental emergence of new genetic combinations through reproductive cloning" is to be understood as "disregard for the dignity accorded the human race" (L. Witteck/C. Erich). Here, human dignity suddenly becomes the dignity of a molecular structure: the likelihood of a connection between two haploid chromosome sets accrues in the rank of a constitutional guarantee, safeguarded, and therefore infallible, by the eternity clause of Art. 79 (3) Basic Law.

At large, it seems that the dignity of species, like the idea of man, uses a construct which conveys the peculiar relative values and convictions directly to the highest constitutional level making these ideas immune to all objections. This is, moreover an expression of the, perhaps very

German, tendency to "nurture deceptive certainty through the omni-present appeal to human dignity" (G. Frankenberg).

III. Therapeutic Cloning

The goal of therapeutic cloning or research cloning is, as mentioned at the beginning, not the birth of a new human being, genetically identical to the cell donor. Instead, the long-term objective is the production of tissue structure or entire organs as a cure for serious degenerative diseases (brain and nerve afflictions, Alzheimer's, Parkinson's). The reference to research cloning conveys that, for the time being, the attainment of fundamental academic knowledge about the development and (re)programming process of pluripotent stem cells and their control is necessary. Practically, in the Dolly method, a body cell is implanted into an unfertilised egg cell hereby making it possible to breed a blastocyte, from which one, in turn, seeks to extract stem cells. These can then be further developed into replacement tissue or even organs. For the time being, only the first step is possible, as was recently demonstrated by South Korean scientists through the production of a clone embryo.[2] The bioethical and constitutional objections correspond in part with the objections against research on (surplus or specifically produced) early embryos (see 1.). They relate partly to the fact that if events had transpired differently, new ground would be broken for the general use of incriminated reproductive clones (2.).

1. The Question of Status

The fundamental question is whether during the period until the destruction of the blastocyte, i.e. within the first three to five days, the clone is even given the status as a personal bearer of human dignity at all. Can a human life also be viewed as granted with human dignity in a prenidation stage? Is the cellular bond to be considered a carrier of human dignity in the eight-cell stage or as a blastocyste?

These are serious and difficult questions. They have so far constantly arisen in the bioethical discussion and have been a controversial object

---

[2]   Science 303 (2004), 937.

of debate. In my opinion, we have to answer the question in the negative both in the case of natural production, and likewise for in the case of artificial impregnation or that of (reproductive as well as therapeutic) cloning. I want to use three examples from a constitutional perspective in order to substantiate this.

a) Constitutionally, it is important to clarify that those answering in the affirmative cannot rely upon case law of the German Federal Constitutional Court. Until now, in the two pertinent judgements relating to abortion, the Court has explicitly set the limit by the period after nidation. Subsequent conclusions are therefore profoundly speculative. Seeking support from the Constitutional Court is, or would be, Karlsruhe astrology. Incidentally, if the nasciturus were to be given the full protection of human dignity before nidation, the decisions of the German Federal Constitutional Court regarding the legitimacy of devices preventing nidation – abortions within the first twelve weeks without justification (supposedly unlawful, but tolerated by the legal system) – would be incomprehensible with reference to so-called medical indication.

b) As it is, a further objection against the personal extension of the human dignity guarantee to life during prenidation, is that the ideas and constitutional provenance of Art. 1 (1) Basic Law clearly relate to born persons. The unborn were not considered, and, thus, prenidation could not have been contemplated.

c) Furthermore, the current theories of human dignity – that are not restricted to the negative definition of human dignity – such as Niklas Luhmann's theory of performance (*Leistungstheorie*) and the so-called theory of communication (*Kommunikationstheorie*), also lead to a negative result. Of the so-called dowry theories (*Mitgifttheorien*), the assumption of the human dignity capacity of life during prenidation is supported best of all by the Christian version – this of course against the background of an eventful history of dogma and, without exception, only in the official reports of the Roman Catholic Church. Within the theological discussion and the many protestant and reformist churches, the contents of discussion are portrayed heterogeneously. Militating against an immediate reference to Kant is the fact that his concept of person only applies to prenatal (or even prenidation) life, by using an extensive misinterpretation of the intentions and requirements of his philosophy. Incidentally, a special enquiry is always to be subjected to the question whether the existence of an injurious act can be affirmed, even if one should approve the question of personal capacity regardless of any doubt.

Overall, due to a lack of legal capacity, it can hardly be justified that therapeutic cloning breaches the guarantee of human dignity.

2. Indistinguishability from Reproductive Cloning?

A somewhat different objection to therapeutic cloning is that if the first steps (Dolly method, the development of an unfertilised egg cell implanted with a somatic cell until it becomes a blastocyst) had transpired differently (namely, by implanting the blastocyst in the woman's womb, pregnancy and birth), the path would be paved for reproductive cloning.

This objection is also not convincing. Firstly, it is to be observed that according to current knowledge, reproductive cloning of human beings (understood as the entire process until the birth of a genetically identical human being) represents, from the point of view of science and of medicine, an objective impossibility; even the Korean researchers were only able to pursue the process up until the blastocyte. Insofar, already the definite possibility to take the step from therapeutic to reproductive cloning is lacking. Secondly and finally, intent is also lacking. In therapeutic cloning, as in other contexts, the finality of action is accorded utmost importance. The manufacturer of a scalpel, with which a surgeon can carry out a life-saving operation, must not have it held against him that a subsequent use (and inasmuch as events transpire differently) could be to utilise the scalpel to commit a deceitful murder. Cell bonds produced for the cell nucleus are not intended for further development beyond the blastocyst stage. Therefore, the uniqueness of human individuality is not denied, but instead, tissue engineering for healing serious degenerative disorders is carried out. As a result, therapeutic cloning does not clash with the Basic Law and the guarantee of human dignity. On the contrary: as the State is admittedly obliged to protect the life and health of its citizens, it must support measures that aid the fight against diseases.

Back to Kant! An Interjection in the Debate on Cloning and Human Dignity

Wolfgang Graf Vitzthum, Tübingen

Legal scholarship and jurisdiction in post-war Germany define "human dignity" in terms of constitutional-violation procedure. The scope of protection is defined negatively: evidence derives from the fact of its negation[1] (e.g., the state-ordered execution of the mentally ill or Germany's temporary departure from the ranks of civilised nations from 1933 to 1945). Thus, the treatment of a human being as the mere object of state, scientific, or economic action infringes the inviolability of human dignity. Relevant as it is to any interpretation, this specific historical background alone is insufficient. Above and beyond it, human dignity is "the very status of being, which 'is' independent of time and space, and which 'should' be realised through the law,"[2] – a universal value on the level of impartiality and equality.

---

[1] Groundbreaking *G. Dürig*'s early works, culminating in his commentary on Arts. 1 and 2 in Maunz-Dürig, Grundgesetz (1958). This publication remains challenging, after 45 years, and still draws differing opinions. On Dürig's approach, see *W. Graf Vizthum*, Die Menschenwürde als Verfassungsbegriff, JZ 1985, 201 et seq.; an earlier version of the following sketch in Henne/Riedlinger (eds.), Das Lüth-Urteil in (rechts-) historischer Sicht (forthcoming 2004).

[2] *G. Dürig*, Der Grundrechtssatz von der Menschenwürde, AöR 81 (1956), 117, 125. Cf. also *C. Enders*, Die Menschenwürde in der Verfassungsordnung (1997); *P. Häberle*, Die Menschenwürde als Grundlage der staatlichen Gemeinschaft, in HdbStR, Vol. II (3rd ed., 2004), 317 et seq.; *T. Geddert-Steinacher*, Menschenwürde als Verfassungsbegriff (1990), 164 et seq. With stronger emphasis on the reason-postulate behind the value-postulate, see *E. Picker*, Menschenwürde und Menschenleben (2002); *id.*, in Schweidler et al. (eds.), Menschenleben – Menschenwürde (2003), 197 et seq. Dürig's "object formula" (*Objektformel*), canonized by the Federal Constitutional Court, is ultimately

But are the Basic Law's human dignity provision and its rationale still valid, given modern demarcation issues such as biological and genetic engineering, research on human embryos, and cloning of human geno- types? The Basic Law has established fundamental bastions against the exploitation of early forms of human life: constitutional limitations, such as principles of necessity, suitability, and proportionality, as well as the prohibition of arbitrariness. But these seem to fall when confronted with those elementary (in the truest sense of the word) processes, in which the individual human development of the embryo is precluded from the outset. As international research continues to surpass its own successes, as research goals are elevated, and as alternative scientific ap- proaches become less effective, the question becomes increasingly ines- capable: based on the Basic Law's right to life in Article 2, paragraph 2, Sentence 1 and its fundamental, constitutional basis in Article 1, para- graph 1,[3] where are the boundaries for research?

Even if (therapeutic) cloning of human cells merely facilitated progress toward healing serious diseases, the human-dignity norm itself would be put to the test. Could it be the basis for consensus among a plurality of international and national values? Can the fundamental, defining provision of the Basic Law draw boundaries where the natural sciences draw certainties into question?[4] When conclusive evidence and consen- sus are absent, normative recourse to human dignity's origins in the philosophy of values and transcendental philosophy is required. A rela- tivisation or pluralisation of the concept of human dignity not only en- dangers human life in its vulnerable early (or late) stages, but also calls the very basis of the basic rights into question. Without a groundwork

---

an adaptation of Kant's practical imperative, based on the principle of reciproc- ity. The negative definition arises only where evidence already exists.

[3]   All article and paragraph references are to the German Basic Law (Grundgesetz), except where otherwise noted. An English translation of ex- cerpts of the Basic Law is reprinted in the annex of this volume, under V 21.

[4]   Thus, it apparently becomes difficult to maintain the thus far ethically important distinction between pluripotence and omnipotence of cells (in the sense of capability to create a whole). It seems that adult stem cells can create more organ systems than previously assumed. Indeed, the certainty that adult stem cells cannot be omnipotent seems to have been lost. Only the genetic trig- ger for the potency to create a whole is not yet known. Embryoid bodies re- semble embryos but stop developing after a certain stage. If the trigger for the potency to create a whole were discovered, and if it could be turned to "off," it would solve key ethical problems of therapeutic cloning. But as long as we do not know the connection, these problems are all the more urgent.

that is *not* amenable to a pluralistic definition, human dignity and the rule of law cannot fulfill their normative function.

I. Human Dignity as a Normative Principle

The historical origin of the Basic Law itself clarifies these relations. The philosophy of values contributed to the spiritual reconstruction in 1948-49, following the damage to the foundations of the community by the NS-Regime. It contributed significantly to the constitutional identity of the Federal Republic of Germany. By setting absolute boundaries for state power not subject to weighing of values, Article 1, paragraph 1 – as the foundational norm of the entire legal order – met the demands of a generation. After the devastation of the Third Reich, especially its idolisation of the state, it was essential for this generation to reestablish the human being as the personal bearer of value, capable of freedom, and as the purpose and center of the commonwealth. The respect due to every human individual had to be established also for the scientific community, parts of which, in the context of "racial research", had excluded entire groups of peoples from the community of citizens with rights. The system of values and claims embodied in the Basic Law needed to be normatively strengthened; the inviolability of human dignity in the "following basic rights" (Art. 1, para. 3) needed to be given shape. This was realised by the concept that the basic rights were not merely subjective rights for protection against the state, but also the expression of an objective system of value – with Article 1, paragraph 1, as its basis and as the *tertium comparationis* for the weighing of legal rights and interests,[5] for the "harmony of inviolable human dignity and legally shaped protection of life" (P. Kirchof).

---

[5]   The proximity of the given legal interest to human dignity is decisive. BVerfGE 39, 1, 43; BVerfGE 35, 202, 225: The more elementary a particular freedom is, the greater the realization of the basic right must be, in terms of practical concordance (the strengthening function of Art. 1, para. 1). For example, as the data from a genome analysis becomes more individualized and personalized, the need for data privacy and protection increases correspondingly. And vice versa: the basic rights indeed have "their respective roots in Art. 1 but find their various explications and prerequisites in a specific area of civil liberties." *P. Kirchof*, Genforschung und die Freiheit der Wissenschaft, in Höffe et al. (eds.), Gentechnik und Menschenwürde (2002), 9, 19. In other words, the guarantee of human dignity has its "grounding" and initial development "espe-

This concept lent itself to non-liberal ideas of the state's fundamental duties of protection, as well.[6] It also concerns the cloning of human genotypes in the current constitutional and legal-political debate.[7] Article 2, paragraph 2, contains the twofold duty (cf. Art. 1, para. 1, Sentence 2) of the dignity-conscious state: firstly, to protect human life, including both unborn life[8] and life still in the petri dish (which is of course controversial due to the definitional debate on what a human being is and when its existence begins) and, secondly, to forbid the construction of human beings, regardless of which and whose notions that construction might follow. The grave dissonance between the protection of the life of the embryo *in vivo* and that of the embryo *in vitro*[9] is well established and need not be developed here.

---

cially in the right to life, that is, in the prohibitions of the death penalty, torture [etc.]." *M. Borowsky*, F.A.Z. of 17 October 2003.

[6]   See BVerfGE 1, 97, 104; BVerfGE 39, 1, 37, 41; BVerfGE 88, 203, 252. Formulated at an early point by *Dürig*, supra note 1 (Art. 1, No. 2), this approach was eagerly received in the literature. See, for example, *D. Dörr*, "Big Brother" und die Menschenwürde (2000), 38 et seq. (discussing the limits of duties of protection, as well). Of course, protection of life is also a term, influenced by values.

[7]   Generally, "reproductive cloning" (i.e., cloning in order to procreate a child) is differentiated from "therapeutic" or scientific cloning (though the very possibility to make such a distinction is debated). Some expect that cloned embryonic stem cells, for example, could later be used for tests of prescription drugs. Already, one anticipates the creation of "designer babies" with eugenic selection of intelligence, sex, and personality and the eventual progression into a "post-human future," in which we can alter humanness at its core. Admittedly, no one seriously supports reproductive cloning, particularly with its horrendous medical risks (apparently, adult donor cells pass on their genetic age). Some say therapeutic cloning has a more realistic chance for development, even if it is still in its infancy.

[8]   BVerfGE 88, 203, 204 (l.r. 10), 261: "Moreover, the protection mandate obligates the state to vitalize the right to protection of unborn life and to keep it in the general consciousness" (2d Abortion Decision). On the conception of the duty of protection, see, for example, *G. Hermes*, Das Grundrecht auf Schutz von Leben und Gesundheit (1987), 43 et seq. On the dogmatics of "sphere of protection" and "object of protection," see *P. Lerche*, HdBStR, Vol. V, para. 121, No. 11 et seq.; *J. Isen*see, ibid., para. 111, No. 40 et seq.

[9]   Compare, on the one hand, illegal but not punishable abortion until the twelfth week of pregnancy – certainly not a powerful protection of unborn life – with, on the other hand, the inadmissibility of using leftover, test-tube embryos, say, for the production of pancreatic tissue cultures. Put another way

The *nasciturus*, protected for its own human dignity, relies on the protection of the mother for the realisation of its right to life. During the pregnancy, she and her child compose a "duality in unity." This will be addressed below.

From the beginning, (post-war) argumentation based on necessarily vague values had made many legal scholars uneasy.[10] Voluntative choice-making, decisionism, subjective values, even a "tyranny of (Christian, occidental) values" might now, it was feared, displace rational, comprehensible reasoning. Case-law jurisprudence was written on the wall; predictability of value judgements was placed on the list of casualties. The fear that (secular) values might be consumed and discarded or that human dignity might be downgraded to commonplace included a tendency "to bring the sanctuaries into the forecourts" (H. Ridder). The prognosis was an infiltration of ethical, religious, or world-view elements into legal-political value assessment and its juridical interpretation.[11]

Basic rights are indeed (to single out one aspect) value judgements, with validity in all areas of the law. But the basic rights of the German Basic Law are not primarily Christian rights. They are asserted and denied, violated and defended in an increasingly pluralistic, secularly determined social context. While the categories of ethics are essentially and functionally universal, the normative content of the basic rights is cul-

---

(with regard to prohibited PID): how do legal dogma and politics get around the contradiction of values that an embryo may be killed without penalty (and often financed by medical insurance) after up to three months in the womb, while a newly created embryo may be neither analyzed nor singled out.

[10] Cf. *H. Goerlich*, Wertordnung und Grundgesetz (1973). *Geddert-Steinacher*, supra note 2, 6, refers to the danger of a "fundamentalization" of the argument for human dignity, ibid., 27 et seq. (discussing also the openness of the term dignity). On the ambivalence of the argument for human dignity, see *C. Hillgruber*, Der Schutz des Menschen vor sich selbst (1992), 104 et seq.; *W. Graf Vitzthum*, Gentechnologie und Menschenwürdeargument, ZRP 1987, 33 et seq. Art. 1, para. 1 is the emergency brake in the constitutional system of protection of legal interests, the Basic Law's ironclad reasoning, reserved for instances of grave endangerment. Note also the fact that especially European states (as with Germany) see dignity as a normative principle, emerging after liberation or revolution, in response to an oppressive, inhuman regime (Italy, Greece, Spain, Portugal, etc.).

[11] Cf. *R. Alexy*, Theorie der Grundrechte (1985), 136 et seq., 142 et seq. (responding to criticism for subjectivity and supporting a "soft" value order). Naturally, every norm contains a bit of voluntarism or decisionism.

turally contingent on a specific space and time (K.W. Nörr). If particular schemata were to claim absolute validity for all, fundamental constitutional consensus would be called into question. In other words, the
core of self-evident agreement would disrupt, if, for example, traditional, Judeo-Christian concepts (R. Spaemann), or pointedly "post-
metaphysical" systematics (N. Luhmann), or discourse theory (J.
Habermas, R. Alexy), were to claim the position of generally binding
"supreme standards."

To avoid becoming the executive organ either of a specific school of so-
ciology or of the Vatican congregation of faith, the constitutional law-
yer must be mindful of the rationalising, commonsense function of con-
stitutional-law dogmatics, which is for its part culturally dependent. At
the same time, recourse to the guarantee of human dignity's inviolability must remain reserved to that grouping of negative circumstances,
which challenge the fundamental consensus of the constitution itself.
The relation between Article 1, paragraph 1, and Article 79, paragraph
3, supports this as well. This systemic component opposes a relativistic
definition of human dignity, simply because such a definition would
shield the fundamental norm from the disposition as democratic sovereign. This can only be justified transcendental-logically.[12] Self-esteem
and autonomy cannot, in principle, be relinquished without also dis-
carding democracy itself (and the claim to personal respect). That
would be contradictory. This "normativism" highlights the problem of
cross-system recognition of values and allows legal scholars to meet the
cascade of philosophical-historical explication of the term human dignity. In this respect, on the philosophical side it is Kant with his concepts who comes closest to the categories of legal scholars, especially
with his justification for the law: "und wenn's ein Volk von Teufeln
wär, das Recht täten sie wohl brauchen..."

II. Human Dignity Based on Transcendental Philosophy

Back to the basic, post-war approach to human dignity! It was Janus-
faced: based both on the philosophy of values and on transcendental
philosophy. The latter approach proved to be longer-lived than the

---

[12]   Kant's sense of transcendental philosophy is the doctrine of *a priori* conditions of human cognition. In the context of human dignity, this philosophy is
used where consensus fails.

former, at that time the "modern" approach. In a secularised society, whose value-basis had been shaken, forces – such as Europeanisation, postmodernity, and globalisation – pushed toward a relativisation of the personal endowments of the human being. Human dignity became a highly demanded export beyond our own cultural sphere, but not based on its value-content, let alone its (metaphysical) roots in the Christian doctrine of the inalienable worth of each human individual, created by God in his own image. Rather, the demand for export was driven by the fact that human dignity was located in the realm of ethical axioms, by its transcendentallogical accentuation, as it was expressed in Kant's "end in itself" formula.

Of course, even this genealogy and rationale did not assure *general* acceptance of the dignity norm. It is, indeed, universal and transcendental, but its interpretation and execution, as stated above, contingently occur in cultural differentiation. This dependence on culture draws boundaries for anthropological approaches to the justification for human rights as well.

III. Relativisation of Human Dignity?

Lately, there have been tendencies to expose the absolute protection, safeguarded by the commitment to the inviolability of human dignity, to relativisation. Increasingly, the embryo in the petri dish is "awarded"[13] only the (statutorily qualifiable) protection of life, but not

---

[13]   Cf. *B. Zypries*, Federal Minister of Justice, speech on 29 October 2003 in Berlin, reprinted in this volume, pp. 107 et seq. Indeed, protection of life from fertilization (such has already been advanced for example by *R. Herzog*, JR 1969, 441), but, because impregnated egg cells have "solely the prospect to cultivate [...] the constitutive elements of human dignity", they are not "award[ed] human dignity" (p. 112), in the sense of Article 1 (consequently Zypries used the prevailing doctrine and the draft of the EU Constitution to qualify the guarantee of human dignity as a basic right – which could mean the first step toward erosion and the opening of the backdoor for a weighing of values). When human dignity "develops" (after nidation in the uterus (approx. two weeks after fertilization), after organ differentiation (approx. three months after fertilization), after birth?), who "awards" it, under what procedure, and by what legitimization are not answered. As a result, speaking of "mere prospect" or "awarding of human dignity" could represent a step in the direction of an "adoption society," with potentially grave effects for disabled children or the

(unqualified) human dignity. If one were to define the concept of a human not as personalised[14], but as ontological and as of natural law, this relativisation would almost be an "objectification" of embryonic life: third persons, such as scientists, would decide the context of life and death of developing human life. Would this not already be, as in E. Picker's question, the authorisation (if initially only limited) of the exploitation of life of one's "own kind"? Would this not thus be the step into a society, in which ultimately everyone would have the mutual, socio-biological primal fear of not being welcome as a human being, but rather being (mis)used for the purposes or needs of his or her peers?

Every attempt to define the Basic Law's concept of a human more precisely (for instance, by recharacterising the term "human" through paraphrase or circumscription) involves the risk that certain people will be, consciously or unconsciously, excluded.[15] But, as the development of biomedicine poses new, pressing questions, is the current guarantee of human dignity in danger of being pulverised – say, between the Preference Utilitarianism of P. Singer and the postulate of genetic "new construction" of the human by J. Watson? Neither the "law of progress" nor international competition nor the demands of national security could justify "human breeding" or the abandonment of those who lack

---

elderly, who no longer have such "prospect" to "develop as humans" or to "reestablish their humanness," that is, to be "awardable."

[14] From a personalized view, the embryonic stem cell has no history and is far from having the status of recognizable individuality. Stem cells from artificial fertilization (embryonic stem cells) or stem cells extracted from several day old embryos (embryonic germ cells) imply the destruction of the embryo. The extraction of stem cells from human embryos is banned in Germany. The Embryo Protection Law of 1990 (reprinted in the annex of this volume, under V 20) permits artificial fertilization of an egg cell only for purposes of impregnation. With this background, the Stem Cell Act of 2002 (reprinted in the annex of this volume, under V 19) regulates the importation and use of stem cells. It is permissible for high ranking, ethically justifiable research projects, where no other option would suffice – "a taste of the fruit of the poisoned tree"?

[15] The prohibition of defining "worthy" and "unworthy" life became a central component of Article 1, due to its historical development out of the Nazi contempt for human life. On the Basic Law's conception of the "human," cf. BVerfGE 4, 7, 15 et seq.: in principle, there is no priority for the individual's legal position. Article 1, paragraph 1 results from the connection with the basic rights and the rule of law (Art. 79, para. 3), as well as the basis of the Basic Law, in protection of subjective freedom, and the basis of the legitimization of the state and the law.

the autonomous possibility for development and thus would seem useless from a utilitarian perspective. And who would, and under what legitimisation, be permitted to define the goals of such an "optimisation" or the reasons for such a "liquidation"?

IV. Kantian Understanding of Human Dignity

But does the success or failure of human dignity *really* depend on issues such as, for example, somatic cell nuclear transfer into denuclearised, human egg cells? Let us first ascertain the standard: firstly, the Kantian definition of human dignity; secondly, its normative form and meaning according to G. Dürig and in Article 1, paragraph 1; and, thirdly, its canonisation by the Federal Constitutional Court!

"You had to be able, in part, to see as far as Kant," Dürig explained,[16] regarding his now almost half-century-old commentary. The Basic Law's primary article was the attempt "first to fathom the depths, to blaze a few trails, to lay a few runways: it's down that way, friends." What has the philosopher taught the public law scholar? What has the scholar, in turn, taught the Federal Constitutional Court? And what has the Court taught us? Has the doctrine of human dignity, the basis of our community, reached its limits, thus rendering our values obsolete and leaving human dignity violable?[17] Or do biomedical challenges prove the timeliness and durability of a specifically Dürigian value system and of a particularly Kantian understanding of human dignity?

The classic definition of the dignity of the human can be found in *Groundwork for the Metaphysics of Morals* (1785).[18] Kant bases dignity on the endowment of the human being with reason, on the abstract ability of self-determination: "*Autonomy* is thus the ground of the dignity of the human and of every rational nature" (emphasis in original). Dignity is independent from the intellectual or physical character of the specific human entity, from any personal achievements, from success or

---

[16]   Address of thanks on his 65th birthday, JöR 36 (1987), 91, 95.

[17]   Cf. *E.W. Böckenförde*, Die Würde des Menschen war unantastbar, F.A.Z. of 3 September 2003 criticising the new commentary to Art. 1, para. 1 Basic Law in Maunz-Dürig, supra note 1, by *M. Herdegen* (2003).

[18]   All quotations are from *A.W. Wood* (ed. & translator), Groundwork for the Metaphysics of Morals (2002). See also Kant's later work, The Metaphysics of Morals (1797). Parallel passages in *Goerlich*, supra note 10, 159 et seq.

failure of identity formation. According to this non-empirical definition, dignity is not attained; rather, it is assigned irrespectively. Personality, on the other hand, as empirical achievement, results from freedom. Reasonability, Kant asserts, elevates our actions above and beyond empirical (mis)chance; it alone prevents us from becoming the
mere plaything of circumstance. Reason validates universality. Expressed in the law, this yields, *inter alia*, human dignity's claim to universal application. According to this instructive conception, the individual's quality as subject is linked primarily to a participation in the
common reason, in the inherent, abundant endowment of reason on
each individual human being.

Kant differentiates between "price" and "dignity." The then developing,
national economy favoured the term "price," or "value," which was to
some degree up in the air; the moralist and economist Adam Smith died
in 1790. According to Kant's *Groundwork*, values can be correlated
with "equivalents." Exchanging them for one another (*e.g.*, "skill and
industry in labour") yields a "market price." But absolute, incomparable, or inner worth cannot be replaced at another price. It imparts to all
else a relative, derivative worth. Such unconditional worth – which is
not subject to any balancing test and which no equivalent can replace –
is possessed by only one thing on Earth: the human being, endowed
with moral identity, personal responsibility based in practical reason,
and the capability of self-determined ordering of its own life:

> In the realm of ends everything has either a *price* or a *dignity*. What
> has a price is such that something else can also be put in its place as
> its *equivalent*; by contrast, that which is elevated above all price, and
> admits of no equivalent, has a dignity.
>
> That which refers to universal human inclinations and needs has a
> *market price*; ... but that which constitutes the condition under
> which alone something can be an end in itself does not have merely
> a relative worth, i.e., a price, but rather an inner worth, i.e., *dignity*.[19]

Kant asserts that

> every rational being, *exists* as an end in itself (*Zweck an sich selbst*)...
> The human being, however, is not a thing, hence not something that

---

[19]   Groundwork, supra note 18 (here and in the following quotations, italics
in original), 52-53 (= BA 77).

can be used *merely* as a means.... Thus I cannot dispose of the human being in my own person....[20]

Thus the human being is unique, irreplaceable. In contrast to things, humans have no market value and no price (nor an "affective price"); instead, the human being has dignity, that is, personal and inner worth, which cannot be instrumentalised. One need not consider theological premises, although frequent in Kant, who is often in line with Stoic and Christian notions.

It would make sense, then, to construe the system to a "supreme end," to an end that requires no other end as a pre-condition for its realisation (Kant). Dignity – that worth which is not subject to balancing tests, which is irreplaceable, and which distinguishes the human being as such – owes its uniquely primary position to the necessary recognition of all those involved. Support for this position can be found in *Metaphysics*, according to which each person can claim respect for his or her own dignity from fellow humans, and the very concept of the human necessarily requires each to recognise the human dignity in every other human ("*die Würde der Menschheit an jedem anderen Menschen praktisch anzunehmen*").

The recognition of this unconditional worth necessitates no creator-God[21] or world regent, no intersubjectivity, as is the case with contract

---

[20]   Ibid., 45, 47 (= BA 67). Can Kant's overall approach help at all in protecting the embryo and in cloning? Typically, Kant's perspective is used in legal-philosophical essays primarily with respect to general justification of the law and the mutual limitations of everyone's external freedom. And this freedom is always that of a born human. Thus, human dignity and being an end-in-itself seem rather to be within the domain of morality, which – aside from its indefiniteness – carries no compulsive requirements for the law. This, possibly, must be reconsidered. Cf. *K. Kühl*, Strafrecht und Moral – Trennendes und Verbindendes, in Amelung et al. (eds.), Festschrift für H.L. Schreiber (2003), 959 et seq. Of course, Kant differentiated between autonomous "morality" and heteronomous "legality."

[21]   In constitutional law, despite the reference to God in the Basic Law's preamble, the principle of dignity can be substantiated without religion – solely by secular notions. But one can find the existence of a deductive interrelation (Isensee): the idea of human rights was conceived on the ground of Christianity. *H. Heller* already argued for the specifically Christian origin of the idea of human dignity and the equal freedom of all those with "human countenance" in his Staatslehre (1934). The biblical declaration that humans are made in God's image renders the understanding of human dignity independent from currently measurable, social consensus. Such consensus could deteriorate with the fading

models (e.g., Hobbes, Beccaria, Rousseau, Rawls; all of which, at any rate, are only fictional contracts), including Hegel's dialectic on master and servant. Nor is a double anthropology required, with the attendant difficulty of tearing apart the human's reason and its sensuality[22] while simultaneously conceiving of it as an inseparable unity. In order to explain a *rational* social order, as does Kant, one need not presuppose society as the primal fact, from which that explanation derives. Rather, each human must necessarily recognise the dignity of every other, simply because it claims human dignity for itself.[23] Contempt for another is contempt for the self; indeed, one cannot renounce the species of his or her own community, of the same human essence. No rational being, in orienting itself in its world, can help but affirm this dignity schema. It converges in *self*-respect, in which all subjects are equal.[24]

The *state* cannot be an "end in itself." Its "dignity" is rooted less in national than in international law, even if some scholars, and not only in the post-war period, might speculate on a doctrine of "constitutional institutions", in order to elevate this side of the commonwealth (as a condition for the security and freedom of the individual), as well. This is particularly true in Germany, despite the prevalent Hegelian conception of the state: the constitutional state exists not as an end in itself, but as an end for humanity, for the sake of human beings, and the human being exists, in turn, for its own sake.

---

of a common basic value. On the position of the German state churches, cf. *M. Kock*, DRiZ 2002, 199; *K. Lehmann*, ibid., 192.

[22]   Of course, Kant imagines (in recognition of the community of species [*Gattungsgemeinschaft*]) the human as "a rational being, obeying no law but that which he himself also gives" (Groundwork, supra note 18, 67 [= BA 77]) – the individual's unassailable value as participant in a system (of principles for thought) that ultimately transcends human reason.

[23]   This has always seemed, in my opinion, to be an especially enlightening element (species-conserving, since it is life-conserving) of Kant's practical philosophy. According to Kant, the bearer of reason is connected with all of nature *via* her or his institutional world. Practically, reason appears primarily as legal obligation of the will. The human fulfills its purpose by acting according to reason (which is considered as supraindividual in the still current philosophy of enlightenment) and thus by acting ethically correctly.

[24]   The banality of this final statement should not prevent its recognition, especially when defining dignity "reasonably" and secularly.

V. The Personal Scope of the Guarantee of Human Dignity

But what is a human being, and when does its existence begin? Each human possesses dignity (per Art. 1, para. 1, in regard to the personal scope of protection) based on the abstract ability of self-determination and determination of the (own) environment, independent of concrete capability (or incapability). The mentally ill, criminals, and misformed infants, as well as embryos, fetuses, the dying, and those already dead fall under the protection of dignity.[25] Thus, the inability to interact "normally" (*imbecillitas*) is not decisive. Where recourse to individual autonomy (rationality, consciousness) fails, because a given human being no longer possesses it (for example, a patient in a waking coma or one who is already braindead), this human being still possesses the full benefit of humanity, that is the objective quality of a human being, membership in the species Homo sapiens. Species membership[26] prohibits the denial of this human's basic rights for particular reasons – for instance, the inability to take part in conscious or social life (*socialitas*). Actual ability is not decisive; rather, it is the "potential ability, ingrained

---

[25] This is, of course, controversial with regard to the various stages of pre-birth, individual human development. Nature (or the "nature of the object") cannot provide the answer; only law can. Therefore, various qualifications persist, both globally and even among European nations. Only for conceptual naturalists does looking into a microscope replace the legal-political decision and the definitional jurisdiction of the culturally independent legislator (the WHO, for instance, considers a newborn to be an "infant in the first 28 days"). The practical side does offer the normative side certain points of contact, which seem less unfair than others. One example is the beginning of human life and its protective status; here, the merging of egg cells and sperm cells is the least arbitrary criterion.

[26] Even when a human being is *de facto* incapable of self-determination, it remains in the human species, based on its ethic-autonomous potential, protected in a permanent, indispensable core of personality: a generic, species-based understanding of human dignity. "Human dignity … is … the dignity of the human as a person of kind (*als Gattungswesen*). Everyone possesses it. … But the right of respect, which follows from it, is violable." BVerfGE 87, 209, 228. No injury against a particular human being can violate its generally human (capability-independent) value – contingency and transcendence are separate categories.

in human existence from the very beginning": "Where human life exists, human dignity inheres".[27]

"Human life" begins at fertilisation, at the completed merging of female egg-cell with male semen, that is, with the programming of the DNA.[28] (This starting point, as a supposedly "conceptually naturalistic" or even "biologistic" argument, is of course disputed.) The human quality, then, exists with the emergence of the embryo, according to the Federal Constitutional Court, which had previously only dealt with the emerging life *in utero*, not *in vitro*, "at least from the fourteenth day after conception (nidation, individuation)."[29] As a subject, a potential subject, or at least a developing form as subject, the fertilised human egg cell itself is considered a human embryo under the Embryo Protection Law.

---

[27] BVerfGE 39, 1, 41. Some have attempted to delegitimate this key tenet with the first Abortion Judgment. For example, conceptually distinguishing an embryo from an inferior "pre-embryo," a mere cluster of cells. Indeed, former Vice President Zeidler of the Federal Constitutional Court qualified it as a "raspberry-like object."

[28] Counter-argument (H. Markl, R. Wolfrum, et al.): the fertilized human egg cell is indeed genetically individualized and capable of development but not independently and of itself; rather, it can develop only after implantation in a receptive, female uterus and in constant interaction with the mother's body (cf. also the position of the DFG, Humane embryonale Stammzellen (2001)). It is well established that these human zygotes have neither sensory nor motor reaction and thus are not capable of consciousness. From a scientific and medical standpoint, it is only certain that they could develop, while in the mother's womb, into a birthable, viable human. But to consider a zygote a human (with full rights and dignity), simply due to its potential for development, requires further justification. At any rate, consensus certainly asserts that the human being is not to be equated with its genetic make-up. The embryo's potential is finally, inescapably dependent on the pregnancy, an interactive process. Cf. also the DFG's Recommendations for Research with Embryos of 03/05/2001, WissR 34 (2001), 287 et seq.

[29] BVerfGE 39, 1, 41. The implantation of the approximately two week old embryo is the decisive condition for development of its life: the production of the permanent physiological supporting and interactive relationship to a physical mother. A completely extracorporeal development is not possible for any higher mammal. Italy's Embryo Protection Law of December 2003 provides the fetus with human status from the point of procreation. Consequently, PID for the purpose of selection of embryos is criminalized, as are surrogate motherhood, sale of germ cells, and research on embryos. Same-sex partners, singles, and informal, heterosexual couples are excluded from artificial fertilization – on the whole, a victory for political Catholicism.

The fertilised, human egg-cell is neither a "legal commodity," distinct from a human being, nor a creature, a mere biological occurrence, a cluster of cells: partner or object, human being or thing, a who or a what – *tertium non datur*.[30] The protective status for pre-birth, human life certainly cannot be only that of animals or nature! (Not even if Article 20a accords great import to the respect for the animal and plant worlds, or if A. Schweitzer's *Reverence for Life* elevates the animal to the level of an end in itself.) But does its status equal that of post-birth life? The fertilised egg cell of a human is already under the pre-effective protection not only of Article 2, paragraph 2, but also – and this is the core of the controversy – of Article 1, paragraph 1: "human dignity from the very beginning" (Chr. Starck). At least according to German legislators, research with embryos or with totipotent, human stem-cells violates the Embryo Protection Law; other violations include pre-implantation diagnostics (PID), the technically yet unrealised alteration of the human germline, and cloning – that is, genetic copying – of human embryos. Extraction, import, or use of embryonic, human stem cells is in principle forbidden – by stem-cell law, anyway – even for high-ranking research purposes.[31]

---

[30] Where human life exists, it receives the protection of Art. 2, para. 2. Human tissue cells lack the *telos* of eventually becoming a human being. For a critical view of this "conceptually naturalistic" definition of the beginning of life, see *H. Hofmann*, Biotechnik, Gentherapie, Genmanipulation - Wissenschaft imrechtsfreien Raum?, JZ 1986, 258 et seq.; *W. Heun*, Embryonenforschung und Verfassung – Lebensrecht und Menschenwürde der Embryos, JZ 2002, 517 et seq. But see also *C. Starck*, Verfassungsrechtliche Grenzen der Biowissenschaft und Fortpflanzungsmedizin, JZ 2002, 1065 et seq.

[31] PID, which is not yet ready to be used, is a matter of examining artificially fertilized embryos with the intention to identify genetic problems or other characteristics, sort out the sick or undesired embryos, and then only implant the others. Ultimately, this process of prenatal malformation diagnostics, with the possibility of subsequent abortion, is "positive eugenics," the claim of the "right to decide over which human life shall have the right to develop" (*Zypries*, supra note 13, pp. 113 et seq.). Cf. also *S. Schneider*, Rechtliche Aspekte der Präimplantations- und Präfertilisationsdiagnostik (2002). In contrast, the supporters of PID point to flagrant contradictions in in the context of the legal regulation of abortion: greater protection for the embryo *in vitro* than for the embryo *in vivo*, and according to the Stem Cell Act (reprinted in the annex of this volume, under V 19) research is allowed (only) with certain imported stem cells from lines produced before 1 January 2002. This deadline supposedly prevents Germany from being the incentive for further destruction of embryos. Stem cells are extracted from the inside of the morula, that is, from approxi-

VI. Human Dignity and God's Likeness

For the *Christian*, a human being is what it is by God. The human, in
its dignity, is thus inviolable, indispensable, inalienable not "only" because of its species membership or its biological characteristics, but because it is – per biblical declaration – the work of God and *imago Dei*.
An individual cannot be a "non-person" or mere "human material," irrespective of how unworthy of life or how "ready-made" for research
she or he may seem. This obtains when the human pre-condition, based
on the unique relationship to God, is conferred; when the external
(metaphysical) imputation takes place.[32] Therein lies a distinction between human and animal, significant not only from a Judeo-Christian
perspective. Other religions (and legal orders) similarly do not consider
the animal as such to be the image of God and worthy of respect.

The subjective and objective extent of dignity's protection is closely
entangled with species criteria and the "object formula." The human
being inevitably finds itself in a community – an interconnected
grouping of healthy and sick persons, of dying and developing life, of
newborns and those in waking comas. Thereby, human dignity and the
right to life are effectively coupled and inter-reinforced.[33] This premise,
then, is the basis for the system of protections and limitations of basic
rights, as developed in the legal literature. Similarly, it is the basis for
the judicially inherited idea of a human, equally encompassing
individuality *and* community, the potential for development *and* the
reality of death. The entire course of becoming, being, and passing is
protected.

---

mately four day old, human embryos, which die off following the intrusion:
thus, stem cell extraction is also embryo consumption.

[32] Kant's general reason contains the key to the cosmos; even God is bound
by it. The natural endowment of reason on the human opens a rational means
of communicating with God (cf. the theological concept, stating that a newborn
has been known to God since time out of mind). Furthermore, sin does not negate the nature of having been created by God in his image. Human existence in
accord with God is an existence in unity of human and human.

[33] But cf. *H. Dreier*, Stufungen des vorgeburtlichen Lebensschutzes, ZRP
2002, 377 et seq.; cf. also the contrary contributions of *J. Nida-Rümelin* (ed.),
Ethische Essays (2002); *R. Merkel*, Forschungssubjekt Embryo (2002). Those
who reject a multi-tiered protection of pre-birth life adhere to the paradigm of
categorical equality among all stages of human life.

VII. Transnational Protection of Human Dignity

This inherited system is complemented today by European and international human-rights protections, which are admittedly still fragmentary and problematically enforceable. Further, the system is enhanced by the principles of legal interpretation in conformity with human rights (Art. 1, para. 2, Art. 25, Art. 59, para. 2) and European law (cf. Art. 23).[34] The relation between (world) peace and the material guarantee of human rights is particularly accentuated, even after having already shaped the UN Charter (1945) and the Universal Declaration of Human Rights (1948). But this, including the "conditionality of human rights" (W. von Simson),[35] may well be an entirely separate matter.

Various recent, legal-political documents, for example, the Council of Europe's Convention on Human Rights and Biomedicine[36] or the UNESCO Declaration on the Human Genome and Human Rights[37], refer explicitly to "human dignity" as the fundamental point of reference and of limitation[38]: could this be resonance with the philosopher's

---

[34]   The Basic Law's formula – as a value-oriented system with the individual and his or her dignity at the center (BVerfGE 2, 1, 12) – finds support in international and European law, though not displacing the ethical primacy on the EU or UN levels. Cf. *M. Kotzur*, Theorieelemente des internationalen Menschenrechtsschutzes (2001), 217 et seq.; ECJ, Case 29/69, Stauder, ECR 419, para. 6 et seq. (1969) (human dignity protects the individual's self-determination over his living environment). Though still only soft law, the EU Charter of Human Rights (OJ 2000 C 354, 9 et seq.) contains absolute rights as well. These are, *inter alia*, results of the pointed guarantee of human dignity, with which the Charter begins (Chapter 1, heading; Arts. 1-5 EU Charter, reprinted in the annex of this volume, under IV 16), though without definition (or reference to humanity's being in God's image).

[35]   Similarly reserved in the face of contingencies, which limit universalism, *P. Mastronardi*, Menschenwürde und kulturelle Bedingtheit des Rechts, in Th. Marauhn (ed.), Die Stellung des Menschen im Völkerrecht (2003), 55, 73: "Human dignity [...] urgently must be universalized."

[36]   Reprinted in the annex of this volume, under III 15.

[37]   Reprinted in the annex of this volume, under II 13.

[38]   Cf. *L. Honnefelder et al.* (eds.), Das Übereinkommen über Menschenrechte und Biomedizin des Europarats (1999); *J. Taupitz*, Biomedizinische Forschung zwischen Freiheit und Verantwortung (2002); *I. Kamp*, Die Europäische Bioethik-Konvention (2000). Neither the European Convention on Human Rights nor the Treaty on European Union mention the term "human dignity." In European jurisprudence, it leads a life only in the shadows. Not so in the EU

propositions? Perhaps, but the protective status of the embryo has still only been vaguely defined; certainly, any resonance is primarily due to the fact that institutional Europe still constantly faces the continent's *vieux démons* and the collapse of civilisation, especially in questions of basic rights, biomedicine, and obligation to certain values. Europe attempts, essentially, to erect dams in the river of ethical discourse. Indeed, those documents ultimately answer neither whether limitations on human dignity are possible *in principle* nor at which stage of individual development a human being is the bearer of human dignity and rights. The Courts in Luxembourg and Strasbourg have not yet decisively dealt with these delicate questions. For the time being, only strictly secular rationales and derivations of the guarantee of human dignity have prospect for pan-European recognition and implementation. "Here, recourse to Kant and the 'object formula' (*Objektformel*) that is prevalent in Germany, would seem proper" (M. Borowsky).

The EU Charter of Human Rights contains an unfortunate, ambiguous peculiarity in terminology. The German version of the Charter recognizes fundamental rights not for *jeden* ("each"), *jedermann* ("everybody") or *jedem Menschen* ("every human") but for *jede Person* ("every person"). The concept of a distinct "dignity of the person," which not every human possesses, has been advanced primarily in Anglo-American areas. Similarly, in the context of the current, biopolitical debate in Germany, this troubling distinction between "human" and "person" is occasionally made, thereby diminishing protection. But such a differentiation is unknown to German constitutional law. On the contrary, the Federal Constitutional Court, as with Kant and Dürig, has considered species membership alone to be sufficient to trigger the right to human dignity – that is, the right to protection against indignity and instrumentalisation. And the EU Constitution, admittedly not yet finally resolved (much less operative), speaks throughout only of "humans" and not of "persons."

VIII. Towards an International Ban on Human Cloning?

Construction of a constitutional system – of the instrument of government and the Bill of Rights – on the Kantian basis of human dignity as

---

Charter of Human Rights, which accentuates the respect for human dignity and anticipates, *inter alia*, a ban on alteration of the human genetic constitution.

an end in itself remains persuasive. In the debate on communitarism, both political philosophy and constitutional law have rediscovered the vibrancy of human dignity.[39] The bioethics discussion has critically re-assessed the dogmatic productivity and connectivity of that basis, in view of fundamentally new prospects and risks[40]: R. Spaemann has already identified a "scientistic debasement (*Entwürdigung*) of the human," and Chr. Hillgruber has observed an "interpretive deformation of the object of protection." Thus, for example, plans for ("reproductive") cloning of a human being – a highly unnatural form of reproduction – would already be inconsistent with the *cloned* human's dignity.[41] It would be denied,

> what is part of every human existence: to stem from a random combination of the father's and the mother's hereditary construction. Regardless of whether we characterise this genetic combination as random, willed by God or as fate: its independence from human disposal is the basis from which human autonomy and thus human freedom accrue.[42]

The negotiations on an international ban on cloning have not led, in fact, to any tangible result on the UN level and are not set to resume until January 2005. The German Federal Government, here, has been

---

[39]   On the conception of the human in communitarism, see *Mastronardi*, supra note 35, 68 et seq. It is admittedly difficult to fully understand the debate over communitarism (as opposed to liberalism) outside of its U.S. American context.

[40]   As mentioned above, Christianity cannot be the determining fundament, which upholds the system of the Basic Law. It does, however, offer a "constitutional girder" (P. Kirchof). What has been abandoned are "the religious notions of the human in God's image as a theological counterpart to human dignity and of translating the holiness of life into secular terms" (M. Borowsky).

[41]   Cloning further results in an unnatural parent-child relationship. A cloned child would be both child and twin sibling of the parent, whose genes were cloned. The child would not be the offspring of the other parent. Nonetheless, this parent would be expected to help raising a younger version of his or her spouse.

[42]   *Zypries*, supra note 13, p. 116. Zypries resists therapeutic cloning with the "flood-gates argument" that she otherwise avoids: "how can we be sure that these techniques will not be used to allow this embryo to mature beyond three or four days?" The more urgent question is to what degree this cloning crosses the boundary into consumption – or cannibalization – of human life. Cf. *J. Taupitz*, Der rechtliche Rahmen des Klonens zu therapeutischen Zwecken, NJW 2001, 3433 et seq.

"strikingly restrained" (M. Böhmer). But the overarching issues still require much open consideration and systematic reflection[43]: on the respect for and protection of the dignity of the human being within the constructs of a pluralistic, open society[44]; on the freedom of the individual; on the fast development of biomedicine and human genetics with all their possibilities and risks for human life. Facing the increasing tendency to separate, and thereby dilute, the protections of human dignity and of human life, the rallying cry must be: "Back to Kant!"

---

[43] Compare *M. Herdegen*, Die Menschenwürde im Fluß des bioethischen Diskurses, JZ 2001, 773 et seq. with *Böckenförde*, supra note 17. The latter rejects the "trial-like treatment," which would have dignity emerge and evolve (e.g., pre- versus postnatal protection of dignity). Böckenförde also rejects the criticism that dignity would finally be surrendered to a weighing of values, as with every other legal position (a "sliding scale"). Cf. also *Zypries*, supra note 13, who in fact is much closer to Herdegen/Dreier, for example, than to Böckenförde/Kirchhof.

[44] Here, European integration leads to particular problems in so far as the EU could support research projects that are prohibited in Germany.

From Procreation to Generation?
Constitutional and Legal-Political Issues in Bioethics

Brigitte Zypries, Berlin [*]

The great advances in genetics and biomedicine have increased the "individual's course of action" immensely. This opinion is expressed by the sociologist Hans Jonas and he adds that, up until now, we have lacked the specification of our values necessary to make this choice. This means, more precisely, that the more we are able to do things that surpass what so far has been impossible, the more we have to be sure whether we wish to do everything that we could do – and why we may deliberately refrain from doing some things. Constitutional and bioethical issues cannot be viewed separately. The importance of this issue is currently particularly demonstrated by pre-implantation diagnosis, research with embryos and embryonic stem cells, and by anonymous donation of semen. I would like to make you acquainted with these three topics, and present my thoughts on fundamental bioethical and constitutional issues.

I. Protection of the Embryo and the Basic Law

The decisive step from procreation to generation was, which becomes clearer in hindsight, the birth of Louise Brown 25 years ago. She was the result of the first successful *in vitro* fertilisation (IVF). Until then,

[*] Lecture held at the Humboldt Forum, Humboldt University of Berlin on the 29th of October, 2003.

the process of fertilisation was kept separate from human intervention and monitoring, as the process occurred inside the body of the mother. From this moment on, the decisive stage of the process could be relocated to the petri dish; a technical process replaced a natural one. Procreation could, in a sense, become generation. This development brought with it new questions: Is childlessness fated? Alternatively, is it perhaps a medical condition or an obstacle which can be technically overcome?

The connection between the embryo and the mother, which exists from the outset in the case of natural fertilisation, develops without outside assistance and leads, in a small percentage of cases, to the nidation of the embryo. In the case of *in vitro* fertilisation, however, this connection is achieved by a deliberate, highly-engineered and error-prone act of a third person, the physician. This act, namely the implantation of the embryo, can be omitted or it can be carried out only after screening, the so-called pre-implantation diagnosis (PID). Still not technically feasible, yet conceivable, is the instance whereby the implantation of the embryo precedes its genetic modification. Even if the embryo is not implanted, it can still be kept alive without establishing the connection to the mother – that is by freezing it. This has the consequence that the embryo can also be utilised for other purposes. It can be donated and hence implanted into another woman, or it can be used for research purposes, in which it can, for example, be destroyed in order to extract stem cells.

The affected couple's course of action (or the course of action of the mother) is, thus, not only expanded by technical assistance to achieve pregnancy. The couple is also given the opportunity to select the embryo, to discard the embryo, to make the embryo available for another couple or to allow its destruction for research purposes. In addition, there are visions of improving the embryo genetically, or even to attempt to create a genetic copy of another person.

It is doubtful whether these visions will ever be technically possible. Nevertheless, they also require a "specification of our values", and rules based thereupon, not least in order to ward off that which conflicts with our values.

The German "Act for the Protection of Embryos" (*Embryonen-schutzgesetz*)[1] established a clear definition of values: every production

---

[1]   English version reprinted in the annex of this volume, under V 20.

and every use of a human embryo is illegal unless it is for the procurement of a pregnancy of the woman concerned.

The legislator has thus decided to narrow the woman's course of action (or that of the affected couple), as well as that of the doctor and the researcher. This means at the same time that the legislator infringes upon their basic rights. One cannot lose sight of the fact that not only the embryo's, but also the parents' and the scientists' basic rights are affected by regulations for the protection of the embryo. In a liberal society, an extension of the course of action is fundamentally synonymous with an increase in the protected, although not wholly unconstrained, constitutional freedoms of citizens. Despite all manner of scientific development, parents do not have a right to a child carrying their own genes or a right to a healthy child. The reason for this is that nobody can guarantee the fulfilment of anyone's desire to have a child, or the health of the child. Nevertheless, the German Basic Law (*Grundgesetz der Bundesrepublik Deutschland* – hereinafter "Basic Law") does protect parents' freedom to decide for themselves whether to seek medical support in fulfilling their wish to have a child. This also includes the available biomedical diagnosis before and after the implantation. And a scientist can invoke the freedom of research as guaranteed under the Basic Law, a freedom that constitutes a significant element of our democratic legal order. Only the infringement of the rights of a third party may justify any restraints on the parents' freedom of action or on the freedom of research. In my opinion, we must not *a priori* exclude embryonic stem cell extraction from the protection of the freedom of research, for it is a part of the research process and essential for the pursuit of particular scientific goals. We are forced to consider all colliding basic rights. Therefore, I will not be able to present you with simple solutions today.

When the legislator – as in the case of the Act for the Protection of Embryos – infringes upon the basic rights of parents and researchers, he must present justifiable reasons. These are found, insofar as the basic rights of others are concerned, primarily with regard to the embryo.

We hence come to the issue of whether or to what extent an embryo *in vitro* enjoys protection under the Basic Law. Hardly any question is as controversial in both society and the doctrine of constitutional law, and not without reason. The issue is not merely a question of simple legal reasoning. Instead it involves philosophical, religious or ideological aspects as well as scientific and legal facets, and all of these are closely bound up with one another. Not only the valuations but also the insights concerning the beginning and end of human life are vague. Chances and risks in biomedicine are largely undetermined.

Against this difficult background, I am sceptical whether categorical responses should be derived from our Basic Law, considering that the current issues concerning biomedicine were not foreseeable when the Basic Law was drafted. The fact that the mothers and fathers of the Basic Law could not anticipate the current issues does not release us from the task of interpreting the Basic Law in light of these new problems. The Basic Law is equipped for this purpose. It is not a rigid constitution, but can and should be interpreted where necessary. Particularly the interpretation of the basic rights is, in light of new dangers and conflicts, open for development – also without an explicit amendment of the text. This has consequences for the methods of interpretation; if the text and the history of the Basic Law do not provide a clear answer, then it is not only legitimate, but also necessary, to consider the varying consequences of different alternatives of interpretation. The issues surrounding biomedicine are complex and, as a consequence of continual scientific progress, subject to constant change. Furthermore, these issues are widely disputed in our own society. Legal comparison shows that such issues are treated in many different ways in states with a similarly liberal constitution. In my opinion, this indicates that the legislator must have the right to maintain some discretion in order to fulfil his duty to protect human life – a discretion which must be exercised with caution, however. The German Parliament has done this in the past with extreme seriousness and care. Call to mind the debates and decisions regarding induced abortions or the protection of embryos! In my opinion, we have no reason not to have sufficient confidence in the legislator, never mind to distrust him.

What are the constitutional guidelines that the legislator must follow when fulfilling his responsibilities? His task is to adjudge the conflicting basic rights in bioethical issues. One specification is certainly to be found in Art. 2 (2) Basic Law – the right to life – a right which also entails a duty of the state to protect human life. This duty extends also to unborn life, as stated by the Federal Constitutional Court in its decision concerning Article 218 of the Criminal Code. But when does this duty commence? When does human life commence? Is an *in vitro* embryo also protected? The Federal Constitutional Court did not have to answer this question in its decisions concerning induced abortion because the legal issues associated with induced abortion only emerge at the completion of nidation of the impregnated egg. The Court stipulates, however, that it seems self-evident that human life commences upon completion of the fusion of the egg and sperm, in other words with the formation of the embryo. I believe that it is correct to allow the constitutional protection under Art. 2 (2) Basic Law to commence at this earliest possible point in time. An embryo, even one *in vitro*, is not an arbitrary group of cells over which parents, doctors and researchers can exercise control at their discretion. They are not allowed to exercise their constitutional freedom irrespective of the responsibility owed to the embryo. An unconstrained authorisation of preimplantation diagnosis and the extraction of embryonic stem cells would exceed the legislator's constitutional discretion.

As formulated by the Federal Constitutional Court, the right to life is not, however, protected absolutely – even if it represents a foundational value within the constitutional order. This right may be infringed upon, if the infringement is based upon a law. This legal reservation allows for the protection of life to be graded, to accrue in accordance with gradual materialisation, such as the legislator did under Articles 218 et seq. of the German Criminal Code for naturally conceived life. The right to life therefore accords some discretion for considerations of the basic rights of parents and researchers.

On the other hand, human dignity is protected absolutely. According to the prevailing opinion, it is not amenable to subsequent considerations. I agree with this. The commitment to the inviolability of human dignity is the foundation of our constitution. Part of its inviolability is that it cannot be balanced with other basic rights. Due to this absolute protection, we must particularly closely examine the issue, whether the *in vitro* embryo enjoys the right to human dignity. In fact, some authors of legal scholarship want to accord human dignity to the embryo, but wish to keep the protection open for relativisation. In my opinion, this is an erroneous approach. It is, however, somewhat excessive to carry this dispute into the feature pages and – as Ernst Wolfgang Böckenförde did in the *Frankfurter Allgemeine Zeitung* under the heading "Human dignity *was* inviolable"[2] – to insinuate the end of human dignity. You may have followed his dispute with Matthias Herdegen on Herdegen's new commentary of Article 1 Basic Law. Those who deduce a comprehensive ban of PID and of embryonic research from the inviolability of human dignity must ask themselves this: Are the attempts to relativise the protection of human dignity not also a result of a broad interpretation of Article 1 Basic Law?

---

[2]   F.A.Z., 3 September 2003, p. 33. Emphasis added. ‑

Since the advent of this basic right, the concept of human dignity has been controversial. It manifestly includes the respect of the intrinsic value of every person and every individual existence. This also applies to the possibility of personal responsibility and individual self-determination. Every person has his dignity and the right to respect for it. This is the case independent of his psychological or physical development, of personal achievement or the successful formation of an identity.

The impregnated egg cell, the embryo in the petri dish, has solely the prospect to cultivate that which I have just described as the constitutive elements of human dignity. The question is now: Does this potential suffice to constitute a recognition of human dignity in the sense of Article 1 Basic Law? Please allow me to identify the fundamental considerations that will lead us to this answer: the first consideration relates to the function of the basic rights. They constitute a protection against state action and they are an expression of our order of values. However, they also establish an obligation of the state to protective action. The *in vitro* embryo would be directly depending on this duty to protective action in order to materialise its human dignity. It would, however, not only be dependent on the state, but more importantly on a woman willing to carry the embryo to term. The state cannot force anybody to carry out this task. This becomes clear when we, secondly, point out that this constellation not only exists with embryos produced *in vitro*, but also, for example, in the application of the contraceptive coil. In this case, too, the impregnated egg cell is prevented from implanting and developing. We must thus be careful not to centre the protection of basic rights on something that we cannot realistically fulfil. As long as the embryo remains *in vitro*, it lacks an essential requirement to independently develop into a human being or – as the Federal Constitutional Court formulated it in its latest decision concerning Article 218 Criminal Code for the foetus – to develop "as" a human being. The mere abstract possibility of it continuing to develop in this sense does not, in my view, suffice for awarding human dignity.

Thus, our constitution drafts a framework for biomedicine, a framework which one can (and must) dispute in each individual case. However, we cannot leave it at the constitutional issues. For the constitution does not provide us with more than a framework. We cannot simply look up the "right" answers to bioethical issues in the Basic Law. Instead we must be at pains to carefully analyse and deliberate the chances and risks of biomedicine for every particular topic area. Anything less would do justice neither to the topic nor to the constitution.

II. Pre-Implantation Diagnosis

Please allow me to use the example of pre-implantation diagnosis (PID) to outline exactly what I mean by this. PID is concerned with the genetic analysis of impregnated embryos in the petri dish. The objective of this is to detect genetic disorders or other characteristics, and to separate the genetically impaired or unsuitable embryos so that the remaining ones are implanted.

At the moment, PID is prohibited. However, some members of the National Ethics Council, for example, are calling for it to be allowed. The supporters of PID correctly state, as I have already pointed out, that the prohibition of this diagnosis infringes upon parents' freedom of decision. It is chiefly argued that this prohibition practically forces a woman to have a potentially genetically-impaired embryo transplanted. Later, following prenatal-diagnosis, the foetus may be aborted on the basis of medical indication. However, this entails significantly greater strain and health dangers for the woman. I find these reasons for permitting PID to be creditable.

A further argument supporting PID is that so-called "late abortions" could hereby be avoided. Nevertheless, I consider the reference to late abortions to be problematic.

According to this view, PID would practically equate to bringing forward a prenatal diagnosis. However, I see two clear differences between prenatal diagnosis and PID and thus also between PID and the case of abortion. Firstly, an abortion is the last resort in an unresolvable conflict between the interests of the woman and those of the child. Please bear in mind that our law does not recognise embryopathic indication. Even though the reality occasionally differs from our legal values and perhaps sometimes even seems to clash with the law, we should not depart from our basic principles of law. These principles are specified as follows: a genetic impairment of an embryo itself does not justify an abortion. Additionally, there have to be profound adverse affects for the woman. Only this situational conflict will make an abortion acceptable. The artificial generation of embryos on the other hand, in order to subject them to PID, is responsible for causing the conflict, which is then resolved at the expense of the embryo.

Secondly, as opposed to prenatal diagnosis, the actual objective of pre-implantation diagnosis is not the rejection of impaired embryos, but rather the selection of suitable ones - thus positive eugenics. By using PID we claim the right to decide over which human life shall have the right to develop. So far, we have not – in my opinion for good reasons – trusted ourselves to do this.

It creates, namely, another question: How will it affect our society if we permit PID in respect of particular genetic dispositions? One must not lose sight of the following: even if one could use PID to ensure that in the future all children grow healthily in the womb, one would still not be able to guarantee that they would also be born healthy and remain healthy. The issue of how to deal with disabilities and sicknesses is not resolved by PID, but by eliminating human life with particular genetic features the answer would, in a way, already have taken shape. This I consider disquieting.

How are we supposed to behave when interacting with somebody who has these characteristics, if human life by law, in this disposition is declared as - and I deliberately formulate this drastically – "worthy of elimination"? How should a person with these characteristics feel? Must a mother justify herself for accepting a handicapped child and thereby potentially imposing burdens upon society? Is she ultimately placed under a duty to produce a healthy child as a quasi "quality product"? Taking into account that recent studies in the USA have shown that over 80% of all parents would abort a pregnancy if they knew that their child was genetically predisposed to obesity, this issue becomes more pressing.

In my deliberations up until now, I have assumed that PID is thought of as a possible solution for particular situations of conflict. The perception that is automatically associated with this is that we could restrict the legal authorisation of PID to these particular situations. Here, however, I envisage a subsequent, irrecoverable problem that I consider decisive against a legalisation of PID: experience shows that such a restriction cannot be maintained in practice, regardless how it is formulated.

This can be seen most evidently in the example of prenatal diagnosis. Originally, it was only intended for a few medical indications. Nevertheless, it has today become one of the standard preventive medical examinations, and I am certain that PID would, no matter what is written in the law, within a few years likewise become standard screening for *in vitro* fertilisation. Please remember that reproductive health professionals, who would be responsible for determining the precise application of this procedure, would probably tend towards an extension of PID. Firstly, the application of PID generally increases the success rate of *in vitro* fertilisation. Secondly, it could help to prevent complications such as the possibility of multiple births. Both motives are, as such, honourable. If we were to permit PID, it would in all probability become extremely difficult for a physician to refuse a couple their request to carry out PID regardless of any special medical indications. Perhaps this is also a reason why the German Doctors' Council opposed the authorisation of PID.

However, not only due to the probable relaxation of legal criteria would we experience a considerable increase in the applicable instances of PID than come to mind when laying down the criteria. No, we would also provoke further instances of application of another sort, as a simple consideration makes clear: PID is linked to extracorporeal fertilisation, which was in turn only originally intended for fertility disorders. Now there are couples with genetic risks who, on the one hand, fulfil the criteria with which we possibly associate the implementation of PID, but who, on the other hand, do not have fertility disorders. Permitting PID would, therefore, inevitably force the affected woman to resort to *in vitro* fertilisation, something which is not entirely unproblematic for her and which was itself originally intended for other circumstances – another thought that I cannot come to terms with.

In my mind, the reasons for maintaining a ban on PID ultimately prevail. Naturally, I am aware of the fact that we are not dealing with a mere abstract legal issue, but with a subject touching the life plans of affected couples. However, permitting PID unavoidably affects an embryo's right to life and entails fundamental implications for society's dealings with sickness and disability. Permitting PID could not guarantee the fulfilment of the wish for a healthy child, since healthy-born children can also fall ill. I recognise that parents desiring children also express through their desire a readiness to assume responsibility for future consequences. In this constellation, however, responsibility for the future requires the parents to sacrifice their wish for a child genetically their own because the price to be paid is too great. As difficult as it may be for the individuals concerned, there are cases in which childlessness is a fate that, despite all manner of scientific and technical possibilities, we cannot and should not try to escape.

III. Research with Embryos and Embryonic Stem Cells

I would now like to introduce a related topic – research with embryos and embryonic stem cells. Germany introduced the Act on the Protection of Embryos in 1991. It prohibits every use of embryos which does not aim at procuring pregnancy. The German Government has not presented any initiatives to change the Act on the Protection of Embryos. Even if the law is unclear on some peripheral matters, and even if the rapid development within genetic engineering constantly poses new questions, the law is still manageable in its present form. Nevertheless, we must continue to follow scientific developments closely.

I consider the prohibition on human cloning to be inviolable. To undertake clone attempts on humans is not only condemnable in light of the high rate of miscarriages and serious defects witnessed in cloned animals. It is also incompatible with the human dignity – more specifically the dignity of the born human – to deny him what is part of every human existence: to stem from a random combination of the father's and the mother's hereditary construction. Regardless of whether we characterise this genetic combination as random, willed by God or as fate: its independence from human disposal is the basis from which human autonomy and thus human freedom accrue.

I am also sceptical of the calls to permit so-called therapeutical cloning, i.e. cloning that allows the cloned embryo to mature for a few days, only to be destroyed in order to extract its embryonic stem cells. This is problematic because the protection of the embryo's life can only be realised when the initial generation is already prohibited. And it is here that we must pay particular heed to the indirect consequences. Even though I believe that one should only reluctantly use the so-called "flood-gates argument", which is often raised in bioethical debates, I believe we should carefully consider it here. If we permit techniques to be developed which allow the cloning of human life, how can we be sure that these techniques will not be used to allow this embryo to mature beyond three or four days. The legislator should be cautious when considering these peripheral issues.

New scientific studies provide an indication as to how we can deal with this ethical dilemma. It may become possible to extract autologous (i.e. stemming from the patient) stem cells, without having to pursue the path of cloned embryo generation. This may be wishful thinking. For it is not yet clear which discoveries science will make and which reprogramming techniques it will develop. On one point researchers agree however: in order to understand the development processes of the human body and its cells, and in order to find out which therapeutic potential the varying kinds of stem cells have, all kinds of stem cells must be analysed: adult stem cells, stem cells from umbilical cord blood or from aborted foetuses – and also embryonic stem cells.

Therefore, the German Parliament, following extremely intensive debates in June 2002, passed the German Stem Cell Act (*Stammzellgesetz*)[3], which permits research with certain imported stem cells. This law thus provides the opportunity to pursue basic research and to fathom the potential of stem cells in Germany. This is to occur by importing stem cells that are extracted out of so-called surplus embryos produced following artificial fertilisation. It is confined to the extraction of surplus embryos so that the production of embryos exclusively for research purposes is also not supported abroad. The German Parliament also decided upon a key date solution: only stem cells that were deposited from lines before 1st January, 2002 can be imported; this key date was introduced so as not to provoke an incentive emanating from Germany for an increase in stem cell extraction.

I realise that many researchers are not satisfied with the Stem Cell Act. They are correct in pointing out that every restriction on the freedom of research requires particular justification. They fear that many prominent scientists will head abroad, where stem cell research is less restricted and where, in particular, new stem cell lines can be deposited and used. They fear that Germany will not be able to keep pace with medical-scientific advances. The Central Ethics Commission for Stem Cell Research, established in July 2002, has received seven applications for permission for projects to this date. Five of these applications have so far been approved by the Commission. Nevertheless, the Commission believes that one cannot determine whether the low degree of interest is due to the Stem Cell Act not permitting research to the desired extent. The applications concern basic research projects that are financed by the German Research Foundation and the Max Planck Society. One application approved came from a pharmaceutical firm. I believe we have to pay very close attention to this development.

Not only as far as Germany as a research location is concerned, but rather the entire present bioethical debate is characterised by the fact that it cannot be carried out without a glance across national borders. An international prohibition against cloning at the UN level is currently being negotiated. The EU will have to decide within the forthcoming weeks how it wishes to proceed with the furtherance of stem cell research in the EU from 2004. The German Parliament has looked into these issues a number of times and has insistently drawn attention to the inherent protection of human life. On 16th October, 2003 the German Parliament affirmed once more that the joint research of the

---

[3]   English version reprinted in the annex of this volume, under V 19.

EU must avoid placing pressure on Member states' divergent legal positions. Thus, the German Government should work towards keeping research support restricted to projects with existing stem cell lines. And this is exactly what the Government is committed to doing in Brussels.

I place particular importance on one aspect: as the extraction of stem cells always requires the destruction of embryos, i.e. it affects human life, every decision in this field requires a particularly careful consideration of the affected rights. This requires a "most considerate balancing" ("*möglichst schonenden Ausgleich*") of the conflicting rights, as stipulated by the German Federal Constitutional Court. The right of researchers to the freedom of research must not be invalidated. And we cannot lose sight of the legitimate societal interest of improving the fundamental scientific principles for transplant medicine or the fight against cancer. Also in this issue, politics must be committed to play its part. For stem cell research this means: Are the stem cell lines produced before the key date 1st January, 2002 sufficient for current basic research? Are new stem cell lines required at present in order to understand the development process and to plumb the depths of the therapeutic potential?

The Stem Cell Act opens up opportunities. These should be used by researchers. Both Government and the legislator will then be required to scrutinise whether a relaxation of the Stem Cell Act is necessary. This is certainly not forbidden constitutionally.

IV. Heterologous Insemination

Matters regarding the "Procreation or Generation" of a child also come into question with artificial insemination – even if this example more closely resembles "procreation" when compared with the aforementioned issues. Depending on whether the transferable semen comes from the husband (or partner) of the woman or a third party, one must distinguish between homologous and heterologous insemination. Of particular precariousness in this context is the issue whether this "third man" is able to remain anonymous – with the consequence that the child will not be able to identify his or her biological father.

Due to the renewed discussion over the legitimacy of "anonymous semen donors", an article appeared in the *Spiegel magazine* with the provocative headline "Sperm for the Do-it-yourselfer". The article reported on an English firm's efforts to set up anonymous sperm banks in Berlin and Munich. The target groups are, in particular, lesbian couples and single women, whom they hope to help realise their desire to have children.

Of course, nobody should be denied their desire to have children. This desire is an expression of the free development of the personality. The freedom of action, under Art. 2 (1) Basic Law, protects the freedom of a woman seeking to reproduce, and the right to do so in every possible manner. Nevertheless, we must ask ourselves how it will affect the rights of a child created in this manner, particularly with regard to the right to knowledge of parentage. We must weigh up the affected rights and draw our conclusions therefrom. Because of the described societal and technological developments, we see ourselves confronted with new challenges.

Until now, there has been no statutory regulation on anonymous semen donors. The German Medical Association's current guidelines on the "implementation of assisted reproduction" only permit heterologous inseminations for married couples and for non-married couples in a steady relationship. Moreover, the physician is required to inform the semen donor that he is bound to provide the child with his name and that in this respect the physician cannot invoke his or her duty to maintain confidentiality. The physician is also required to comply with the required documentation.

The question remains whether a prohibition of anonymous semen donors is constitutionally necessary. Firstly, the German Federal Constitutional Court determined in its fundamental judgement in 1989 that the general personal rights enshrined in Art. 2 (1) Basic law, in conjunction with Art. 1 (1), also encompass the right to knowledge of one's own parentage. The starting point is that the free development of the personality requires, amongst other things, knowledge of one's own parentage. This interpretation of the Basic Law assumes that not only the social, but also the biological ancestry and the individual's knowledge thereof are critical for achieving individuality and self-awareness. Admittedly, Art. 2 (1) Basic Law, in conjunction with Art. 1 (1), does not convey a right to obtain information about one's own parentage, it merely safeguards against attainable information being withheld.

If the state fails to prevent anonymous semen donation, this does not give rise to a state infringement of the child's right to knowledge of its parentage. However, a state duty relating to the guarantee of the constitutive requirements for the development of the personality and thus knowledge of one's own parentage does arise from the child's basic rights. How is the duty to protect the right of the child to knowledge of

its parentage to be aligned with the freedom of action of the reproduc-
tion-seeking woman and the potential semen donor, as well as possible
operators of "internet sperm banks" and physicians?

In my opinion, a consideration of affected basic rights leads to a state
commitment to prevent the artificial generation of children using
anonymous semen donation. According to the previous decisions of the
Federal Constitutional Court, the knowledge of one's own parentage is
accorded a high significance – the importance of achieving personal
individuality and self-awareness mentioned earlier supports this. The
freedom of action of the woman and the semen donor, as well as the
freedom in the exercise of a profession of other participants, must, in
my opinion, take second place behind the former. And I do not think
that the path of infertile parents to a child will be made more difficult as
a result of such a – howsoever articulated – prohibition. For most semen donors the most important issue will be the issue of not being
legally recognised as the father of the child with the inherent obligations this entails. This objective can be achieved, however, without forcing the semen donor into anonymity: it merely requires preventing him
from having to assume the legal role of the father and the duties involved as such. section 1600 (2) German Civil Code, introduced in the
last legislative period via the Act for the Improvement of Children's
Rights, already heads in this direction. According to section 1600 (2),
the right of the legal father or the mother to contest paternity is excluded if the child has been conceived by means of artificial insemination using the semen donated by a third party. Only the child can appeal against the legal paternity. A further alternative would be, for example, the general exemption of semen donors from statutory paternal
duties. Then the semen donor would still be obliged to recognise his
position as biological father. Furthermore, for child welfare reasons it
should be ensured that the child has, where possible, two parents – even
if they are not the biological parents – who take on the legal responsibility of the child. Until now, this has been guaranteed in the cases of
artificial insemination because heterologous insemination only takes
place where a partnership already exists.

For legal certainty reasons, I support statutory regulation, which prevents generation using anonymous semen donors.

V. Conclusion

When Johann Wolfgang von Goethe wrote Faust II almost 200 years ago, it was beyond all technical possibility to generate humans artificially. Nevertheless, "Homunculus", an artificially created creature with human-like features plays a major part in this work. Encased in a glass vial, he hovers brightly before Faust and Mephistopheles seeking to become a natural body himself. In doing so he shows Faust, who is concerned with deep, existential questions, the way to a number of philosophers and to antiquity settings. I believe this scene is also a good example of the importance of the specification of values, which I discussed at the beginning of this article. The transition from procreation to generation – here vividly embodied by Homunculus – throws light onto our own existential questions and values. For Goethe this remained in the realm of human imagination. Nowadays, in light of the advances in genetics and biomedicine, it is necessary to articulate them in reality. The "specification of values" is a constant process which has not yet been concluded. In order for it to be successful, the pro-cess requires the participation of as many citizens and specialists as possible.

Part 4

Limits to Human Cloning in International Law

International Legal Limits to Human Cloning

Hans Lilie, Halle

Recent debate on cloning explicitly shows that the discussion on medical-legal and bioethical questions has long since moved beyond traditional separate disciplines to become an international issue. Whereas bioscience lawyers[1], philosophers and theologians look for solutions in national discourse, doctors and biologists work in a global network of laboratories. The globalisation of biomedical research, in particular cell biology, is set against highly fragmented national law which is scarcely even transparent for the experts in the individual countries. Particularly in the area of cloning, the international legal situation is very diverse and has reached very different levels of development in different countries.[2] During the current phase, it has been subjected in most countries to an unreliable and incomprehensible legislative activism. The legal diversity in individual countries provokes a need for action under international law to enact international legal instru-

---

[1]   *H.-L. Schreiber*, Rechtliche Bewertung der im Zusammenhang mit der Gentherapie auftretenden Probleme, in Bayertz/Schmidtke/Schreiber (eds.), Somatische Gentherapie - Medizinische, ethische und juristische Aspekte des Gentransfers in menschlichen Körperzellen (1995), 251-283; *idem*, Biotechnik. Rechtlich, in Korff/Beck/Mikat (eds.), Lexikon der Bioethik, Vol. 1 (1998), 395-397 (in conjunction with Henning Rosenau); *idem*, Die Würde des Menschen - eine rechtliche Fiktion?, in Elsner/Schreiber (eds.), Was ist der Mensch? (2002), 231-247.

[2]   For a summary of the situation in Europe see *H. Lilie*/C. *Mandla* in Beyleveld/Frazer/Lilie/Mandla, The Regulation of Embryo Research in Europe, in Solter et al. (eds.), Human Embryo Research in Pluralistic Europe (2003); for the German discussion cf. *H. Rosenau*, Reproduktives und therapeutisches Klonen aus juristischer Sicht, in Festschrift für Hans-Ludwig Schreiber; most recently *R. Neidert*, Das überschätzte Embryonenschutzgesetz, ZRP 2002, 467 et seq.

ments. The rapid relocation of biomedical research is risk-filled.[3] The more restrictive the national legislation is, the greater is the pressure on individual research scientists to go where the research is less restricted.[4]

On the national level in most countries, the questions of biomedical research are already viewed differently from medical, legal and ethical angles.[5] Laws and legislative bills are, therefore, frequently shaped by compromises which are closely linked to social, political and religious pre-understandings. However, if one looks beyond the national level, one sees that different national concepts are leading to a greater interweaving of approaches and masking viable solutions. Economic development is taking place in a broad spectrum of ethical diversity of post-modern societies and is caught in their dependencies. Hence, it is hardly surprising that attempts are made to break through – often national – limitations, in order to establish binding standards for existing or future international law provisions.

Precursors and trailblazers for the regulation of biomedical research under international law are the ten principles of the Nuremberg Code declared by the American military court in conjunction with the Nuremberg trials of doctors.[6]

When it comes to research involving human beings, the Declaration of Helsinki calls for the highest priority to be given to the safety of the persons concerned by carefully assessing the predictable risks and foreseeable benefits. The well-being of the test person must always prevail over the interests of science and society. Informed consent is another method to obtain consent for persons who are unable to state their accordance. In these cases, the

---

[3]   Ibid., 209 with further extensive notes.

[4]   Ibid.

[5]   For the German discussion from ethical and legal perspectives cf. *Rosenau*, supra note 2; *J. Taupitz*, Therapeutisches und reproduktives Klonen aus juristischer Sicht, Zeitschrift für ärztliche Fortbildung 2002, 449 et seq.; *idem*, Import embryonaler Stammzellen, ZRP 2002, 111; *C.F. Gethmann*, Ethische Anmerkungen zur Diskussion um den moralischen Status des menschlichen Embryos, DRiZ 2002, 204 et seq.; *C.F. Gethmann/F. Thiele*, Moral arguments against the cloning of humans; Poiesis & Praxis, Vol. 1 (2001), 35-46; *T. Harks*, Der Schutz der Menschenwürde bei der Entnahme fötalen Gewebes, NJW 2002, 716; *R. Zuck*, Wie führt man eine Debatte? Die Embryonennutzung und die Würde des Menschen, NJW 2002, 869; *H. Lilie/D. Albrecht*, Strafbarkeit im Umgang von Stammzelllinien aus Embryonen, NJW 2001, 2774.

[6]   *E. Deutsch*, Die zehn Punkte des Nürnberger Ärzteprozesses über die klinische Forschung am Menschen, in Festschrift für Wassermann (1985), 69 et seq.; *H. Pichlmayr*, Haltung und Verantwortungsbewußtsein der deutschen Ärzte, 50 Jahre nach dem Nürnberger Ärzteprozeß, F.A.Z., 13.10.1997.

legal guardian gives the consent. Evidently, these general principles apply in the case of research on human reproductive cloning.[7]

Contrary to what is said in the Declaration of Helsinki, a number of international human rights and professional code provisions address reproductive cloning.[8] The Universal Declaration of UNESCO on the Human Genome and Human Rights should be particularly mentioned.[9] Article 11 explicitly prohibits reproductive cloning. For research on the human genome, it postulates a priority for the respect of human rights, the fundamental freedoms and the human dignity of individuals over research and research applications. The Resolution on Cloning of the World Medical Association of November 1997 also calls on doctors and other research scientists

---

[7] *E. Deutsch/J. Taupitz*, Deklaration von Helsinki des Weltärztebundes, in Winter/Fenger/Schreiber (eds.), Genmedizin und Recht, No. 527 et seq..

[8] UNESCO: Universal Declaration on the Human Genome and Human Rights, 11 November 1997 (reprinted in the annex of this volume, under II 13); UN General Assembly: Resolution 53/152 on the Human Genome and Human Rights, 9 December 1998; UN Commission on Human Rights: Resolution 1993/91 on Human Rights and Bioethics, 10 March 1993; WHO: Resolution WHA 51.10 on Ethical, Scientific and Social Implications of Cloning in Human Health, 16 May 1998 (reprinted under II 12); Resolution WHA 50.37 on Cloning in Human Reproduction, 14 May 1997; Council of Europe: Convention for the Protection of Human Rights and Dignity of the Human Being with regard to the Application of Biology and Medicine, 4 April 1997 (reprinted under III 15); Additional Protocol to the Convention for the Protection of Human Rights and Dignity of the Human Being with regard to the Application of Biology and Medicine, on the Prohibition of Cloning Human Beings, 12 January 1998 (repinted under III 14); Council of Europe, Parliamentary Assembly, Order No. 534 (1997) on Research and the Cloning of Human Beings, 23 September 1997; Council of Europe, Parliamentary Assembly, Recommendation 1046 (1986) on the Use of Human Embryos and Foetuses for Diagnostic, Therapeutic, Scientific, Industrial and Commercial Purposes, 24 September 1986; European Union: European Council, Declaration on Banning the Cloning of Human Beings, 16 June 1997; European Parliament, Resolution on Human Cloning, 7 September 2000 (reprinted under IV 17); European Parliament, Resolution on Human Cloning, 15 January 1998; European Parliament, Resolution on the Cloning of the Human Embryo, 22 November 1993; further comprehensive notes on „International instruments concerning the reproductive cloning of human beings" are contained in this document from the Secretary of the „Ad Hoc Committee on an International Convention against the Reproductive Cloning of Human Beings".

[9] UNESCO-Deklaration über das menschliche Genom und Menschenrechte, in Winter/Fenger/Schreiber (eds.), Genmedizin und Recht, No. 500 et seq. English version reprinted in the annex of this volume, under II 13.

to exercise constraint in reproductive cloning until all ethical and legal problems have been solved and every necessary control has been guaranteed.

The catalogue of international provisions explicitly prohibiting reproductive cloning may be continued. The efforts of the General Assembly of the United Nations to achieve an international convention against reproductive cloning should particularly be mentioned.[10] Today I would like to focus on the Additional Protocol to the Convention for the Protection of Human Rights and Dignity of the Human Being with regard to the Application of Biology and Medicine, on the Prohibition of Cloning Human Beings. This additional Protocol builds on provisions of the Convention on Human Rights and Biomedicine, the so-called Oviedo-Convention.[11] Hence, one must consider the additional Cloning Protocol as well as the relevant operative articles of the Oviedo Convention. The explanatory report of the Cloning Protocol stresses that the prohibition on cloning human beings is within the scope of the protocol.

First, I would like to briefly summarise the reasons supposedly justifying reproductive cloning. Similar to therapeutic cloning, the focus here is on medical needs: the cloned human being could act as a donor for organs and tissue.[12] Hereditary diseases could be better understood and thus become treatable. After all, there is a desire to improve the opportunities for treating infertility or replacing a dead child. In particular, men who do not produce gametes could have children who inherit their genome. In such cases, if the egg came from the wife, the couple would not have to involve a sperm donor in the creating their child. Women, who do not produce eggs, could likewise have children carrying their genetic information.

In the case of reproductive cloning, the questions of self-interest and benefits for others create specific problems.[13] All these scenarios raise ethical, legal and social questions. Therefore, the Council of Europe could not find a sufficient ethical justification for the cloning of human beings. Since a naturally occurring genetic recombination is likely to create more freedom for the human being than a predetermined genetic make-up, the additional protocol to the Oviedo Convention was urgently needed.

---

[10]   United Nations, General Assembly Doc A/AC.263/2002/INF/1/Rev. 1.

[11]   Convention on Human Rights and Biomedicine ETS Oviedo, 4 April 1997 (CHRB) (signed on 7 May 1999), reprinted in the annex of this volume, under III 15.

[12]   *W. Höfling*, Verfassungsrechtliche Aspekte des so genannten therapeutischen Klonens , Zeitschrift für medizinische Ethik 2001, 277.

[13]   *J. Taupitz*, Therapeutisches und reproduktives Klonen aus juristischer Sicht, ZaeFQ 2002, 449 et seq.

We now have to ask whom the Oviedo Convention, and especially the additional protocol, protects. Whose rights could be violated by cloning and which are these rights? If we look at the person who wishes to be cloned, then at first sight it is difficult to classify reproductive cloning if the clone is to serve later as a donor for organs and tissues. This also applies indirectly to those cases in which the goal is to avoid genetic hereditary diseases. This means that it is the interests of others that is to be served, unless the person to be cloned himself expresses the wish for reproductive cloning out of self-interest. From the viewpoint of the person to be cloned, the creation of a twin would then not solely benefit another person. Without the request of the person to be cloned – i.e. without his explicit demand – the scientists concerned would not have the option of cloning. If, in the case of reproductive cloning, one were only to look at the person to be cloned, then this would indeed lead to a distortion of the situation. On the other hand, at least there is consensus today that the emphasis of assessment is on the scientific-experimental character. This way of viewing the situation masks the far more serious risk for the clone. Such an approach will, of course, have the consequence that the concrete benefit for the person being cloned is of lesser importance here. Also in the case of infertility treatment it is hardly possible to talk about a benefit for others in this context. Here it is a matter of the further development of biomedical science. This is and remains the decisive aspect which is presently cited as the justification for reproductive cloning.[14]

The first consideration is the scientific acceptability of the procedure; i. e. the expected progress must be weighed against the risk which the clone is exposed to in order to determine whether one then could speak of an acceptable risk. The main criterion for the admissibility of cloning is the scientific admissibility or acceptable risk. It requires that the person concerned be only exposed to a commensurate relationship between risk and benefit.[15]

There is an obvious difficulty in trying to apply this principle to the human experiment of reproductive cloning: the life and health of the person involved in the respective experiment must be protected. This corresponds to the old principle of *primum nil nocere*.[16] This non-maleficence principle is interpreted in such a way that a certain degree of risk is admissible. However, cloning becomes inadmissible when the risk is no longer defendable since the person concerned runs the risk of serious injury. The additional

---

[14] *J. Gross*, FAZ-Magazin, Notizbuch, Neue Folge 91; also cited from *E. Deutsch*, Embryonenschutzgesetz in Deutschland, NJW 1991, 721 (725); see also Die Zeit No. 49 (27 november 2003), 43.

[15] *A. Laufs*, in Laufs/Uhlenbruck (eds.), Handbuch des Arztrechts, para. 130, No. 24.

[16] Ibid., para. 63, No. 8.

protocol wants to exclude the weighing up of general well-being against the concrete risk for a specific person. On one side of the scale, we have the somewhat vague progress of medical research and on the other side the related healing interests. However, the very thought of cloning individual human beings leads to major concerns because there is a risk that this technology could be used for breeding, i. e. for eugenic purposes. It still has not been clarified what health risks and possible deformities the clone may encounter. Scientific research on reproductive cloning in other mammals shows that there is a markedly higher incidence of foetal disorders and loss throughout pregnancy.

There is also great concern over so-called big offspring and malformation as well as death among newborns. There is no reason to suppose that the outcome would be different in humans. That means that there would be a serious threat to the health of the cloned individual, not just at birth but potentially at all stages of life, as there is obviously no compensating benefit to the individual bearing this threat. Hence, for reproductive cloning, it is a matter of laying down the boundary for acceptance of the risk and scale of dangers which society and the legal order is willing to bear. Risks may be accepted when they are closely linked to the interests of the person concerned. In this context, the decisive yardstick is the high probability of therapeutic advantage resulting from reproductive cloning. Of course, the instrumentalisation of human life cannot be legitimated when the procedure mainly involves research to help others. This would amount to instrumentalisation if there were intentional plans to breed human beings with specific traits, particularly as the clone created in this way would carry in itself the risk of genetic damage from the very outset. Against a truly scientific background, the creation of genetically identical twins could be considered acceptable where, as in the case of the natural development of twins, the result would be genetically identical human beings. A frequently heard argument is that, as in nature, a monozygotic twin could be artificially created through cloning[17]. However, this targeted allocation of the same genetic predetermination is the marked distinction to the natural development of twins. On the other hand, given the risk, it cannot be accepted because the artificial creation of more than one child cannot be deemed a relevant progress in medicine. Viewed in isolation, this is not an important ethical goal of research. At the same time, it means that the creation of even one embryo for the sole purpose of use as an organ donor violates the rights of this embryo in such a fundamental way that the interests of science and society could not justify this procedure.

The additional Protocol wants clear barriers against the misuse of human embryos. If the human experiment of reproductive cloning goes in the direc-

---

[17] *Taupitz*, supra note 13, 452

tion of instrumentalising the clone as an organ donor, then already by virtue of this principle there is an insurmountable obstacle. We have to take into consideration "that concern for the interests of the subject must always prevail over the interests of science and society"[18].

The additional Protocol aims at protecting human dignity in two different but related ways. This kind of instrumentalisation of human beings undermines the clone's right to an individual course of life and forces the clone to behave in a manner which is strongly influenced by others only because of having been cloned.

Another aspect seems to be important: reproductive cloning could at best be deemed a human experiment. Unsurprisingly, central ethical and legal aspects of research stand in the way of its admissibility. In particular, the expected danger is not in any relationship to the expected advantage offered by this form of research. The preconditions of informed consent cannot be met by reproductive cloning. This means that this procedure also violates all preconditions of the Declaration of Helsinki and must be rejected on this basis without applying the controversial argument of dignity from the very outset.

If one tries to apply the preconditions of informed consent to the cases of reproductive cloning, one should first look at the clone. Since it does not yet exist, it is not in a position to give its own consent. One could consider applying the principles of consent by proxy consent. The proxy could at best be the person who is going to be cloned. However, because of the existing conflict of interest, particularly in the case of one-sided interests, he will be excluded from this representation from the very outset. However, the person to be cloned also cannot agree to such a procedure in his own right. It is not just his personal interests and objects of legal protection that are up for debate. In the case of reproductive cloning, the interests of the clone must also be taken into account. This leads to the failure of the legal admissibility of reproductive cloning as a human experiment at the latest when it comes to consent. That means that also the issue of autonomy would arise, if a person's DNA were used to create one or more copies without that person's permission or even without his or her knowledge.

There is another important element. Reproductive cloning is dependent on fertilisable ova. According to the current level of knowledge, a large number of ova is required for a successful cloning procedure. It has been reported from animal experiments that between 30 and 100 ova are required. For this it would be necessary to hyperstimulate the ovaries of many women. There are fears that women in developing countries would be abused for the purposes of harvesting ova. The interests of science and

---

[18]   *Laufs*, supra note 15, para. 2, No. 8.

society cannot justify such a wide scale instrumentalisation of women of a child-bearing age.

Already for these reasons, the additional protocol still appears to be a blunt sword. As long as there is no implementation in the single states that bans any intervention seeking to create a human being genetically identical to another and as long as there are no penal sanctions, we cannot claim that there is reliable protection for the rights and interests mentioned above.

Who Is Protected by Human Rights Conventions? Protection of the Embryo vs. Scientific Freedom and Public Health

Rüdiger Wolfrum/Silja Vöneky, Heidelberg

I. Introduction

As we have seen, there exist different ethical and religious concepts concerning the notion of human being or concerning the question of who is entitled to human dignity: only the human being after completion of birth or also the embryo and if so from which stage? The different approaches considered or advocated in Judaism, Buddhism, Islam and Christianity are obvious; they may be decisive in answering the question whether therapeutic and reproductive cloning can or should be allowed or have to be ruled out by a future international agreement or national legislation. The different approaches referred to may even have to be taken into account when interpreting the respective human rights standards, in particular the protection of human dignity, under the proviso, however, that it is considered appropriate to have recourse to extralegal considerations in the interpretation of human rights standards at all.

The existing binding instruments in international law which deal with biomedical issues are rather vague and are limited in scope, especially in respect of therapeutic cloning. Professor Lilie has pointed out[1] the difficulties concerning the interpretation of the Council of Europe Biomedicine Convention[2] and its Protocol[3]. Apart from that we would

---

[1]   See his contribution in this volume.

[2]   Convention for the Protection of Human Rights and Dignity of the Human Being with regard to the Application of Biology and Medicine: Conven-

like to refer to the very small number of states which have become parties to the Biomedicine Convention and its Protocol.[4] Therefore, it is problematic to consider the standards established by this convention as generally applicable guidelines for biomedicine research in general and cloning in particular. In fact, international law has not yet developed adequate rules concerning biomedicine.

Even international instruments concerning biomedicine research which do not bind the states formally – so-called soft law rules – are clear only in regard to reproductive cloning and do not cover therapeutic cloning expressly. The UNESCO Declaration on the Human Genome of 1997[5] states in Article 11:

> "Practices which are contrary to human dignity, such as reproductive cloning of human beings, shall not be permitted."

This wording labels reproductive cloning of human beings as a violation of human dignity and, by singling out reproductive cloning in this respect, indicates that there may be other forms of cloning which violate human dignity, but it does not go any further. Generally speaking, international law, at least so far, does not explicitly prohibit cloning of human beings, in particular not therapeutic cloning.[6] Whether a universal convention against cloning of human beings will come into existence, and in particular its future scope, is still an open question.[7] Ms.

---

tion on Human Rights and Biomedicine, 4 April 1997, ETS No. 164, reprinted in the annex of this volume, under III 15.

[3] Additional Protocol to the Convention for the Protection of Human Rights and Dignity of the Human Being with regard to the Application of Biology and Medicine, on the Prohibition of Cloning Human Beings, 12 January 1998, ETS No. 168; reprinted in the annex of this volume, under III 14.

[4] As of 24 May 2004, 17 states have ratified the Convention and 14 states ratified the Additional Protocol on the Prohibition of Cloning Human Beings.

[5] Universal Declaration on the Human Genome and Human Rights, 11 November 1997, UNESCO Doc. 29 C/Resolution 16; reprinted in the annex of this volume, under II 13.

[6] See e.g. *J. Taupitz*, Der rechtliche Rahmen des Klonens zu therapeutischen Zwecken, NJW 54 (2001), 3433, 3439.

[7] Item included in the agenda of the UN General Assembly's 59th Sess., 2004 after an agreement could not be reached at the 58th Sess., 2003; see UN Doc. A/58/PV.72, 9 December 2003.

Arsanjani informed us about the problems concerning the respective negotiations.[8]

The question therefore arises, and our presentation will focus on this aspect, whether *traditional human rights agreements* could fill in this presently existing lacuna. To ask this question seems to be odd, at first glance, as there are certainly no express rules in the traditional human rights treaties dealing with cloning of human beings or the protection of embryos. Nevertheless, human rights standards may provide some guidance, which even the new agreement on cloning of human beings may have to respect, at least if it does not want to deviate from established international human rights standards.

We will attempt to show that international human rights agreements, although not expressly dealing with cloning, embody relevant concepts in regard to cloning of human beings: these concepts embrace the protection of human dignity and life, public health, scientific freedom and parental rights. The most promising, but at the same time most ambiguous concept – here as well as in national law – is that of human dignity. We will concentrate thereon.

II. The International Protection of Human Dignity: a Restriction on the Cloning of Human Beings?

If one has a look at the various draft resolutions concerning the international convention against cloning[9] it is striking how many times the notion of human dignity appears in the preambular formulations. We will not go into detail on this topic, but allow us some introductory remarks.

The Draft Resolution concerning an universal Convention against *Reproductive* Cloning of 2003[10] mentions the notion of human dignity – with some variations – *seven* times. This resolution was supported by

---

[8] See her contribution in this volume.

[9] E.g. UN Doc. A/C.6/57/L.3/Rev.1; UN Doc. A/C.6/57/L.8; UN Doc. A/C.6/58/L.2; UN Doc. A/C.6/58/L.8. All documents reprinted in the annex of this volume, under I 3, 4, 6 and 7.

[10] International Convention against the Reproductive Cloning of Human Beings, Draft Resolution, 2 October 2003, UN Doc. A/C.6/58/L.8, reprinted in the annex of this volume, under I 3.

states such as – for instance – China, Japan and the UK. The Draft
Resolution of the opposing group, concerning a convention against *all
forms of human cloning*[11] names "human dignity" or "the dignity of the
human race" at least five times. The latter resolution is supported by
states so different as – inter alia – the United States, Nauru, Panama,
Tajikistan and Tanzania. This, in our view, is a clear indication (1) that
there is an *opinio iuris* that human dignity is a valid principle in international law; (2) that some forms of cloning constitute a violation of this
principle; (3) that the notion of human dignity is flexible enough to
bridge cultural, religious and ethical gaps, as it is supported as decisive
in regard to questions of cloning by states all over the world; and (4)
that there is, however, only limited consensus about the scope or content of the principle of human dignity.

The concept of "human dignity" as such is a rather new concept embodied expressly in international treaties or resolutions. The Charter of
the United Nations was one of the first documents in international law
referring to this concept.[12] The second preambular paragraph of the
UN Charter states that the Peoples of the United Nations are determined "to reaffirm faith in fundamental human rights, in the dignity
and worth of human person". This reaffirmation of the faith in human
dignity in the Preamble follows just behind the confirmation of the
purpose to save succeeding generations from the scourge of war. Thus,
human dignity is one of the primary ends of the United Nations, and it
is – at the same time – its fundamental basis and accordingly that of the
present international legal order.

Similar formulations as in the United Nations Charter are to be found
in the Universal Declaration of Human Rights of 1948.[13] Its Preamble
even starts with the emphasis on human dignity. It reads:

> "Whereas recognition of the inherent dignity and of the equal and
> inalienable rights of all members of the human family is the founda-
> tion for freedom, justice and peace in the world."[14]

Article 1 of this Declaration provides:

---

[11] International Convention against Human Cloning, Draft Resolution, 26
September 2003, A/C.6/58/L.2; reprinted in the annex of this volume, under I 4.

[12] Previously, human dignity had been referred to by the 1944 Philadelphia
Declaration of the ILO, reprinted in AJIL Supp. 38 (1944), 203.

[13] Universal Declaration on Human Rights, UN Doc. A/Res.217 (III), UN
Doc. A/810 at 71, 10 December 1948.

[14] Ibid., preambular para. 1.

"All human beings are born free and equal in dignity and rights."

The UN Charter and the Universal Declaration – as fundaments of the new world order – emphasise and confirm the significance of the concept of human dignity for the international order after the Second World War.

Both references to human dignity in these documents remind in some way of the German Basic Law (*Grundgesetz*) of 1949[15] and the post-war Constitutions of the German *Länder*[16]. This is no coincidence as the drafters of the German Basic Law were aware of the UN Charter and the Universal Declaration of Human Rights.[17] The deeper reasons, however, for this parallelism are certainly the barbarous violations of human dignity during the Nazi regime.[18] In rejection of this period, Germany had to establish a new constitutional (state) order; equally, on the international level the community of states felt it necessary to lay down the fundament for a new and peaceful world order. For both orders – as they were counter-drafts to the Nazi ideology – the reaffirmation of the concept of human dignity was compelling and inherently necessary. Human dignity was seen – and the Universal Declaration states it[19] – as the foundation of freedom, justice and peace in the world.[20] The concept since then has been an *ethical* – and we stress: an *ethical* – cornerstone of the international legal order.

Nevertheless there is an important difference between the concept of human dignity in the German Basic Law on the one hand and the

---

[15] Excerpts reprinted in the annex of this volume, under V 21.

[16] Cf. Article 1 of the Constitution of Hessen of 1 December 1946; Article 100 of the Bavarian Constitution of 2 December 1946; Article 5 of the Constitution of Bremen of 21 October 1947.

[17] *J. Eckert*, Legal Roots of Dignity in German Law, in Kretzmer/Klein (eds.), The Concept of Human Dignity in Human Rights Discourse (2002), 41, 42.

[18] *J.A. Frowein*, Human Dignity in International Law, in Kretzmer/Klein, The Concept of Human Dignity in Human Rights Discourse, supra note 17, 121, 123; *J. Morsink*, The Philosophy of the Universal Declaration, Hum. Rts. Quarterly 6 (1984), 309.

[19] Universal Declaration on Human Rights, supra note 13, preambular para. 1.

[20] *Y. Arieli*, On the Necessary and Sufficient Conditions for the Emergence of the Doctrine of the Dignity of Man and His Rights, in Kretzmer/Klein, The Concept of Human Dignity in Human Rights Discourse, supra note 17, 1, 8.

United Nations Charter or the Universal Declaration on the other. In both of these *international* instruments the concept is *not* laid down as legally binding.[21] The Universal Declaration is a non-binding document although significant parts of it constitute customary international law. The Charter of the United Nations is formally binding only in regard to its operative part; it is *not* formally binding in regard to its Preamble formulations, where the concept of human dignity is spelled out.

Does this mean that "human dignity" is just a "rainbow" on the horizon of international law? Nice to look at from the tough grounds of legal facts and positive law but rather useless? It is not surprising that in international law – even more than in the German law – the specific legal essence of the concept of human dignity is far from clear.[22] The protection of human dignity is a valid principle of international law which has a significant impact on the interpretation of international human rights instruments. It is, as already stated, one of the essential components and the very foundation of the international order. This makes it necessary to develop a clearer understanding of the scope and content of the notion of human dignity. Such understanding can only be gained from international human rights instruments which – at least to a certain extent – concretise the notion of human dignity and the scope of protection it requires.

In most of the general human rights agreements the notion of human dignity is referred to in the operative parts of the treaties. The American Convention on Human Rights of 1969[23] mentions "human dignity" three times expressly; each of the Covenants of 1966,[24] the African

---

[21]   Cf. *J. Eckert*, supra note 17, 42.

[22]   Cf. *J. Martain*, Introduction, in UNESCO (ed.), Human Rights: Comments and interpretations (1973), 7: "We agree about the rights but on the condition that no one asks us why"; *K. Dicke*, Die der Person innewohnende Würde und die Frage der Universalität der Menschenrechte, in Bielefeldt et al. (eds.), Würde und Recht des Menschen, Festschrift für Johannes Schwartländer zum 70. Geburtstag (1992), 161, 180.

[23]   American Charter on Human Rights, entered into force 18 July 1978, O.A.S. Treaty Series No. 36, 1144 U.N.T.S. 123.

[24]   International Covenant on Civil and Political Rights, UN Doc. A/6316 (1966), 999 U.N.T.S. 171, entered into force 23 March 1976; International Covenant on Economic, Social and Cultural Rights, UN Doc. A/6316 (1966), 993 U.N.T.S. 3, entered into force 3 January 1976.

Charter on Human Rights of 1981[25] and the Arab Charter on Human Rights of 1994[26] refer to it once. Only the European Charter on Human Rights of 1950[27] does not mention it expressly.[28]

However, in those agreements where human dignity is referred to expressly, the scope of the concept of human dignity is limited. Only *prohibitions* of certain acts are laid down in regard to it in the Covenant on Civil and Political Rights[29] and in Articles 5 and 6 of the American Charter of Human Rights.[30] They state that all persons deprived of their liberty shall be treated with respect for the inherent dignity of the human person.

The African (Banjul) Charter of Human Rights is aimed in the same direction. It contains a broad formulation stating in Article 5 that "every individual shall have the right to the respect of the dignity inherent in a human being".[31] However, this broad approach is limited by the subsequent sentence which says that "all forms of exploitation and degradation ... shall be prohibited".

Equally a rather broad formulation is to be found in Article 11para. 1, of the American Charter of Human Rights which states that:

"Everyone has the right to have his honor respected and his dignity recognized."

However, the scope is limited as well, as it is linked solely to the right to privacy.

---

[25]   African [Banjul] Charter on Human and Peoples' Rights, adopted 27 June 1981, OAU Doc. CAB/LEG/67/3 Rev. 5, 21 I.L.M. 58 (1982), entered into force 21 October 1986.

[26]   Arab Charter on Human Rights, adopted by the League of Arab States, reprinted in Hum. Rts. L.J. 18 (1997), 151.

[27]   Convention for the Protection of Human Rights and Fundamental Freedoms, 4 November 1950, ETS No. 005.

[28]   But the jurisprudence of the organs has recognised it as a fundamental value by interpreting certain rights of the charter on the basis of human dignity, as for instance the prohibition of torture (Article 3), the right to freedom and security (Article 5), and the right of privacy (Article 8) (the rights of prisoners, the problems of personal or sexual identity).

[29]   International Covenant on Civil and Political Rights, supra note 24, Article 10.

[30]   American Charter on Human Rights, supra note 23, Article 5 para. 2; similar Article 6 para. 2 (3).

[31]   Arab Charter on Human Rights, supra note 26, Article 5 para. 1 (1).

Human dignity is perceived from a different point of view in the International Covenant on Economic, Social and Cultural Rights.[32] There human dignity is connected with a so-called social right: the state parties agree that education shall be directed to the full development of "the human personality and the sense of its dignity."[33]

Looking at those examples it becomes evident that in the operative parts of human rights treaties human dignity is not a nice rainbow but rather a hidden sunflower: nice to see as well, but limited in scope.

However, sunflowers and rainbows are quite useful: the first one produces seeds and the latter one shows where the rain and the sun are. The same is true in regard to the concept of human dignity in international law. As already indicated, some of the human rights standards are a direct reflection of the overall obligation of states to protect human dignity. Just some examples will suffice to make the point: the prohibition of torture, the right of everybody to juridical personality, the prohibition of slavery and the prohibition of marriages without consent of both sides. Both the general concept, included in the treaty Preambles and the declarations, as well as the principle which is the very foundation of the positive standards of human rights in the operative parts are to be considered as guidelines, not only for the interpretation of human rights standards as such, but also for the development of new international human rights standards.

The broad and general concept of "inherent dignity" in the Preambles of the human rights treaties and the Charter of the United Nations indicates that the concept is historically contingent; however, it is not limited to its historical meaning. In international law the historical circumstances are only a supplementary means of interpretation.[34] This is even more true in regard to a fundamental principle which by its broad and universal language avoids any limitation to a certain ethical or religious concept. A dynamic interpretation of the notion of human dignity is possible, and in so interpreting it is necessary to take into account the considerations common to the various cultures and religions.

Consequently, the notion of human dignity is first of all an objective value rather than a subjective human right. It would constitute a misin-

---

[32]   International Covenant on Economic, Social and Cultural Rights, supra note 24.

[33]   Ibid., Article 13.

[34]   Article 32, Vienna Convention of the Law of Treaties, 1155 UNTS 331.

terpretation of the notion of human dignity, however, to assume that it is only an objective principle in international law and may not as well have an impact upon subjective rights.[35] As we have already indicated, the obligation to protect human dignity may transform into a subjective (human) right. Such transformation has been brought about by the respective international standards.

The question remains whether they provide for the prohibition of cloning of human beings. Several arguments have been advanced so far which we will attempt to summarise briefly. It has been argued that cloning would result in an infringement of the right to privacy, namely that the privacy of the cloning recipient would be violated on the basis of the knowledge of the genetic life of the donor.[36] Further, it has been argued that cloning may undermine the conditions of autonomy of the child given the child's knowledge that it has only one genetic parent.[37] It has also been argued that cloning may give the recipient a sense of non-individualisation.[38] Finally, the argument has been made that cloning would be a step in the direction of the commodification of life or, in other words, that life would be reduced to production, rendering it similar to objects.[39] This touches upon Kant's definition of human dignity, according to which individuals are not to be perceived or treated as instruments or objects of the will of others.[40]

We consider these arguments as not being fully convincing. In particular, they cover predominantly reproductive cloning and to a lesser extent therapeutic cloning. Apart from that it is telling that references are always made to the individual rather than to the embryo. This is under-

---

[35] *O. Schachter*, Human Dignity as a Normative Concept, AJIL 77 (1983), 848, 853.

[36] *F.C. Pizzulli*, Asexual Reproduction and Genetic Engeneering: A Constitutional Assessment of the Technology of Cloning, S. Cal. L. Rev. 47 (1973/74), 476, 498.

[37] Ibid., 498.

[38] *L.B. Andrews*, Is there a Right to Clone? Constitutional Challenges to Bans on Human Cloning, Harvard J.L. & Tech. 11 (1998), 643, 657.

[39] E.g. *J.C. Heller*, Religious Based Objections to Human Cloning: Are They Sustainable?, in Cole-Turner (ed.), Human Cloning: Religious Responses (1997), 153, 169; *T. Peters*, Cloning Shock: A Theological Reaction, in ibid., 12, 21.

[40] *I. Kant*, Groundwork for the Metaphysics of Morals, ed. by A.W. Wood (2002), 45 et seq. See on this topic, the paper of Graf Vitzthum in this volume.

standable since those arguing against cloning have no intention to re-
open the discussion on abortion, which would be inevitable if the embryo were considered to be fully covered under the obligation to protect human dignity.

Therefore it is, in our view, impossible to abstractly deduce the content
of a subjective right – namely, the right not to be the result of cloning –
from the broad concept of human dignity in international law. Equally
there is no basis in international human rights agreements to argue that
the embryo is protected as an individual. There is also no basis to argue
to the contrary.

It would be wrong, though, to assume that state parties of the international human rights instruments are free to decide what does affect the
dignity of a human being and what does not. The United Nations
Charter speaks of the "reaffirmation" of the faith in the dignity of the
human person.[41] This shows that human dignity has a pre-normative
character.[42] Accordingly the scope and content of the notion of human
dignity cannot be defined by states; human dignity can only be discovered by them.

Whereas there was a quick and unanimous consensus amongst states
that *reproductive* cloning is a violation of the dignity of human beings,[43]
several states (for instance China and the UK) doubt that *therapeutic*
cloning constitutes any such violation. What could be the solution to
the question of therapeutic cloning with regard to the concept of human dignity as it is included in the human rights treaties? Only states,
by engaging in a substantial dialogue which, preferably, should include
the civil society, can "find" the scope and content of human dignity
concerning cloning techniques. As long as there is no consensus between states, the mere concept of human dignity cannot be the basis for
further prohibition or state obligation. The dialogue referred to above
will first have to consider the very elements of the notion of human
dignity, in particular whether or to what extent it covers the human
embryo. In that respect the various cultural, religious and ethical approaches will be of relevance. Additionally, the positive as well as negative aspects of therapeutic cloning will have to be weighed. Here again
the various cultural, religious and ethical considerations are of relevance. On that basis it is doubtful whether a universal standard in re-

---

[41]   Charter of the United Nations, preambular para. 2.

[42]   E.g. *Dicke*, supra note 22, 176.

[43]   See UN Doc. A/57/51, 8 para. 11.

spect of therapeutic cloning can be established. If not, rules are necessary which provide for an accommodation between the various standards which may emerge.

The Negotiations on a Treaty on Cloning: Some Reflections

Mahnoush H. Arsanjani, New York[*]

I. Introduction

The prescriptive function of international law, like domestic law, is to signal to states and other actors, including individual human beings, approved codes of behaviour. While multilateral treaty making has always been one way of making and clarifying what the law on a particular subject is, it was not until the establishment of the United Nations Charter system in 1945, that multilateral agreements slowly became a preferred mode of clarifying or making international law.[1] The increasing concentration on concluding multilateral agreements began to reduce the incidence of customary development of the law and the general principles of law as two important sources of international law under Article 38 of the Statute of the International Court of Justice. There are other factors that contributed to the ascendance of treaties and decline of custom.[2] But the consequence has been the increase in reliance

---

[1] Article 13 (a) of the Charter has often been used to encourage states in that direction. This Article is basis for the establishment of the International Law Commission.

[2] Since the 1970s and the end of the decolonisation process and the increase in the membership of the United Nations, many newly independent states questioned the validity of certain rules of international law based on custom to the development of which they did not contribute. The notion of equal sovereignty of states led to the notion of democratisation of international law, hence the need for consensus and compromise. There is also the general view among

on states' express collective views and, as a result, the necessity of securing consensus on particular issues.

Those who have spent their careers in multilateral treaty making process are familiar with the so-called standard requirements for selection of a topic as appropriate for multilateral treaty making. They include the pressing need for the regulation of the subject-matter, preferably substantial state practice or at least some state practice, some degree of consensus among states about the general direction of the topic, political commitment on the part of a significant number of states to spend the time and energy necessary to work on the topic, and a handful of committed experts to provide the intellectual and expert leadership in shaping the development of the subject and resolving the technical and policy questions which inevitably emerge in any codification process. In more recent years, the interest and participation of non-governmental organisations have sometimes emerged as critical factors. For topics affecting a substantial segment of industry, or a special interest group, of course, their participation (or their opposition) can influence the process substantially. A treaty need not promise to "solve" a problem, but it must appear to be a potentially effective instrument in dealing with it. Finally, there are those occasionally unforeseen factors that can mortally wound a process or, on the contrary, breathe life into a seemingly moribund exercise.[3]

---

many newly independent, smaller and developing states that, in case of doubt or conflict, they might do better to resolve their dispute by judicial means. This view has even become popular with many European states. This attitude reduces the norm-generative power of state behaviour and increases correspondingly the norm-generative power of judicial decisions. Similarly, the proliferation of courts and judicial bodies and the specialisation of international law which has led to the establishment of dispute settlement mechanisms compel states parties to the treaties to resort to those mechanisms.

[3]   The codification of international criminal law in the last decade and a half is a good example representing both the standard and classical requirements for codification as well as the unconventional factors affecting that process. The proposal for drafting the Rome Statute for the International Criminal Court was made before the Yugoslav Tribunal was established. That proposal was not viewed as feasible. It did not enjoy political support from critical states, there was no consensus among states on the general direction to the topic, and there was no pressing need, in the view of many governments, for the establishment of such a court. But two years later, the Balkan conflict and atrocities committed in that conflict changed the political mood. When the Statute of the Yugoslav Tribunal was drafted, there was political commitment on the part of critical states for an international criminal tribunal, not necessarily by enthusiastic

II. Cloning Human Beings[4]

1. Background in the Sixth Committee

In the fall of 2001, France and Germany proposed to the General Assembly the topic of an international convention against reproductive cloning of human beings.[5] When the issue was first discussed in the Sixth Committee of the General Assembly, there appeared to be a broad consensus on the scope of a convention against the reproductive cloning of human beings.[6] The broad consensus (or the absence of a strong

---

choice, but as a result of having no alternative. Expert reports were prepared by a handful of states which assisted the drafting of the Statute of the Yugoslav tribunal by the Secretariat of the United Nations. For the Rwanda Statute, the pressure from the non-governmental organisation was also a factor, not to mention the gruesome pictures of dead and maimed civilians publicised by the media and embarrassing the political leaders for lack of preventive actions. The two processes bred life into the proposal of drafting the Rome Statute. By then, there were models for similar statutes indicating some general and broad consensus among states as to the substance of such a treaty. It became more difficult for those states that had supported the two ad hoc criminal tribunals now to fiercely oppose a similar statute for a standing tribunal. An additional factor was the commitment of a good number of experts in criminal and humanitarian law who provided the intellectual and technical leadership for the development of the subject. There was also a growing active support by more than 200 organised non-governmental organisations using various modalities for influencing the process in favour of the creation of the court. In short, the convergence of a number of factors bred life to a process which appeared hopeless at the start.

[4]   Cloning and stem cell research are defined by the Inter Academy Panel as:

"Cloning of an organism commonly involves a technique called somatic cell nuclear transfer, where the nucleus of an egg cell (containing its genetic material) is removed and replaced with the nucleus of a somatic cell taken from the body of an adult. If the reconstructed egg cell is then stimulated successfully to divide, it may develop to the pre-implantation blastocyst stage. In reproductive cloning, the cloned blastocyst is then implanted in the uterus of a female and allowed to continue its development until birth. However, in cloning for research or therapeutic purposes, instead of being implanted in the uterus the cloned blastocyst is converted into a tissue culture to make a stem cell line for research or clinical applications."

[5]   A/56/192.

[6]   General Assembly Resolution 56/93 adopted on 12 December 2001. Reprinted in the annex of this volume, under I 8.

opposition) may have been the result of the lack of familiarity of many delegations with the subject. In fact, during initial discussions, it became clear that the topic was too novel for delegates of the Sixth Committee. The strong scientific and technical elements of the topic were not matters that many international lawyers are familiar with or can quickly comprehend and master. During the first meeting of the ad hoc committee in the spring of 2002, the organisation of a day-briefing by an expert group on the scientific, technical and ethical issues of the topic was helpful but insufficient to provide the delegations with a thorough understanding of the subject. Only a handful of industrial states had reached a scientific and technical level that required them to consider and establish national positions. For many other states, the topic had very little, if any, practical and immediate significance.

During the initial discussions on the topic in the ad hoc committee in the fall of 2002, the novelty of the subject and the lack of immediate concern of the topic to many states limited the dialogue to a smaller group of states with sharply divided views. Some delegations supported a comprehensive ban on all forms of cloning while some other delegations strongly and categorically opposed banning therapeutic cloning or even discussing therapeutic cloning at all. This was a matter, they felt, that should be left entirely to domestic law. Other states did not have any particular position on the subject.[7]

A number of important changes took place between the fall of 2002 and the fall of 2003. The Franco-German proposal had led to national debates or debates at the governmental level in a number of countries both in Europe and in other regions on the issue of cloning. The Working Group of the Sixth Committee that discussed the issue in the fall of 2003 was well attended by delegations, many of whom had come from their capitals specifically for this issue and had scientific advisors. The views expressed by delegations indicated a much better understanding of what was involved and more reasoned explanations for supporting one view or opposing another.

The composition of delegations for and against a comprehensive approach was also more broadly defined by the time the subject was discussed in the Sixth Committee in the fall of 2003. Costa Rica was now leading a group of 68 states supporting a comprehensive approach.[8] The

---

[7]   See the report of the Ad Hoc Committee in document A/57/51.

[8]   A/C.6/58/L.2. Reprinted in the annex of this volume, under I 4. The sponsors of the draft resolution proposed by Costa Rica rose to 68 states. See A/58/520, section II (A).

United States, the Holy See, Spain, Italy, Portugal, and a number of Latin American states, as well as some states with substantial Moslem populations such as the Philippines, Ethiopia and Nigeria, supported a comprehensive ban. A limited ban proposed by France and Germany had also gained more support. Some states, initially opposing any discussion on therapeutic cloning, agreed, at a later stage of the discussion, to its inclusion in a convention not on banning but only on regulating the practice. Many European states, including the United Kingdom, Belgium, some Nordic states, as well as China, Japan, India and Singapore agreed in principle to work on that basis. The group of states members of the Islamic Conference also supported only banning cloning for reproductive purposes and thus joined the approach suggested by France and Germany.[9] A modified Franco-German approach was subsequently proposed by Belgium and 22 other states which called for a ban on cloning for reproductive purposes and called on states to either ban, regulate, or impose a moratorium on therapeutic cloning.[10]

A working group of the Sixth Committee in September/October of 2003 failed to bridge the gap between the two competing views.[11] During the Sixth Committee consideration of the item, it became clear that there was no possibility for a consensus decision. It also became clear that some delegations were considering procedural motions in order to delay making a decision on the substance of the issue until later dates. On 6 November, the last day of the Sixth Committee meeting, Iran, on behalf of the states members of the Organisation of Islamic Conference, made a motion to adjourn the consideration of the item until the sixtieth session of the General Assembly in 2005.[12] The motion was carried

---

[9]   Sierra Leone and Uganda, members of the Islamic Conference, dissented from that view and supported complete banning of all forms of cloning.

[10]   A/C.6/58/L.8. Reprinted in the annex of this volume, under I 3.

[11]   For the report of the Working Group see A/C.6/58/L.9, reprinted in the annex of this volume, under I 2.

[12]   In explaining the reasons for the motion, the representative of Iran listed the lack of consensus among delegations on how to proceed on substance and uncertainty among the scientific community about the utility of therapeutic cloning. He stated the motion was intended to be without prejudice to any positions that delegations may have on either the proposal on a comprehensive ban as proposed by Costa Rica in A/C.6/58/L.2 or the partial ban proposed by Belgium in A/C.6/58/L.8. See A/C.6/58/SR.23.

by a vote of 80 in favour, 79 against and 15 abstentions.[13] The General Assembly, however following further consultations among delegations, decided to include the item at its next session (fifty-ninth session), in 2004.[14]

---

[13]   The following states voted in favour of the motion: Algeria, Argentina, Armenia, Azerbaijan, Bahamas, Bahrain, Belarus, Belgium, Botswana, Brazil, Brunei Darussalam, Bulgaria, Cambodia, China, Comoros, Croatia, Cuba, Cyprus, Czech Republic, Democratic Peoples Republic of Korea, Denmark, Djibouti, Egypt, Estonia, Finland, France, Gabon, Germany, Greece, Hungary, Iceland, India, Indonesia, Islamic Republic of Iran, Japan, Jordan, Kuwait, Latvia, Lebanon, Liechtenstein, Lithuania, Luxembourg, Malaysia, Maldives, Mali, Mauritania, Mauritius, Mexico, Monaco, Morocco, Myanmar, Namibia, Netherlands, New Zealand, Niger, Oman, Pakistan, Qatar, Republic of Korea, Russian Federation, Saudi Arabia, Senegal, Singapore, Slovenia, South Africa, Sri Lanka, Sudan, Swaziland, Sweden, Switzerland, Syrian Arab Republic, Thailand, Tonga, Tunisia, Turkey, United Arab Emirates, United Kingdom of Great Britain and Northern Ireland, Viet Nam, Yemen and Zimbabwe.

The following states voted against the motion: Albania, Andorra, Angola, Antigua and Barbuda, Australia, Austria, Barbados, Belize, Bolivia, Bosnia and Herzegovina, Burundi, Central African Republic, Chile, Costa Rica, Democratic Republic of Congo, Dominica, Dominican Republic, Ecuador, El Salvador, Equatorial Guinea, Eritrea, Ethiopia, Fiji, Gambia, Georgia, Grenada, Guatemala, Guinea, Guyana, Haiti, Honduras, Ireland, Israel, Italy, Kazakhstan, Kenya, Kyrgyzstan, Lesotho, Madagascar, Malawi, Malta, Marshall Islands, Micronesia (the Federated States of), Nauru, Nepal, Nicaragua, Nigeria, Norway, Palau, Panama, Papua New Guinea, Paraguay, Philippines, Poland, Portugal, Rwanda, Saint Kitts and Nevis, Saint Lucia, Saint Vincent and the Grenadines, Samoa, San Marino, Sao Tome and Principe, Sierra Leone, Slovakia, Solomon Islands, Somalia, Spain, Suriname, Tajikistan, Timor-Leste, Trinidad and Tobago, Tuvalu, Uganda, United Republic of Tanzania, United States of America, Uzbekistan, Vanuatu, Venezuela and Zambia.

The following states abstained: Bangladesh, Bhutan, Burkina Faso, Cameroon, Canada, Cape Verde, Colombia, Jamaica, Peru, Republic of Moldova, Romania, Serbia and Montenegro, The Former Yugoslav Republic of Macedonia, Ukraine and Uruguay. See A/C.6/58/SR.23.

[14]   Costa Rica proposed a slightly revised resolution that it had proposed in the Sixth Committee to the General Assembly (A/58/L.37). Following further consultations among delegations, the General Assembly decided to include the item at its next session and not take any action on either the recommendation of the Sixth Committee or the draft resolution proposed by Costa Rica. See A/58/PV.72, 9 December 2003. The United Kingdom in explanation of position after the vote stated that it will neither participate in drafting a convention that would ban therapeutic cloning, nor becomes a party to such a treaty. See ibid.

2. Basic Issues

a) Religious and Cultural Diversity

Human cloning inevitably raises religious issues. Of course, reconciling religious beliefs with international standards and the emotional and occasionally passionate discourse that attends this process are not new to international negotiations. A number of treaties in the human rights area, dealing, for example, with the protection of children and discrimination against women, forced many delegations to work out their national and religious positions in compromise language that all sides could live with.[15] In the context of cloning, such a compromise seemed impossible.

All states supported banning cloning for reproductive purposes, though for different reasons. For some states, the process of creating human beings through the technique of cloning is objectionable because it is asexual and is a threat to the conception of a family. Others have policy reasons unrelated to religious beliefs prohibiting such a practice.[16] But what delegations could not agree on was the definition of a "human being." For some delegations, the early human embryo, not yet implanted

---

[15]   These issues also came up during the 1998 Rome Diplomatic Conference in the context of definition of crimes against humanity.

[16]   See also Leon Kass, Chair of the President's Council on Bioethics, who argues against cloning for reproductive purposes on the following ground:

"We are repelled by the prospect of cloning human beings not because of the strangeness or novelty of the undertaking, but because we intuit and feel, immediately and without argument, the violation of things that we rightfully hold dear. Repugnance, here as elsewhere, revolts against the excesses of human willfulness, warning us not to transgress what is unspeakably profound."

L.R. Kass, The Wisdom of Repugnance, in The Ethics of Cloning (published for the American Enterprise Institute, 1998), 19. A somewhat similar view is expressed by Howard Markel, a pediatrician and historian of medicine at the University of Michigan. In his view "The political problem with the manufacture of human embryos, however early in their development, is not just that it upsets opponents of abortion. It is that it shifts a barrier that might become porous, weakening the sacral quality of the human. And once that takes place, the slippery slope becomes far more slippery. Where are lines to be drawn? Will human life forms ultimately be harvested for the sake of other humans?" See H. Markel, Life in a Bottle, in The New York Times Book Review, March 28, 2004. See also Being Human: Readings from The President's Council on Bioethics (The President's Council on Bioethics, Washington DC. December 2003).

into a womb, is a human being, with a human life, already evolving as an autonomous organism toward its full potential. Destroying this embryo results in a deliberate suppression of an innocent human life. Therapeutic cloning requires the production of millions of human embryos with the intention of destroying them as part of the process of using them for scientific research. For these states, a partial ban would challenge the very basic religious presumption that life begins with a human embryo. This understanding is central to their religious beliefs and any compromise on this issue would be a capitulation to other religious or non-religious beliefs.

For other religious practices in which the conception of life, as such, is not essential to their belief system and practices, or they have not taken a view on this issue from which they cannot dissociate, accepting any view based on a particular set of religious teachings would be unacceptable. During the discussion, Iran, speaking on behalf of the states members of the Islamic Conference supported a ban only for human cloning for reproductive purposes and stated that the states of the Islamic Conference had not taken a collective view on stem cell research and were not prepared to go along with its ban at this time. It based its position on the potential scientific benefits of stem cell research. Its statement was devoid of any religious reasoning. It was the most explicit separation from Catholicism which the Islamic countries had taken on the issues of the origin of life or abortion.

Other states, approaching the matter from a non-religious perspective, objected to any imposition of a religious perspective at the universal level. The opposition to therapeutic cloning on religious grounds was compared to arguments against the use of anaesthetics on the basis of the Old Testament's Book of Genesis, where God is reported to have said that women are supposed to endure pain in childbirth because of Eve's sin in the Garden of Eden. In-Vitro Fertilisation (IVF) technology was called immoral and illicit. As against this, it was argued that, as with IVF technology, it is inappropriate in a world comprising diverse peoples, with diverse beliefs and circumstances, for one value-system or religion to impose its tenets on the rest of humanity, particularly on such a sensitive issue. One cannot speak of sanctity of life without also considering the victims of debilitating illness. They too are entitled to life. Representatives of these states repeatedly asked for respect for diversity of religious beliefs and practices.

To overcome this sharp division of views, suggestions were made to use a terminology similar to the 1998 Additional Protocol on the Prohibition of Cloning Human Beings in which the definition of "human beings" is left to domestic law. But the proposal was unacceptable to those supporting a comprehensive approach.

The basic difficulty therefore was how to reach an agreement on a mandate for a convention on human cloning that recognises cultural, moral and religious diversity and does not prejudice the desire to respect individual freedom and to allow people to live according to their own cultural, moral and religious beliefs.[17]

b) Human Rights Dimensions

A number of issues raised in the discussion also had human rights dimensions. One on which all delegations seemed to agree, is the individuality of human beings and their dignity. Any human cloning for reproductive purposes would, it seems, violate that dignity. Human dignity was not defined[18], and the conclusion that human dignity would be violated by reproductive cloning was expressed more as a given rather than based on any particular reasoning, although for those supporting a comprehensive ban the issue was more closely linked to the asexual creation of human beings. Some states also expressed concerns about the fate of children born from cloning whose inalienable rights may be whittled away by social stigma and ill health arising from cloning defects, causing them considerable anguish and ultimately physical and psychological trauma. Suggestions were also made that cloning could devalue individual human beings since they could be easily replaced.

Protection of the embryo was also raised as an important element. The supporters of a comprehensive ban viewed the embryo as a human being and hence entitled to all the protections available to persons. For this group, production of embryos with the intention of their destruction after research would violate the human rights of the embryos and

---

[17]   See an editorial by *D.C. Dennet*, Brights of the World, Stand and be Counted, in International Herald Tribune, 15 July 2003, 9. He defines a "Bright" as "a person with a naturalist as opposed to a supernaturalist world view." In his definition "Brights" "don't believe in ghosts or elves or the Easter bunny – or God." According to a 2002 survey by the Pew Forum on Religion and Public Life, there are 27 million Americans who are either atheist or agnostic or have no religious preference.

[18]   McDougal, Lasswell and Reisman define "human dignity" in the context of their jurisprudential theory of Law, Science and Policy as referring to a conception of the person as autonomous, a value in himself or herself equipped for making choices, and not as a means to an end.

was therefore unacceptable. They argued that therapeutic cloning would exploit tiny human lives, cells that carry the full genetic code of a human being, treating them as a mere resource to be mined and exploited, eroding their human dignity in the process.

Those supporting a partial ban rejected, implicitly or explicitly, both the notion of an embryo as a human being and that it is entitled to the same degree of protection. They argued that IVF treatment, certain forms of birth control such as the intra-uterine contraceptive device and abortion all involve destruction of embryos. There is therefore no justification to ban therapeutic cloning on that ground while those other procedures are allowed. For this group of states, therapeutic cloning could be allowed under strict regulations, including monitoring mechanisms. Some states referred to their internal law which allowed therapeutic cloning under certain limited conditions and restrictions for the first 14 days of a fertilised egg.

Some arguments focussed on the freedom of thought and of research as supporting therapeutic cloning.[19] It was stated that the techniques of cloning have already been used on DNA, genes and cells in the manufacture of vaccines and diagnostic and pharmaceutical products without any negative ethical consequences. Considering the potential benefit from therapeutic cloning, these proponents argued, there is no justification for banning it altogether. On the contrary, all types of cell research including therapeutic cloning should be encouraged to maximise the chances of medical breakthroughs.

For those supporting a comprehensive ban, the potentials of therapeutic cloning were highly exaggerated and medical experimentation should instead focus on "adult" stem cells, a process that raises no profound ethical issues. Therefore a complete ban on cloning would not prevent scientific research.

One other argument in favour of banning cloning for reproductive purposes is that, at this stage of experimentation with other mammals, there is a high incidence of fatal disorders and lost pregnancy as well as deformation after birth involving pain and suffering. In addition there would be a serious danger to the health of a woman carrying the cloned

---

[19]   See Article 12 (b) of the Universal Declaration on the Human Genome and Human Rights (1997). See also Articles 18 and 19 of the Universal Declaration of Human Rights (1948), which provide for the freedom of thought and expression; and Article 15 (3) of the International Covenant on Economic, Social and Cultural Rights (1966), which requires states to respect the freedom indispensable for scientific research.

embryo. Considering that there is no benefit to such experimentation, the danger that individuals are exposed to is unjustifiable.

c) Commercialisation of Embryos

One argument advanced in favour of a complete ban was the commercialisation of human embryos and the degradation of the status of women. It was argued that permitting therapeutic cloning would in-crease demand for human eggs or oocytes. The process of obtaining these eggs is not without risk, and would use women's bodies as mere reservoirs of oocytes. Hormonal treatment for the production of a large number of eggs in a given cycle carries risk which can be life threaten-ing in certain circumstances. There was already substantial demand for such eggs for fertility purposes, and permitting therapeutic cloning would lead to an even greater demand. Poor women and women from developing countries could be the likely target as paid egg donors. This would be one other form of exploitation of poor women and of devel-oping countries.

Those supporting therapeutic cloning believed that proper regulation and monitoring would adequately address these issues and would pre-vent abuse.

d) Unity of Techniques

The technique for therapeutic cloning is the same as that for reproduc-tive purposes. Therefore permitting therapeutic cloning would allow the technology to develop, and, once cloned human embryos are avail-able, it would be difficult if not impossible to fully control what is done with them. The fear that has been expressed by supporters of a compre-hensive ban is that, at that stage, there would be no way to prevent the birth of a cloned baby. This concern touches on two issues. First, that in fact there will be demands by individuals who would like to have cloned babies despite any prohibition. Once healthy cloned babies are born, the social stigma and the regulatory prohibitions would then be undermined if not completely ineffective in discouraging more cloned babies. The second issue is the fear of unscrupulous scientists. Once the technology is effective, it would not be difficult for a determined scien-tist to find means of implanting a cloned embryo in the womb of a woman and producing a cloned baby. Therefore those supporting a complete ban aim at stopping the advancement of the technology in this area altogether.

Those supporting a partial ban do not necessarily deny that there may be a temptation, both on the part of certain individuals as well as scientists, to produce cloned babies but view the law and the regulatory mechanism as means of controlling behaviour. Technology cannot be condemned or considered immoral for the sole reason of potential abuse. A complete ban, which amounts to banning certain technologies and scientific experimentation, was an unreasonable response to a fear of potential abuse.

e) Universal Acceptance

Supporters of a partial ban argue that only a universally accepted convention would have any chance of universal application and consequently of preventing the birth of cloned babies. The aim is to foreclose any safe haven for scientists who could move to states that are not parties to a convention on a ban. The serious divergence of views among states would not make it possible to reach an agreement on a comprehensive ban, hence support for a partial ban limited to cloning for the purposes of producing children. This argument is particularly pertinent in view of the fact that a number of states with advanced technology and which are already experimenting with therapeutic cloning, such as the United Kingdom, China, Japan and Singapore, are unwilling to stop their experiments and would only agree to a partial ban.

Supporters of a comprehensive ban, while preferring a universally acceptable convention, would not compromise on what is for them an issue of principle. They would be willing to go ahead with a convention that is ethically and morally defensible, but not universally accepted.

f) Non-Governmental Organisations and Scientific Associations

Negotiations on a convention on human cloning did not attract much attention from non-governmental organisations. While there were more non-governmental organisations active and present in the fall of 2003, as opposed to the fall of 2002, only a handful supported in principle a comprehensive ban on all forms of cloning. Their influence, if any, was not noticeable.

The possibility of a ban on therapeutic cloning had certainly interested the scientific community. The InterAcademy Panel on International Affairs (IAP), an association of 60 national academies of science from various parts of the world, issued a statement on 22 September 2003 supporting banning cloning for reproductive purposes while opposing any ban on therapeutic cloning.[20] The IAP suggested that policies on cloning for research and therapeutic purposes should be reviewed periodically in the light of scientific and social developments. Those supporting a partial ban repeatedly quoted the IAP position. But there was no indication, at that time, that the IAP position had influenced the views of governments. The President of the IAP also sent a letter to the Chairman of the Sixth Committee together with the statement by the IAP requesting that the importance of scientific research and the development of potential therapies using cloning be given due consideration when the Committee considers the subject.

III. Possible Forms of a Convention on Cloning

Although the discussions in the Sixth Committee focussed on the scope of the convention on cloning, certain issues relating to the content of and approach to an eventual convention were also raised. The issue was primarily whether banning and regulation of cloning should be approached within the context of a human rights instrument or a law enforcement instrument, or whether other approaches should be explored.

The European Convention for the Protection of Human Rights and Dignity of the Human Being with regard to the Application of Biology and Medicine of 1997 is what might be called a "least interventionist

---

[20]   IAP took the position that

"Research studies using nuclear transfer techniques could be important for improving our basic knowledge of, for example, how the cell nucleus can be reprogrammed to switch on the set of genes that characterizes a particular specialized cell, or for understanding the genetic basis for human diseases, or for enhancing our understanding of re-programming faulty human genes. A more long-term goal would be to learn how to re-program somatic cells into stem cells and thus provide a way of obtaining stem cells, genetically compatible with the patient without any need for the use of eggs and embryos. It is, of course, only justified to carry out this research using human eggs where animal studies fail to provide a suitable alternative."

approach" in national jurisdictions. It prohibits or imposes certain conditions on scientific research and leaves implementation to states. It does not criminalise an act nor does it deal with sanctions. Domestic laws will have to deal with these issues. The European convention is much closer to a form of human rights instrument or even guidelines for unification of national laws. The Additional Protocol to the Convention on the Prohibition of Cloning Human Beings follows the same pattern. Domestic laws are given substantial latitude with interpretation or they may elect to take a more stringent approach.

As for the discussions within the Sixth Committee, Costa Rica, in April 2003, submitted a draft convention on the prohibition of all forms of human cloning including therapeutic cloning.[21] The draft convention views the subject more in the context of a criminal law and law enforcement instrument, following the structure of a prosecute or extradite treaty. The draft is influenced much by the International Convention for the Suppression of the Financing of Terrorism. It defines the crime and sets out an obligation on states parties to adopt domestic legislation to criminalise the act and empower their courts to exercise jurisdiction with respect to individuals who commit such a crime. Following the anti-terrorism conventions, it requires states to confiscate funds of individuals and institutions involved or implicated in the crime. Paragraph 4 of the Article of the proposed draft defines "victim" as:

> ...both the person whose genetic material or oocyte is used without permission to commit an offence set forth in Article 2, paragraph 1, and the *living organism created by the commission of the offence set forth in Article 2, paragraph 1.*[22]

The definition of "victim" is for the purposes of establishing jurisdiction and awarding possible damages.

A state party to the convention is obliged to either prosecute the offender promptly or extradite the offender to another state that is prepared to institute prosecution. The draft does not allow reservations to Articles 1, 2 and 3 on the scope of the convention and criminalisation of the act of cloning.

During negotiations, other possibilities were directly or indirectly raised as a way of imposing a stricter regulatory regime for therapeutic cloning, short of a complete ban. These suggestions were based on do-

---

21   Document A/58/73. Reprinted in the annex of this volume, under I 5.

22   Ibid. Emphasis added.

mestic law models requiring some form of a reporting and monitoring mechanism. In some domestic laws, any embryo research, whether in the private or public sector, is subject to licensing. Before issuance of such a license, the requests are subjected to a robust system of case-by-case consideration. Research is only allowed for the specified limited purposes and no research is allowed on embryos over 14 days old. A monitoring mechanism at the international level, such as a reporting requirement, could help to enhance domestic compliance. The convention could also be subjected to review after a number of years to make certain that it has not been outdated in view of further scientific and social developments.

IV. Is Cloning Human Beings an Appropriate Subject for a Convention?

As a "good/appropriate" topic for a multilateral treaty, human cloning, at this stage, lacks some of the criteria identified at the beginning of this paper. There is no clear evidence that there is pressing need to address this topic at the global level. Scientists have viewed claims by a few doctors that they are on the verge of cloning babies with scepticism. Reproductive cloning in other mammals has not been completely successful. Dolly the sheep, while scientifically valuable, is not considered a successful experiment for the cloning purposes. It is not likely that, until experiments with other mammals are successful, there will be experimentation on human cloning, so the argument that unless there is a global convention banning reproductive cloning soon there will be cloned babies fails to persuade.

The subject of international bioethics is itself new to international law. Human cloning is even newer. Hence there is very little in terms of precedents or state practice. Aside from the 1997 Universal Declaration on the Human Genome and Human Rights with a very general statement on inherent dignity and inalienable rights of all members of the human family, there is no other global instrument. As for regional instruments, there is only the 1998 Additional Protocol (to the European Convention) on the Prohibition of Cloning Human Beings. There are no other international agreements, state practice or judicial decisions.

The topic is also new in domestic legislation. As of now, there are about 30 countries that have adopted national legislation, which explicitly or implicitly prohibits human reproductive cloning, and about 20 countries that are in the process of elaborating regulations.[23] As for therapeutic cloning, 16 countries have domestic legislation, 5 of which are in favour of and 11 against therapeutic cloning.[24]

Nor does the topic rate high on the scale of priorities. For many countries confronted with more tangible and immediate problems of economic development like hunger, lack of health care, and peace and security, the possibility that a scientist may produce a cloned baby somewhere in a laboratory seems comparatively minor compared with their pressing life-and-death issues.

Nor is there any general consensus among states on the direction of the topic. On the contrary, the views of states are sharply divided and there seems to be no possibility of consensus on a direction acceptable to all. But were states to agree on a common direction, there would be no shortage in providing the necessary intellectual and technical leadership for the development of the topic.

As for the activities of non-governmental organisations and other special groups, the topic will certainly attract attention among those organisations active in the pro-life campaign as well as in the scientific community and the pharmaceutical industry at the national level.

V. Possible Future Scenarios

To recommend a particular course of action, policy makers project future scenarios. For the purposes of exploring whether a multilateral agreement, with a comprehensive ban or a partial ban, on cloning human beings is necessary or likely to be successful, I will propose two scenarios.

One scenario simply projects the current lack of convention on either type of ban.

At the present time there are a limited number of states that have sufficient technological and scientific resources to experiment with cloning embryos. These countries either already have a ban on all forms of cloning or on cloning for reproductive purposes or are in the process of adopting such domestic laws. It is possible that those scientists, who are

---

[23]   Information provided to the Working Group of the Sixth Committee by UNESCO on 29 September 2003.

[24]   Ibid.

involved or would like to be involved in stem cell research and are in countries with legislation banning all forms of cloning, would migrate to countries which allow for such research. As for pharmaceutical companies, it might be more difficult to join or create some form of partnership with other companies in countries permitting stem cell research without being subject to investigations in their own state of registration.

Countries that have the technology to allow therapeutic cloning either have in place legislation banning cloning for producing children or are in the process of adopting such legislation. Attempts to produce cloned babies in these countries will be difficult and will confront criminal and civil suits. It is also unlikely that a reputable scientist, scientific institution or pharmaceutical company will establish a laboratory in a country that does not have domestic law banning cloning for reproductive purposes purely for purposes of that form of experimentation. The possibility of reputational costs and criminal actions in other locations against the institution or the individuals involved would be too high to warrant the risk.

The second scenario projects a universal convention banning all forms of cloning.

Some states have made it very clear that they will never join a treaty banning all forms of cloning. These countries have the technological know-how to continue with research. Such a convention may be ratified by a large number of states, but not by all. In addition, the process of drafting a convention and then preparing domestic ratification requiring implementing legislation will take years before the entry into force of a treaty and even more before a large number of states ratify or accede to it. So the universality of a convention is a goal that will take years to become a reality, if it ever does. Meanwhile, there would be states that have not ratified the convention and countries that would allow stem cell research while banning human cloning.

While successful cloning of a baby is not possible now, scientists do not deny the possibility that sometime in the future scientific knowledge may advance to the point where reproductive cloning could be accomplished. Still the criminal and other administrative actions in the first scenario are available and may be taken against those involved. In particular, if the experimentation is unsuccessful, leading to birth of a baby with deformation or other serious medical problems, or health problems for the mother who carried the pregnancy to term, the condemnation and various civil and criminal actions available under the first scenario would be a strong and serious disincentive for future experimentation. These actions would have to be taken under domestic law whether or not a state is a party to a convention banning all forms of cloning or only cloning for reproductive purposes. For those states which have no domestic legislation whether or not they are parties to the convention, no action would be taken. A convention may allow other states parties to take actions under certain circumstances.

Problems encountered

The lowest common denominator between the two scenarios is the attempt to prevent producing cloned babies. If science and technology develops so much that a healthy child is born clandestinely and illegally, both scenarios will encounter serious problems. Despite whatever civil or criminal actions may be taken against the scientist, the affiliated institution or company, the very fact that a healthy child has been born could defeat the stigma associated with the practice. Once the experiment is successful, there would be demand for it. Like other social issues dealing with abortion, definition of family, marriage between homosexuals[25], adoption of children by homosexuals and single parents,

---

[25]   On 18 November 2003, Massachusetts' highest court ruled that gay couples have the right to marry under the state's constitution, and it gave the legislature 180 days to make same-sex marriages possible. "Marriage by Gays gains big Victory in Massachusetts," New York Times, November 19, 2003, A 1 and A 24. On June 26, 2003, the Supreme Court of the United States decided that Texas statute making it a crime for two persons of the same sex to engage in certain consensual intimate sexual conduct was unconstitutional. *Lawrence v. Texas*, 123 S.Ct. 2472. In that case, the Supreme Court referring to an earlier decision stated:

"It must be acknowledged, of course, that the Court in *Bowers* was making the broader point that for centuries there have been powerful voices to condemn homosexual conduct as immoral. The condemnation has been shaped by religious beliefs, conceptions of right and acceptable behavior, and respect for the traditional family. For many persons these are not trivial concerns but profound and deep convictions accepted as ethical and moral principles to which they aspire and which thus determine the course of their lives. These considerations do not answer the question before us, however. The issue is whether the majority may use the power of the State to enforce these views on the whole society through operation of the criminal law. 'Our obligation is to define the liberty of all, not to mandate our own moral code.'"

The European Court of Human Rights in 1981 also declared that the laws of Northern Ireland forbidding homosexual conduct among consenting adults were invalid under the European Convention on Human Rights, *Dudgeon v. United Kingdom*, Eur. Ct. H.R. 45 (1981), 52.

etc., social adjustments in a sufficient number of countries would temper and diminish the unacceptablity of the practice.[26] Cloned persons or their supporters would become active and agitate to remove any stigma or to change the law. No criminal sanctions and financial costs imposed on those associated with the birth of healthy cloned babies would change the trend. In this context, there is merit in the argument of those supporting a complete ban on the fear that one successful attempt would undermine the law. But there is no certainty that even a universally subscribed convention on a complete ban on all forms of cloning could arrest the trend once a single healthy cloned baby is born.

---

[26] Leon Kass arguing against human cloning illustrates the difficulty with the culture of rationalism:

"…It has become harder, not easier, to discern the true meaning of human cloning. […] We have become accustomed to new practices in human reproduction: not just in vitro fertilization, but also embryo manipulation, embryo donation, and surrogate pregnancy. Animal biotechnology has yielded transgenic animals and a burgeoning science of genetic engineering, easily and soon to be transferable to humans.

Even more important, changes in the broader culture make it now vastly more difficult to express a common and respectful understanding of sexuality, procreation, nascent life, family, and the meaning of motherhood, fatherhood, and the links between the generations. Twenty-five years ago, abortion was still illegal and thought to be immoral, the sexual revolution (…) was still in infancy, and few had yet heard about the reproductive rights of single women, homosexual men, and lesbians. […] Today, defenders of stable, monogamous marriage risk charges of giving offense to those adults who are living in "new family forms" or to those children who, even without the benefit of assisted reproduction, have acquired either three or four parents or one or none at all. Today one must even apologize for voicing opinions that twenty-five years ago were nearly universally regarded as the core of our culture's wisdom on those matters. In a world whose once-given natural boundaries are blurred by technological change and whose moral boundaries are seemingly up for grabs, it is much more difficult to make persuasive the still compelling case against cloning human beings." See *Kass*, supra note 16, 6-8.

On the question of morality, Svend Ranulf and Harold Lasswell have suggested that legislating morality was initiated by one social class to suppress another ascending cultural formation in an effort at social control. See *S. Ranulf*, Moral Indignation and Middle Class Psychology (1938, reprinted 1964). See also the Introduction to Ranulf's book by *H. Lassewell*, ibid., ix, xii.

VI. Some Reflections

The fact that there might be breaches of multilateral treaties has never reduced the utility of concluding treaties. Indeed legislation creates breaches. Nor does the violation of a treaty, per se, reduce the normative value that has been set out by the treaty. Human rights treaties have and are being violated on a daily basis. The violations have not reduced the importance and the authoritative character of the treaties. Sanctions either in the form of compensation, restitution, or criminal penalties have been used to reinforce the norms set out by treaties. Monitoring bodies have become guardians of standard setting treaties by exposing states that breach their obligations. Similarly, terrorism conventions have not stopped acts of terrorism. But terrorism has not undermined the authoritative character of these conventions nor has it made terrorism acceptable. The reasons in both situations are the abhorrent consequences and effects of human rights violations or acts of terrorism.

But banning cloning human beings is different from prohibiting acts of violating human rights and terrorism. It is hard to imagine many ordinary people condemning the product of successful cloning, whether therapeutic or for producing children. The promise of a breakthrough for treatment of serious and debilitating disease, if it materialises, will be applauded and not condemned. It would be difficult even for those who oppose therapeutic cloning on religious and ethical grounds to remain firm in their condemnation. If cloning for producing children is successful, the very outcome – a healthy child – would make it difficult to condemn the practice.

Twenty-five years ago, Louise Brown, the first "In Vitro Fertilisation" baby, became famous for being the first child conceived outside the body. The arguments and the doubts about the immorality of the procedure subsided after her successful birth. Today, IVF is conventional and there is nothing spectacular about it. One percent of the babies born in the United States are the result of IVF.[27] There are still those who do not agree with the IVF procedure for religious and cultural reasons and would not use it. Even though IVF still remains an inexact science, involves high costs and is not affordable for low income families, and even though the production of twins, triplets and even higher mul-

---

[27] See *M. Duenwald*, 25, In Vitro Fertilization has come of Age, in International Herald Tribune, 17 July 2003, 10. For a review of early controversy over research in in vitro fertilization see *R.M. Henig*, Pandora's Baby: How the First Test Tube Babies Sparked the Reproductive Revolution, 2004.

tiple pregnancies may cause persistent problems often causing premature deliveries, low birth weights and other health problems, there is no condemnation of the procedure and it is being improved and developed continuously. Will therapeutic cloning – and even cloning human beings – go through the same process?

A Convention on Cloning – Annotations to an almost Unsolvable Dilemma

Spiros Simitis, Frankfurt

I. Premises

"By all accounts we have entered upon a golden age for biology, medicine and biotechnology"[1]. The President's Council on Bioethics could hardly have been more emphatic. In an equally categorical manner the American National Science Foundation had only shortly before also spoken of a "unique moment in the history of technical achievement" at which an "improvement of human performance becomes possible" introducing "a golden age that would be a turning point for human productivity and quality of life."[2] No other technique has, indeed, since the early days of information technology raised so many hopes, stirred so many fantasies and instigated so emotional debates as biotechnology. The times in which ailments such as Alzheimer's or Parkinson's were regarded as a terrible but unchangeable fate, or in which children were the result of "a random, unpredictable meeting of sperm and egg"[3] seem to be definitely over. All in all, nothing appears more appropriate than a simple and unequivocal affirmative answer to James Watson's question:

---

[1]   Beyond Therapy – Biotechnology and the Pursuit of Happiness, A Report of The President's Council on Bioethics (October 2003), 5.

[2]   National Science Foundation, Converging Technologies for Improving Human Performance: Nanotechnology, Biotechnology, Information Technology and Cognitive Science (2003), 6.

[3]   *G. Stock*, Redesigning Humans: Our Inevitable Genetic Future (2002), 200.

"If we could make better human beings by knowing how to add genes, why shouldn't we?"[4].

But what for many is the daily confirmation of an unstoppable advance in science, constitutes for others an unmistakable sign of a radical negation of fundamental principles of any society that claims to respect human dignity and individual self-determination. Therefore, all further reflections should focus more than ever on the ethical, social and political implications of biotechnology. Opinions such as those of the German National Ethics Council on the import of stem cells[5] or the preimplantation genetic diagnosis[6], of the French National Ethics Committee on reproductive cloning[7] or on the duty of a familial genetic information[8], and of the European Group on Ethics in Science and New Technologies to the European Commission on genetic testing in the workplace[9], the inquiry of the President's Council on Bioethics into the potential implications of using biotechnology for "better children, superior performance, ageless bodies, and happy souls"[10], and the proposals of the European Commission on the use of embryonic cells for research purposes[11] as well as the ensuing controversies in the Council of Ministers[12] illustrate the growing desire to place biotechnology back in

---

[4]   Quoted in *T. Wheeler*, Miracle Molecule, 50 Years On, Baltimore Sun, 4 February 2003, 8A.

[5]   German National Ethics Council, The Import of Human Embryonic Stem Cells (2001).

[6]   German National Ethics Council, Genetic diagnosis before and during pregnancy (2003).

[7]   Comité Consultatif National d'Éthique, Réponse au Président de la République au sujet du clonage reproductif, Avis No. 054, 22 April 1997.

[8]   Comité Consultatif National d'Éthique, À propos de l'obligation d'information génétique familiale en cas de nécessité médicale, Avis No. 076, 24 April 2003.

[9]   European Group on Ethics in Science and New Technologies to the European Commission, Opinion on the ethical aspects of genetic testing in the workplace, Opinion No.18, 28 July 2003.

[10]   Supra note 1, 27, 101, 159.

[11]   Proposal for a Council Decision amending decision 2002/834/EC on the specific programme for research, technological development and demonstration: "Integrating and strengthening the European research area" (2002-2006), 9 July 2003, COM (2003) 390 final.

[12]   Cf. especially the report on the 2550th Council meeting – Competitiveness – (Internal market, Industry and Research) Brussels, 3 December 2003,

its social context and, thus, to redefine the premises of all reflections on the conditions of its development and application, also and mainly with a view to establishing a series of binding regulatory principles.

However, as different as the issues discussed and the respective reactions may be, two aspects characterise the entire debate. It, first, deals with the implications of a particular technology. The interest in biotechnology is, secondly, exactly as in the case of information technology, by no means a purely national phenomenon. Consequently, none of the questions arising out of its evolution and its potential implications addresses problems confined to a specific country. The state of the technology may differ, the policies and projects vary, but hopes and worries are nevertheless determined by one and the same technology, despite the indisputable fact that conflicts originate most of the time in a national context and reflect considerations often motivated by typically national concerns. Thus, for example, the controversy on the import of stem cells was triggered by the strict limitations on embryonic research established by German law. Similarly, the remarks of the President's Council in its aforementioned report on "choosing in", i.e. the selection of embryos for genetic engineering[13], were in response to plans of American scientists. And, finally, the obligation of the French National Ethics Committee to also treat issues brought up by questions or complaints of medical doctors, researchers or any other interested person emphasises the national affinity even more. Still, the national context is just the surface of a truly international issue.

Therefore, the German National Ethics Council declared shortly after its establishment that the problems caused by biotechnology can ultimately only be successfully dealt with on an international level. In precisely this spirit the Council sought a close cooperation with the French Committee that, for instance, led to the adoption of a common document on biobanks[14] preceding the respective national opinions[15]. The

---

15531/03 (Presse 355); but also Federal Ministry of Education and Research, Press Release No. 230/2003 of 3 December 2003.

[13]   Supra note 1, 40.

[14]   Ergänzende gemeinsame Erklärung des Nationalen Ethikrates und des Comité Consultatif National d'Éthique zu ihren Stellungnahmen über Biobanken, 24 July 2003.

[15]   Cf. Comité Consultatif National d'Éthique, Problèmes éthiques posés par les collections de matériel biologique et les données d'informations associées: "biobanques", "biothèques" (Ethical problems caused by the collection of biological material and the associated data bases: "biobanks", "biotheques"), Avis

case of the Icelandic Health Sector Database is another noteworthy example. What at first was regarded as a clearly national project quickly proved to be the starting point of a broad international debate also, if not mainly, conducted in countries without similar plans for such a database. And it was this increasingly international dispute that finally resulted in the ongoing critical review of the original design. A different but equally important aspect of the internationality of biotechnology is illustrated by the advent of the pre-implantation genetic diagnosis, the growth of biotourism. Tests strictly forbidden in Germany, for example, can be easily carried out in Belgium. Furthermore, embryonic research that obviously contradicts the goals of French, Italian or German legislators is perfectly legal in the United Kingdom or the Scandinavian countries.

The internationality of the implications of biotechnology certainly does not exempt national regulatory authorities from further reflections on the necessity and the content of domestic rules. Internationality is in other terms not a valid justification for national passivity. On the contrary, an accurate determination of the national standpoint is the indispensable first step towards an international regulation. But as crucial as a clarification of the national attitude is, it must also be understood as an incentive to seek an international approach. Only then can a truly efficient reaction be achieved. Once the need for internationally acknowledged requirements is admitted, all further reflections seem, at least as far as the regulatory instrument is concerned, to be determined. One or more conventions appear to be the sole way to counteract effectively the consequences of biotechnology and, thus, to respond to an international challenge with equally international expectations.

 ## II. Experiences

The quest for an international accord has a well-known precedent. Similar demands were already expressed in the early eighties. The first to react was the Council of Europe. The result was the adoption of the 1997 Biomedicine-Convention[16]. Moreover, a simple glance at the text

---

No. 077, 20 March 2003; Nationaler Ethikrat, Biobanken für die Forschung, Stellungnahme, 17 March 2004.

[16] Convention for the Protection of Human Rights and Dignity of the Human Being with regard to the Application of Biology and Medicine: Conven-

shows that the agreement contains provisions on many of the issues currently discussed, as alone the examples of the articles on the human genome (Art. 11 et seq.) or research (Art. 15 et seq.) illustrate. But while the text should certainly not be neglected, both the history of the Convention and the aftermath of its adoption are definitely more interesting for all considerations on the importance and the impact of international accords. The original proposals were modified time and again in a decade of cumbersome, sometimes even painful debates that reached their highpoint after the secrecy of the deliberations was broken by a "democratic indiscretion"[17]. Twenty-one out of the 40 Member States of the Council of Europe finally signed the Convention.

However, the conflicts that marked its beginning were never overcome, notwithstanding the elaboration of a series of additional protocols, intended to either clarify and detail existing provisions, as in the case of transplantation, or amplify the agreement by including, as in the case of cloning, additional issues. Interestingly, the latest attempt to rescue the Convention, is an additional protocol that in fact amounts to a comprehensive revision of central parts of the original text[18]. Nevertheless none of these efforts has noticeably increased the acceptance of the Convention. To this day, only 16 states have ratified the agreement, another 15 having signed it. The readiness to ratify or at least sign the additional protocols is equally remarkably low. Even where, as in Germany, governments after years of hesitation cautiously indicated their intention to adhere to the Convention[19], the negative parliamentary reactions quickly forced them to a hasty retreat.

The experiences of the Council of Europe are by no means unique. Thus, the European Commission has encountered quite comparable difficulties, for example, in connection with the transposition of the

---

tion on Human Rights and Biomedicine, signed on 4 April 1997, ETS No. 164, reprinted in the annex of this volume, under III 15.

[17]   Cf. *R. Röspel* (ed.), Biologie am Horizont der Philosophie. Der Entwurf einer europäischen Bioethik-Konvention (1997); *T. Degener*, Chronologie der Bioethik – Konvention und ihre Streitpunkte, KritV 81 (1998), 7.

[18]   Council of Europe, Steering Committee on Bioethics (CDBI), Draft additional Protocol to the Convention on Human Rights and Biomedicine, on Biomedical Research, 23 June 2003, CDBI/INF 6.

[19]   Cf. Federal Ministry of Justice, Das Übereinkommen zum Schutz der Menschenrechte und der Menschenwürde im Hinblick auf die Anwendung von Biologie und Medizin – des Europarats vom 4. April 1997, Januar 1998/2, 18.

Directive on Biotechnological Inventions[20]. The reticence of the Member States is conspicuous. Some, as especially the Netherlands supported by Italy and Norway, openly contested the Directive by seeking, however without success, a correction through an intervention of the European Court of Justice[21]. Others, as Germany, chose to wait until the very last moment, stressed the need of a review and prepared a draft[22] literally under the threat of an appeal by the Commission to the European Court[23]. The conflicts follow the lines of the controversies accompanying the Council of Europe's Biotechnology Convention. Hence, questions such as the handling of the human genome, the ban on cloning or the limits of research dominate once more the debate[24].

The failure of the United Nations to reach an agreement on human cloning is another equally significant example of the hindrances and complications inevitably arising whenever issues related to biotechnology are treated. The apparent consensus on a prohibition of reproductive cloning promptly broke down. While a clear majority of countries repeatedly affirmed their categorical opposition to any attempt to directly or indirectly tolerate reproductive cloning, the same states were obviously unwilling to underscore their position by a common resolution. Paradoxically, all texts tabled on two successive occasions insisted on a ban. Thus, it was exactly this expectation that in the fall of 2002 was not only in the centre of the ultimately unsuccessful Franco-German initiative[25], but also a main element of the parallel proposals

---

[20]   Directive 98/44/EC of the European Parliament and of the Council on the legal Protection of Biotechnological Inventions of 6 July 1998 (OJ No. L 213/13).

[21]   Cf. the Judgement of the Court of Justice in Netherlands v. Parliament and Council, Case 377/98 (2001) ECR I-7079.

[22]   Draft Statute on the Legal Protection of Biotechnological Inventions (Entwurf eines Gesetzes zur Umsetzung der Richtlinie über den rechtlichen Schutz biotechnologischer Erfindungen), Printed Matter (*Bundestagsdrucksache*) 15/1709, 15 October 2003.

[23]   Cf. also Report from the Commission to the European Parliament and the Council, Development and implications of patent law in the field of biotechnology and genetic engineering, 7 October 2002, COM (2002) 545 final, 7, 30.

[24]   Cf., for example, German Bundestag, Plenary Protocol of the 53rd session, 26 June 2003, Stenographic Report 15/53, 4456-4461.

[25]   Cf. United Nations, General Assembly, Fifty-seventh session, Sixth Committee, Agenda item 162, International Convention against the Reproduc-

co-sponsored by the United States and Spain[26]. And when a year later, in November 2003, the United Nations Legal Committee in its Ending Session reconsidered the chances of a prohibition, both draft resolutions were unmistakably in favour of a convention to precisely this purpose[27]. In the end, the Committee approved by a narrow vote (80 in favour to 79 against, with 15 abstentions) a motion carried by Iran on behalf of the Organisation of the Islamic Conference supported by Belgium and India to recommend that the General Assembly defer for two years the question of an international accord and resume the debate at its sixtieth session in 2005[28].

The persistent hesitations to condemn reproductive cloning are in view of the 1997 UNESCO-Declaration on the Human Genome and Human Rights[29], the 1998 resolution of the United Nations General Assembly endorsing this Declaration[30] and the 2002 report of the Ad hoc Committee on an International Convention against the Reproductive Cloning of Human Beings[31] even more puzzling[32]. Indeed, nothing would have, against this background, appeared more consistent than a clear ban. However, the stumbling block is in reality not dissent against

---

tive Cloning of Human Beings, A/C.6/57/L.8, 18 October 2002, reprinted in the annex of this volume, under I 7.

[26]   Cf. United Nations, General Assembly, Fifty-seventh session, Sixth Committee, Agenda item 162, International Convention against the Reproductive Cloning of Human Beings, A/C.6/57/L.3/Rev.1, 18 October 2002, reprinted in the annex of this volume, under I 6.

[27]   Cf. United Nations, General Assembly, Fifty-eighth session, Sixth Committee, 23d Meeting, International Convention against the Reproductive Cloning of Human Beings, Draft Resolutions A/C.58/L.2 (International Convention against Human Cloning) and A/C.6/58/L.8 (International Convention against the Reproductive Cloning of Human Beings), both reprinted in the annex of this volume, under I 3 and 4.

[28]   Cf. United Nations, Press Release GA/L//3246, 6 November 2003.

[29]   UNESCO, Records of the General Conference, Twenty-ninth Session, Vol. 1, Resolutions, Resolution 16.

[30]   Resolution 53/152, 9 December 1998.

[31]   Official Records of the General Assembly, Fifty-seventh Session, Supplement No 51 (A/57/51).

[32]   Cf. also the Resolution 2001/71 on "Human Rights and Bioethics", adopted on 25 April 2001 by the Commission on Human Rights, Official Records of the Economic and Social Council, 2001, Supplement No. 8 (E/2001/23).

the prohibition of reproductive cloning, but disagreement on the range of a possible convention, the latest being from the above mentioned discussions in the Sixth (Legal) Committee of the General Assembly. Countries like the United States, Costa-Rica, Nigeria, Italy, Tanzania, Uganda, the Philippines, or Spain insisted that the ban should be total, in other terms, exclude any form of cloning. Belgium, Sweden, China, Norway, Cuba, the United Kingdom and Switzerland, as well as several other countries agreed on the contrary opinion that the prohibition was to be restricted to reproductive cloning and at the same time be complemented by an obligation to either secure the control of other forms of cloning by specific legal provisions or to subject them to a moratorium. Both groups refused to compromise[33]. The first regarded concessions as a typical example of a slippery slope that eventually would legitimate every type of cloning; the latter considered any step towards a complete ban as an inadmissible overreaction that would especially inhibit important medical research. As a consequence, a postponement of the decision on a convention appeared as the only way out[34].

III. Implications

The negative experiences seem to imply an equally negative conclusion: Issues of biotechnology are, at least to a large and decisive extent, inaccessible to regulation by means of a convention. Documents such as the UNESCO-Declaration on the Human Genome and Human Rights or the various rules and proposals of the EC-Commission do not contradict this supposition. Both are structured and determined by premises clearly different from those governing the adoption of a convention. Declarations have no binding consequences. Therefore, the scope of the negotiations is definitely broader. The participants can agree on points

---

[33]   Cf. UN News Service of 22 October 2003.

[34]   The bitter reaction of the British representative, Ambassador Adam Thomson, in the ensuing debate of the General Assembly, cf. infra note 35, quoted in The New York Times of 10 December 2003, is therefore not at all surprising. In his opinion it "is clear that there is no consensus in respect to therapeutic cloning research, but by ignoring this fact and pressing for action to ban all cloning, supporters of the Costa Rican resolution have effectively destroyed the possibility of action on the important area on which we all agreed – a ban of productive cloning".

they would never accept in the context of a convention, unless they never intended to ratify and really apply the convention and thus never meant for it to be binding. Significantly enough, the UNESCO-Declaration encountered no difficulties in the General Assembly, while in the case of reproductive cloning the best that could be expected was the approval of the postponement proposal. And indeed, the General Assembly reacted in exactly this way, however with a small modification: cloning will be discussed anew a year earlier, in the fifty-ninth session in 2004 instead of the originally envisaged sixtieth session in 2006[35].

Besides, it is certainly not accidental that other decidedly more flexible types of instruments have increasingly displaced conventions. Thus, the International Labour Organisation has progressively shifted the accent from conventions to recommendations and codes of practice[36]. Their advantage is double: The Organisation can reasonably expect to achieve most of its objectives, while the members need not apprehend taking on obligations overly contradictory to their actual national rules.

The relevance of this last aspect is illustrated by an initially rather astonishing development. The more the weight shifted to recommendations, the more the reactions were adapted to those typical for the debates on conventions. The acceptance of a recommendation became increasingly tied to an express reservation related to individual provisions. Needless to say, any such declaration is strictly speaking senseless. Recommendations are probably most characterised by the deliberate avoidance of binding obligations. Hence, reservations have solely a both political and psychological function. They permit timely documentation of the disagreement with a specific proposal and, thus, to greater protection against the growing pressure emanating from the increasing importance of recommendations.

Experiences such as those of the International Labour Organisation indicate not only a general trend, they are also particularly relevant for all reflections regarding agreements related to biotechnology. As necessary as an agreement may appear, rules interfering with labour relations

---

[35]   Cf. the Resolution of the 72nd Plenary Meeting of the General Assembly on 9 December 2003, United Nations Press Release GA/10218, 9 December 2003.

[36]   Cf. *L. Betten*, International Labour Law (1993), 7 et seq.; *S. Simitis*, Zur Internationalisierung des Arbeitnehmerdatenschutzes – Die Verhaltensregeln der Internationalen Arbeitsorganisation, in Festschrift für T. Dieterich (1999), 606 et seq.

affect issues that are both economically and politically amongst the most sensitive. Irrespective of what is at stake – whether the conditions and the scope of collective bargaining, the hours of work, the elimination of discrimination, workers' participation, the prevention of professional diseases or the protection of workers' personal data – any attempt to agree on internationally applicable rules is encumbered from the very beginning by strongly opposed interests, the diversity of the socio-political context, the persistence of cultural and historical traditions and the impact of specific economic and political conceptions. The preparatory talks on the agenda of the International Labour Organisation, as well as decisions to adopt a code of practice[37] for unusually complicated matters, such as the protection of workers' data, instead of attempting to negotiate a recommendation, not to speak of a convention, exemplify both the importance and the consequences of this burden. Where therefore, as in the case of biotechnology, conflicts are, compared to labour relations, generally sharper, reservations deeper and antagonisms nearly irreconcilable, the search for an alternative to conventions becomes even more imperative.

As for the regulations of the European Commission, they are part of a legislative process. Directives, once adopted, are not optional for the Member States. They may offer them alternatives, or even empower them to further develop and specify a particular regulation, but they nonetheless establish a binding framework that necessarily entails a review of the respective national rules. Hence, conflicts such as those on embryonic research or biopatents may reflect substantial differences of opinion between the Member States, but they do not affect the competence of the EC-Commission to determine in each of these cases the rules according to which Member States must proceed. Doubts, objections or disagreements can consequently only be dealt with through the generally applicable procedure.

Thus, the diverging attitudes of the Member States with respect to embryonic research may have forced the European Commission to justify anew the rules, which were already in force, in a meeting of the Council[38]. Nonetheless the failure to agree on a common position does not exclude an application of these provisions. The European Commission is still entitled to fund research, though beginning in

---

[37] International Labour Office, Protection of Workers' Personal Data, Code of Practice adopted at the 267th Session of the Governing Body in November 1996 (1997).

[38] Cf. supra note 12.

January 2004 under significantly stricter conditions, as alone the modalities of the examination and acceptance of a project demonstrate. In sum, even where the object of the controversy and the intensity of the dispute are quite alike, international conventions and regulations of the European Commission are nevertheless incomparable. The regulatory process within the European Union influences and directs both the policies and the comportment of the Member States to an extent that no negotiations in view of a convention can ever equal.

The example of the European Union shows also that the era of regulations, which avoid clear phrasing and precise requirements by taking refuge in conspicuously general statements is over. Neither science nor the pharmaceutical industry waits for the potential regulators to formulate their requirements. As different, though sometimes quite convergent, as their interests are, their common primary aim is to increase knowledge and systematically exploit the chances it offers both for cognitive and pragmatic purposes. Neither the open passivity of the regulators, nor their reticence to interfere, concealed by intentionally cloudy language, is under these circumstances anything but synonymous with a "moratorium" in academic research or the development of new applications of biomedicine or biotechnology.

Therefore, if the actual gap between regulatory requirements and the evolution of research is to be kept at least constant, all regulatory efforts must fulfil two conditions. They should, first, not be confined to mere responses to current conflicts but should try to situate the envisaged reactions in a context that not only addresses actual controversies but also anticipates, primarily against the background of the advances in research, future problems. Thus, scientific work, as in the case of derivation of embryonic cells and male gametes from embryonic stem cells[39], forces on the one hand review of the still obstinate insistence on the apparently absolutely irreplaceable research with human stem cells and compels on the other hand timely reaction to possible implications of a derivation for the development of chimeras. Considerations as those of the President's Council on Bioethics on enhancement and psy-

---

[39] Cf. especially *N. Geisjen/M. Horoschak/K. Kim/J. Gribnau/K. Eggan/ G. Daley*, Nature AOP, published online 10 December 2003, doi: 10.1038/nature02247; *R. Jaenisch*, The Biology of Nuclear Cloning and the Potential of Embryonic Stem Cells for Transplantation Therapy, Appendix N to Monitoring Stem Cell Research, A Report of The President's Council on Bioethics (January 2004).

chotropic drugs[40] are exemplary for such an effort, deliberately transcending the limits of a simple reply to an individual event and attempting to establish the premises for further developments.

Secondly, irrespective of whether currently discussed or future issues are treated, the demands must be as precise as possible. Debates, as those mentioned on biobanks and cloning, demonstrate how urgent a concrete approach followed by equally clear requirements is. Thus, the probably most salient characteristic of the United Kingdom Biobank is the combination of health and lifestyle data. As a result, a collection of personal data will emerge that permits to arrive at unprecedented personal profiles. It may very well be that exactly this combination will also offer unparalleled opportunities in the main research field of the biobank, namely those ailments commonly affecting a specific age group, for instance, heart disease or strokes. However, it is no less obvious that profiles based on the particular details stemming from the biobank are of equal interest to employers, insurance companies, and health or security agencies. Implications as these must be openly addressed. Therefore, it is neither enough to simply stress the importance of such collections and their potential contribution to an amelioration of the health condition not only of particular groups of persons but ultimately of the entire population, nor to put together lists of "Frequently asked questions" describing in an equally abstract way the aims as well as the content of the biobank and a series of other particulars.

The admissibility of such a collection depends finally on the certainty that the data stored and especially the profiles will be exclusively used for the expressly stated purposes of the biobank. The *conditio sine qua non* is in other terms, as underscored by both the German National Ethics Council and the French National Ethics Committee[41], the acknowledgement of a "research secret", guaranteeing the inaccessibility of the data. Expectations such as these collide with the widespread national and international use of legal provisions that establish exceptions ultimately providing access mainly to public agencies. But precisely this experience shows also that biobanks can only be successfully secluded and loopholes can only be truly closed by a regulation that deliberately seeks concrete answers, which go distinctly further than the usual international statements.

---

[40] Supra note 1, 71.

[41] Cf. supra notes 14, 15 and the opinion of the German National Ethics Council on Biobanks, sect. 6.5.

Similarly, a review of the by now common terminology is overdue. The debate has been, as mentioned, largely dominated by the effort to distinguish between unacceptable "reproductive" and possibly tolerable "therapeutic" cloning. However, the choice of the latter term is anything but accidental. In fact, the qualification of certain cloning procedures as "therapeutic" has a definite purpose. Its principal, if not sole, aim is to suggest that cloning can at any rate have an unquestionably positive function, all the more since the therapeutic effect is as a rule related to widespread, largely still incurable diseases, such as Alzheimer's, Parkinson's, leukaemia, and diabetes. In other words, the label "therapeutic" explains and legitimates the quest for an exception. Yet the fragility, to put it moderately, of such an argumentation has progressively led to a change of terms. "Therapeutic" is more and more replaced by "research" or "cognitive" cloning. In short, the attention shifts increasingly from the result to the function.

The wordplay may correct false impressions, but it does not solve the problems resulting from the split of cloning into a good and a bad part. Neither the mere reference to research nor a term such as "cognitive" offers a precise and reliable explanation of cloning purposes. Therefore, the least that can be expected is to abandon all wordplay and to precisely indicate, in which situations exceptions should, if at all, be considered, for what reasons and with what results. Only clear-cut statements excluding all ambiguities and delineating exact and obligatory limits can justify further reflections on a separate treatment of different cloning procedures. As long as this expectation is not fulfilled there is no alternative to an equally clear-cut prohibition.

Another no less far-reaching ambiguity is the systematic avoidance of describing the addressees of the expected rules. Thus, many of the proposals to forbid cloning do not determine whether the prohibition is to be respected by both public and private bodies or is in reality limited to the public sector. The debate in the United States probably best exemplifies this dichotomy. References to the particular legal conditions and especially to the partition of competences in the federal system may explain this attitude; they are nevertheless fully inconsistent with the general and unspecified demands for a ban. In sum, future efforts to regulate cloning must cease to be an exercise in abstract and noncommittal terminology and must instead give plain and binding answers to all questions hitherto raised by the debate.

IV. Outlook

As obvious as the difficulties are, the aim of an international regulation for a definitely international issue can and should not questioned. The long-term objective must nevertheless not cloud the view for short-term steps that could also help to realise the ultimate purpose. Thus, for the Member States of the European Union the way to a really substantial international agreement begins with a regulation transcending their own frontiers and establishing uniform standards for the entire European Union. How necessary a common attitude is has been sufficiently demonstrated by the debates on the prohibition of human cloning in the United Nations as well as by the discussions on embryonic research. Instead of jointly supporting one of the proposals to ban cloning and in spite of the call of EC-Commissioner for Research, Philippe Busquin, for a global prohibition[42], the Member States not only split but also were among the principal instigators of the competing drafts. Moreover, the British representative, openly contradicting the view defended by other Member States, such as Italy and Spain, stressed on the occasion of the General Assembly's decision to postpone the debate for another year, that stem cell research, including therapeutic cloning, should be encouraged. The United Kingdom would therefore never adhere to any convention introducing a universal ban on therapeutic cloning[43]. As for embryonic research, the divergence is equally manifest.

However, as opposed to other international bodies, the European Union has both the duty and the means to promote and enforce a common position. Its Charter of Fundamental rights[44] (Art. 3 par. 2; Art. 8) as well as the Convention's draft for a Constitution[45] (Art. II-3 par. 2; Art. II-8) contain provisions that explicitly forbid reproductive cloning of human beings, prohibit eugenic practices and guarantee the protection of personal data. Surely, each of these documents completes the enu-

---

[42] "Reproductive cloning must be condemned not only for obvious ethical reasons and common values, but also because it is about an utterly irresponsible practice from the scientific point of view.", quoted by Reuters, 9 January 2003.

[43] Cf. supra note 34.

[44] Adopted by the Council on 7 December 2000 (OJ No. C 364/01).

[45] Draft Treaty Establishing a Constitution for Europe, adopted unanimously by the European Convention on 13 June and 10 July 2003 (Office for Official Publications of the European Communities 2003).

meration of fundamental rights by stating that their acknowledgement neither amplifies nor modifies the powers and tasks determined by the Community Treaties and the Treaty on European Union (Art. 51 par. 2 of the Charter; Art. II-51 para. 1 of the draft Constitution). But examples, such as the tense debates on biopatents or embryonic research, demonstrate that the European Union has the necessary powers and is already exercising them[46]. Furthermore, documents such as the Charter and the draft Constitution are the most recent steps in a long process confirmed and accelerated by the Amsterdam and Maastricht Treaties, a slow but unstoppable transformation of an initially economic entity into a manifestly political Union. As a consequence, the European Union is now, more than ever, obliged to measure its policies and decisions against the fundamental values and rights last ascertained by documents such as the Charter and the draft Constitution.

Therefore, the European Union must, exactly as in the case of the Directive on the Protection of personal data[47], in which the Parliament, Council and Commission justified the adoption of common rules securing the protection of privacy by expressly pointing to the individual's fundamental rights (Recitals (1) and (2); Art. 1 par. 2), consider all its regulatory efforts regarding biotechnology issues as a direct result of its duty to respect and guarantee human dignity, the integrity of the individual genetic constitution and the individual's right to determine the purposes and uses of her or his personal data. Hence, it is not the concern about establishing and expanding a "biomarket" and thus ensuring the competitiveness of the European Union but the obligation to confirm and concretise in its daily work the foundations of its very existence that defines and delimits the activities of the European Union in the field of biotechnology, quite in conformity with the previously mentioned, clearly articulated expectations of the Council[48].

For precisely this reason, the chances to move from a supranational to a truly international agreement depend essentially on the readiness to accept and explicitly acknowledge the restraint already provided by the

---

[46] Quite in line with these experiences Commissioner *Busquin*, supra note 42, spoke of a possible "new legislation by year end" and emphasised that the European Union's Charter of Fundamental Rights forbids cloning practices.

[47] Directive 95/46/EC of the European Parliament and of the Council on the Protection of Individuals with regard to the Processing of Personal Data and on the Free Movement of Such Data, of October 24, 1995 (OJ No. L 281, 23 November 1995).

[48] Cf. supra note 12.

Convention on Biomedicine (Art. 27)[49] – namely, the qualification of the rules stipulated by the agreement as minimum standards - and, thus, the implicit ascertainment of the signatories' right to strive for better protection. Similarly, despite the opposition of the European Commission, the Council inserted in the Recitals of the 1995 Directive of the European Union on the Protection of Personal Data a paragraph[50], in which the obligation of the Member States to continuously review and improve data protection is expressly recognised.

Any such statement certainly does devaluate the respective rules. It confines the application of the agreement and at the same time reduces the regulatory powers of the international body responsible for the particular document. Yet the advantages outweigh these indisputable consequences. If the provisions are really to counterbalance a constantly evolving technology, they must legitimate and tolerate reactions especially intended to cope with these changes as well as justify all attempts to find ways and means that implement the premises of the agreement better than its actual text. Moreover, by entitling the signatories to further develop the rules, the international body admits that the regulation adopted is no more than a temporary answer and that therefore its authors are under the obligation not only to closely follow the evolution of the technology, but also to continuously review the decisions they took, an expectation first fulfilled by the 1985 Icelandic Law on the Systematic Recording of Personal Data (Art. 31) and later by regulations such as the 2002 German Stem Cell Act (Art. 15)[51].

---

[49] Cf. supra note 16.

[50] Cf. supra note 47, Recital No 9.

[51] Cf. *S. Simitis*, in Falkenburg (ed.) Wem dient die Technik? (2004), 35 et seq.

Annex

Relevant International and National Documents

I. International Convention against the (Reproductive) Cloning of Human Beings

1. International Convention against the Reproductive Cloning of Human Beings (A/58/L.37)

United Nations, General Assembly
5 December 2003
Original: English

Costa Rica: Draft Resolution

The General Assembly,

Recalling the Universal Declaration on the Human Genome and Human Rights,[1] adopted by the General Conference of the United Nations Educational, Scientific and Cultural Organization on 11 November 1997, and in particular article 11 thereof, which states that practices which are contrary to human dignity, such as the reproductive cloning of human beings, shall not be permitted,

Recalling also its resolution 53/152 of 9 December 1998, by which it endorsed the Universal Declaration on the Human Genome and Human Rights,

Bearing in mind Commission on Human Rights resolution 2003/69 of 25 April 2003, entitled "Human rights and bioethics", adopted at the fifty-ninth session of the Commission,

---

[1]   United Nations Educational, Scientific and Cultural Organizations, Records of the General Conference, Twenty-ninth session, Vol. 1, Resolutions, resolution 16.

Bearing also in mind Economic and Social Council resolution 2001/39, entitled "Genetic privacy and non-discrimination", of 26 July 2001,

Aware of the rapid development of the life sciences and of ethical concerns raised by certain of their applications with regard to the dignity of the human race and the human rights and fundamental freedoms of the individual,

Concerned at recently disclosed information on research into and attempts at the creation of human beings through cloning processes,

Convinced that human cloning, for any purpose whatsoever, is unethical, morally repugnant and contrary to due respect for the human person, and that it cannot be justified or accepted,

Recalling that recognition of the inherent dignity and equal and inalienable rights of all members of the human family is the foundation of freedom, justice and peace in the world, as stated in the Universal Declaration of Human Rights,

Seeking to promote scientific and technical progress in the fields of biology and genetics in a manner respectful of human rights and for the benefit of all,

Concerned about the serious difficulties of a medical, physical, psychological and social nature that human cloning may imply for the individuals involved, and alarmed that it may cause the exploitation of women,

Recalling its resolution 56/93 of 12 December 2001, by which it decided to establish an Ad Hoc Committee, open to all States Members of the United Nations or members of specialized agencies or of the International Atomic Energy Agency,

Determined to prevent as a matter of urgency such an attack on the human dignity of the individual,

1. *Requests* the Ad Hoc Committee to be reconvened for one week during the fifty-ninth session of the General Assembly in order to prepare, as a matter of urgency, the draft text of an international convention against human cloning, bearing in mind that it will not prohibit the use of nuclear transfer or other cloning techniques to produce deoxyribonucleic acid molecules, organs, plants, tissues, cells other than human embryos or animals other than humans, and recommends that the Sixth Committee designate specific dates for the meetings of the Ad Hoc Committee during the consideration of this item at that session;

2. *Also requests* the Ad Hoc Committee to consider, in developing the draft convention, the proposals put forward during the fifty-eighth session of the General Assembly;

3. *Solemnly declares* that, pending the adoption of an international convention against human cloning, States shall prohibit any research, experiment, development or application in their territories or areas under their jurisdiction or control of any technique aimed at human cloning;

4. *Calls upon* States to adopt such measures as may be necessary to prohibit those techniques of genetic engineering that may have adverse consequences on the respect for human dignity;

5. *Strongly encourages* States and other entities to direct funds that might have been used for human cloning technologies to pressing global issues in developing countries such as famine, desertification, infant mortality and diseases, including the human immunodeficiency virus/acquired immunodeficiency syndrome;

6. *Requests* the Secretary-General to provide the Ad Hoc Committee with the necessary facilities for the performance of its work;

7. *Invites* the Ad Hoc Committee to take into consideration the contributions of United Nations agencies and competent international organizations in the process of negotiations;

8. *Requests* the Ad Hoc Committee to report on its work to the General Assembly at its fifty-ninth session;

9. *Decides* to include in the provisional agenda of its fifty-ninth session an item entitled "International convention against human cloning".

2. International Convention against the Reproductive Cloning of Human Beings - Report of the Working Group (A/C.6/58/L.9)

United Nations, General Assembly
Chairman: Mr. Juan Manuel Gomez Robledo (Mexico)
3 October 2003
Original: English

Contents

Annexes

I. Introduction

1.   The General Assembly, in its resolution 56/93 of 12 December 2001, decided to establish the Ad Hoc Committee on an International Convention against the Reproductive Cloning of Human Beings, to consider the elaboration of a mandate for the negotiation of an international convention against the reproductive cloning of human beings, including a list of existing international instruments to be taken into consideration and a list of issues to be addressed in the convention. The Assembly also recommended that the work continue during its fifty-seventh session, within the framework of a working group of the Sixth Committee.

2.   Subsequently, in its decision 57/512 of 19 November 2002, the General Assembly decided that a working group of the Sixth Committee should be convened during the fifty-eighth session of the Assembly from 29 September to 3 October 2003 in order

to continue the work undertaken during the fifty-seventh session.

3.   Accordingly, the Sixth Committee, at its 1st meeting of the fifty-eighth session, on 29 September 2003, established such a Working Group open to all States Members of the United Nations or members of the specialized agencies or of the International Atomic Energy Agency. The Committee also elected Juan Manuel Gomez Robledo (Mexico) as the Chairman of the Working Group.

4.   The Working Group held 5 meetings, from 29 September to 3 October 2003.

5.   The Working Group had before it its report on its previous session (A/C.6/57/L.4), the report of the Sixth Committee during the fifty-seventh session (A/57/569), the revised version of the information document prepared by the Secretariat containing, inter alia, a list of relevant international instruments on human cloning (A/AC.263/2002/INF/1/Rev.1), a draft international convention for the prohibition of all forms of human cloning and a brief explanatory commentary thereon submitted by Costa Rica (see A/58/73) and a paper submitted by the Holy See (A/C.6/58/WG.1/CRP.1).

6.   The Working Group considered and adopted its report at its 5th meeting, on 3 October.

II. Proceedings of the Working Group

7.   The Working Group held a general exchange of views at its 1st, 2nd and 3rd meetings, on 29 and 30 September and 2 October. An informal summary of the general discussion in the Working Group, prepared by the Chairman, is included in annex II to the present report. The summary is intended for reference purposes only, and not as an official record of the discussions.

8.   The Working Group also decided to hear a statement by the representative of the United Nations Educational, Scientific and Cultural Organization (UNESCO) at its 1st meeting, on 29 September.

9.   Discussions were subsequently held both in the Working Group and in informal consultations.

Elaboration of a mandate for the negotiation of an international convention against the reproductive cloning of human beings

10. The Working Group held informal consultations, chaired by Bart Wijnberg (Netherlands), concerning the consideration of the elaboration of a mandate for the negotiation of an international convention against the reproductive cloning of human beings, on 1 and 2 October.

III. Recommendations and conclusions

11. At its 5th meeting, on 3 October, the Working Group decided to refer the present report to the Sixth Committee for its consideration and recommended that the Committee continue the consideration of the elaboration of a negotiation mandate during the current session, taking into account the discussions in the Working Group.

Annex I

Written amendments and proposals submitted by delegations

Paper submitted by the Holy See (A/C.6/58/WG.I/CRP.1)

Views of the Holy See on human embryonic cloning

1. The Holy See strongly supports the advancement of human biological sciences and agrees with the procurement of human stem cells, as long as they are not harvested from live embryos, that is, so-called "adult" stem cells. It also supports the use for research or therapeutic purposes of these "adult" stem cells and of any material derived from them, provided that this use is pursued in a way that does not offend human dignity and, if applied clinically, respects the principle of full informed consent. The procurement, research and potential therapies with "adult" stem cells meet, in principle, these moral criteria, and as far as is known, they also contain a great scientific promise.

2. The difference between "reproductive" cloning and "research" cloning (so-called "therapeutic" cloning) consists only in the objective of the procedure: in "reproductive" cloning one intends to develop a child by implanting the cloned embryo in a womb. In "research" cloning, one intends to use the cloned

embryo in such a way that it is ultimately destroyed. To ban "reproductive" cloning only, without prohibiting "research" cloning, would be to allow the production of individual human lives with the intention of destroying these lives as part of the process of using them for scientific research. The early human embryo, not yet implanted into a womb, is nonetheless a human individual, with a human life, and evolving as an autonomous organism towards its full development into a human foetus. Destroying this embryo is therefore a grave moral disorder, since it is the deliberate suppression of an innocent human being.

3. The Holy See believes that these forms of artificial asexual and agamic reproduction to create human embryos gravely offend the dignity of the human race and the dignity of human life. No one should ever do evil in order to achieve a good. When, in an effort to advance human science or to help human beings in need, one faces a choice between an unobjectionable means, such as "adult" stem cells, and a means that is universally recognized as raising profound ethical questions, such as "research" cloning, prudence dictates choosing only the unobjectionable means. Therefore, even those who do not share the view that the cloned human embryo has full human dignity should still be opposed to all forms of human embryonic cloning.

4. It is the view of the Holy See that any possible attempt to limit a ban on human cloning to that undertaken for reproductive purposes would be nearly impossible to enforce since human embryos cloned for research purposes would be widely available and would have the potential to be brought to birth simply by transfer to a womb using procedures employed for artificially assisted reproduction. Since human reproductive cloning is universally condemned, only a complete ban on all forms of human embryonic cloning would achieve the goal of prohibiting human reproductive cloning.

5. Further, if research cloning were permitted, it would require, to be effective, a large number of human oocytes. The Holy See is concerned by this prospect for several reasons. In the first place, the process would use the body of women as a reservoir of oocytes without any consideration being given to the number of donations and her procreative future. In the second place, the massive demand for human oocytes would

disproportionately affect the poor and marginalized of the world bringing a new type of injustice and discrimination into existence.

6. Human cloning would encourage the development of a trade in cloned human embryos and their derivatives for scientific research or for industrial research and development purposes. Therefore, an explicit prohibition of such exchanges regardless of whether they are commercial or not should be enacted. No intellectual property rights should be granted to information or technologies specific to human cloning.

7. The Holy See seeks a complete and explicit prohibition on all techniques of creating new individual human embryos by cloning, including somatic cell nuclear transfer, embryo splitting and other similar techniques that may develop in the future. This prohibition must also encompass parthenogenesis and the creation of human-animal "chimeric embryos" by nuclear transfer.

17 July 2003

Annex II

Informal summary of the general discussion in the Working Group, prepared by the Chairman

1. Many speakers reiterated their support for the continued consideration of the topic. However, it was noted with concern that, despite two years of discussing the topic in the General Assembly, limited progress had been made. Many speakers stressed the importance of reaching consensus on how to move forward on the issue. States were also called upon to make all efforts to reach such consensus on a negotiation mandate, leading to the commencement of the negotiations soon thereafter, thereby sending an important signal to the international community. Strong support was also expressed for retaining the item in the agenda of the Assembly.

2. However, the general discussion continued to reveal a divergence of views among delegations. Some speakers spoke in favour of an international convention prohibiting all forms of human cloning, as proposed in draft resolution A/C.6/58/L.2. There was concern that developments in the medical sciences and genetic research, despite the possibility that they offered curing diseases, could be used to breach human rights and to

violate the intrinsic dignity of all human beings. Indeed, it was stated that the dignity of human life did not tolerate the testing of human embryos, whatever the objective. In that regard, the view was expressed that an embryo was a human being in the earliest stages of formation and thus the killing of embryos for therapeutic purposes constituted a grave attack on the dignity of mankind. It was also pointed out that human cloning degraded the human being into a mere object of industrial production and manipulation.

3.   The view was likewise expressed that cloning for "therapeutic" or "experimental" purposes was inherently risky, especially for donor women. Indeed, concern was expressed that the demand for human eggs would disproportionately affect the poor and marginalized women, resulting in a new form of discrimination. Similarly, the prospect of the successful development of therapeutic techniques was considered limited, and of dubious value, especially in the light of the serious ethical implications it raised, arising from the deliberate production and destruction of human embryos. Instead, a preference was expressed for adult stem cell research as a viable alternative with proved results. In terms of another suggestion, States were urged to allocate those funds that would otherwise be spent on human cloning techniques, towards other issues such as human immunodeficiency virus/acquired immunodeficiency syndrome (HIV/AIDS), infant mortality and morbidity, famine and desertification.

4.   It was also stated that a partial ban, limited only to cloning for reproductive purposes, would be a false ban, since it would be confusing, ineffective and impossible to enforce. It would also lead to the unacceptable result of embryos' being exploited as commodities for commercial use. Instead, only a complete ban on all forms of human embryonic cloning would achieve the goal of prohibiting human reproductive cloning, and would be more durable. Similarly, an all-inclusive convention would properly allow States to formulate appropriate domestic legislation on human cloning.

5.   Some other speakers were of a different view. It was recalled that the mandate of the Working Group was limited to establishing a negotiation mandate for the elaboration of an international convention against the reproductive cloning of human beings. The Working Group's attention was drawn to

recent announcements of the birth of cloned humans, which, although not confirmed, had highlighted the urgent need for an international ban on reproductive cloning of human beings. It was stated that a lack of universally binding regulations dealing with any type of cloning of human beings constituted an open invitation for certain scientists to undertake the kind of research which was considered by all to be morally repugnant and contrary to human dignity. Indeed, some speakers, supporting a narrower ban on cloning for reproductive purposes, pointed out that their own domestic legislation already banned all forms of cloning. Hence, their support for a narrower approach was based solely on pragmatic reasons: it was viewed as the only possible basis on which to achieve consensus at the international level. Support was thus expressed for the revised Franco-German non-paper espousing a negotiating mandate for a comprehensive convention that would, on the one hand, adopt a strict ban on cloning of human beings for reproductive purposes, while, on the other, seek to regulate other forms of cloning by giving future States parties the option either to ban or impose a moratorium on such types of cloning or otherwise to regulate them by means of national legislation.

6.   Several other speakers also described activities undertaken at the national level, inter alia, through legislation, to regulate human embryonic research for non-reproductive purposes. It was pointed out that the decision to allow such research had followed from an extensive national debate and internal consultation process, and that the legislation in question provided robust safeguards for the protection of the embryo, such as national monitoring mechanisms, while strictly prohibiting cloning for reproductive purposes. The view was expressed that therapeutic cloning research, as such, should be allowed to continue in countries that had reached a national consensus on the issue and had put into place a rigorous and effective system of regulation of embryo research. Indeed, several speakers also pointed to the potential that therapeutic cloning offered for curing disease and improving human life; and reference was made to recent statements, emanating from within the international scientific community, expressing support for a ban on reproductive cloning, while allowing therapeutic cloning to continue. It was observed that, given the

complexity of the issue, an approach that respected the diversity of views and beliefs among States offered the greater chance of success. Such an approach would also enjoy the benefit of taking into account the views of those States whose national laws banned cloning only for reproductive purposes, but allowed research, including on human embryos, for non-reproductive purposes, albeit strictly regulated.

7. Other suggestions included agreeing on a general mandate for negotiation, so as to commence the work, albeit without stipulating at this stage the scope of the future convention; and calling for a moratorium on such activities, although it was cautioned that the General Assembly did not have the authority to impose a binding moratorium on States. It was also suggested that the Working Group consider the economic, sustainable development and human rights implications of the subject, in particular with regard to gender, children and indigenous peoples.

3. International Convention against the Reproductive Cloning of Human Beings (A/C.6/58/L.8)

United Nations, General Assembly

2 October 2003

Original: English

Belarus, Belgium, Brazil, China, Czech Republic, Denmark, Finland, Iceland, Japan, Liechtenstein, South Africa, Sweden, Switzerland and United Kingdom of Great Britain and Northern Ireland: Draft Resolution

The General Assembly,

Recalling the Universal Declaration on the Human Genome and Human Rights,[1] adopted by the General Conference of the United Nations Educational, Scientific and Cultural Organization on 11 November 1997, in particular article 11 thereof, which states that practices that are contrary to human dignity, such as reproductive cloning of human beings, shall not be permitted,

Recalling also its resolution 53/152 of 9 December 1998, by which it endorsed the Universal Declaration on the Human Genome and Human Rights,

Bearing in mind Commission on Human Rights resolution 2003/69 of 25 April 2003, entitled "Human rights and bioethics",[2] adopted by the Commission at its fifty-seventh session,

Mindful of the importance of the development of the life sciences for the benefit of mankind, with full respect for the integrity and dignity of the human being,

---

[1]   United Nations Educational, Scientific and Cultural Organization, Records of the General Conference, Twenty-ninth Session, Vol. 1, Resolutions, resolution 16.

[2]   See Official Records of the Economic and Social Council, 2003, Supplement No. 3 (E/2003/23), chap. II, sect. A.

Aware that the rapid development of the life sciences opens up prospects for the improvement of the health of individuals and mankind as a whole, but also that certain practices pose potential dangers to the integrity and dignity of the individual,

Concerned by the seriousness of problems posed by the development of techniques of reproductive cloning of human beings applied to mankind, which may have consequences for respect for human dignity,

Particularly concerned, in the context of practices that are contrary to human dignity, at recently disclosed information on research into and attempts at the reproductive cloning of human beings,

Determined to prevent, as a matter of urgency, such an offence to human dignity,

Recalling its resolution 56/93 of 12 December 2001, by which it decided to establish an Ad Hoc Committee, open to all States Members of the United Nations or members of specialized agencies or of the International Atomic Energy Agency, for the purpose of considering the elaboration of an international convention against the reproductive cloning of human beings,

Determined to adopt provisional measures at the national level to prevent potential dangers to the human dignity of the individual pending the adoption and entry into force of an international convention against the reproductive cloning of human beings,

1. *Welcomes* the report of the Working Group of the Sixth Committee on its work from 29 September to 3 October 2003;

2. *Decides* that the Ad Hoc Committee shall be reconvened from ___ to ___ February and from ___ to ___ September 2004 in order to prepare, as a matter of urgency and if possible by the end of 2004, a draft international convention against the reproductive cloning of human beings;

3. *Requests* the Ad Hoc Committee, in developing the draft convention, to include the following elements:

   a) An obligation on all contracting parties to ban reproductive cloning of human beings with no possibility of making any reservations;

   b) An obligation on all contracting parties to take action to control other forms of human cloning by adopting a ban or imposing a moratorium or regulating them by means of national legislation;

4. *Also requests* the Ad Hoc Committee to take into consideration the relevant existing international instruments;

5. *Calls upon* those States that have not yet done so, pending the adoption and entry into force of an international convention against the reproductive cloning of human beings and their becoming party thereto, to adopt at the national level a prohibition against reproductive cloning of human beings;

6. *Also calls upon* those States that have not yet done so, pending the adoption and entry into force of an international convention against the reproductive cloning of human beings and their becoming party thereto, to take action to control other forms of human cloning by adopting a ban or imposing a moratorium or regulating them by means of national legislation;

7. *Requests* the Secretary-General to provide the Ad Hoc Committee with the facilities necessary for the performance of its work;

8. *Invites* the Ad Hoc Committee to take into consideration the contributions of United Nations bodies and to closely involve the United Nations Educational, Scientific and Cultural Organization, the World Health Organization and the United Nations Conference on Trade and Development in the process of negotiations;

9. *Requests* the Ad Hoc Committee to report on its work to the General Assembly at its fifty-ninth session;

10. *Decides* to include in the provisional agenda of its fifty-ninth session the item entitled "International convention against the reproductive cloning of human beings".

4. International Convention against Human Cloning (A/C.6/58/L.2)

United Nations, General Assembly
26 September 2003
Original: English

Antigua and Barbuda, Benin, Costa Rica, Côte d'Ivoire, Dominica, Dominican Republic, El Salvador, Eritrea, Ethiopia, Fiji, Gambia, Georgia, Grenada, Haiti, Honduras, Italy, Kazakhstan, Kenya, Kyrgyzstan, Lesotho, Madagascar, Marshall Islands, Micronesia, Nauru, Nicaragua, Nigeria, Palau, Panama, Paraguay, Philippines, Portugal, Saint Kitts and Nevis, Saint Vincent and the Grenadines, San Marino, Sierra Leone, Spain, Suriname, Tajikistan, Timor-Leste, Uganda, United Republic of Tanzania, United States of America, Uzbekistan, Vanuatu and Zambia: Draft Resolution

The General Assembly,

Recalling the Universal Declaration on the Human Genome and Human Rights[1], adopted by the General Conference of the United Nations Educational, Scientific and Cultural Organization on 11 November 1997, and in particular article 11 thereof, which states that practices which are contrary to human dignity, such as the reproductive cloning of human beings, shall not be permitted,

Recalling also its resolution 53/152 of 9 December 1998, by which it endorsed the Universal Declaration on the Human Genome and Human Rights, *Bearing in mind* Commission on Human Rights resolution 2003/69 of 25 April 2003, entitled "Human rights and bioethics", adopted at the fifty-ninth session of the Commission,

Bearing also in mind Economic and Social Council resolution 2001/39, entitled "Genetic privacy and non-discrimination", of 26 July 2001,

---

[1]   United Nations Educational, Scientific and Cultural Organization, Records of the General Conference, Twenty-ninth session, Vol. 1, Resolutions, resolution 16

Aware of the rapid development of the life sciences and of ethical concerns raised by certain of their applications with regard to the dignity of the human race and the human rights and fundamental freedoms of the individual,

Concerned at recently disclosed information on research into and attempts at the creation of human beings through cloning processes,

Convinced that human cloning, for any purpose whatsoever, is unethical, morally repugnant and contrary to due respect for the human person, and that it cannot be justified or accepted,

Recalling also that recognition of the inherent dignity and equal and inalienable rights of all members of the human family is the foundation of freedom, justice and peace in the world, as stated in the Universal Declaration of Human Rights,

Seeking to promote scientific and technical progress in the fields of biology and genetics in a manner respectful of human rights and for the benefit of all,

Concerned about the serious difficulties of a medical, physical, psychological and social nature that human cloning may imply for the individuals involved, and alarmed that it may cause the exploitation of women,

Recalling its resolution 56/93 of 12 December 2001, by which it decided to establish an Ad Hoc Committee, open to all States Members of the United Nations or members of specialized agencies or of the International Atomic Energy Agency,

Determined to prevent as a matter of urgency such an attack on the human dignity of the individual,

1.   *Requests* the Ad Hoc Committee to be reconvened from _____ to _____ 2004 in order to prepare, as a matter of urgency, the draft text of an international convention against human cloning, bearing in mind that it will not prohibit the use of nuclear transfer or other cloning techniques to produce DNA molecules, organs, plants, tissues, cells other than human embryos or animals other than humans, and recommends that the work continue during the fifty-ninth session of the General Assembly from _____ to _____ 2004 within the framework of a working group of the Sixth Committee;

2.   *Also requests* the Ad Hoc Committee to consider, in developing the draft convention, the proposals put forward during the fifty-eighth session of the General Assembly;

3.   *Solemnly declares* that, pending the adoption of an international convention against human cloning, States shall prohibit any research, experiment, development or application in their territories or areas under their jurisdiction or control of any technique aimed at human cloning;

4.   *Calls upon* States to adopt such measures as may be necessary to prohibit those techniques of genetic engineering that may have adverse consequences on the respect for human dignity;

5.   *Strongly encourages* States and other entities to direct funds that might have been used for human cloning technologies to pressing global issues in developing countries such as famine, desertification, infant mortality and diseases, including the human immunodeficiency virus/acquired immunodeficiency syndrome (HIV/AIDS);

6.   *Requests* the Secretary-General to provide the Ad Hoc Committee with the necessary facilities for the performance of its work;

7.   *Invites* the Ad Hoc Committee to take into consideration the contributions of United Nations agencies and competent international organizations in the process of negotiations;

8.   *Requests* the Ad Hoc Committee to report on its work to the General Assembly at its fifty-ninth session;

9.   *Decides* to include in the provisional agenda of its fifty-ninth session an item entitled "International convention against human cloning".

5. International Convention against the Reproductive Cloning of Human Beings (A/58/73)

United Nations, General Assembly
17 April 2003
Original: Spanish

Letter dated 2 April 2003 from the Permanent Representative of Costa Rica to the United Nations addressed to the Secretary-General

I have the honour to transmit to you attached hereto the draft international convention for the prohibition of all forms of human cloning, prepared by the Government of Costa Rica, as well as the text of a brief explanatory commentary to it (see annexes I and II).

The Government of Costa Rica is convinced that this draft will be a constructive contribution to the negotiation process currently being carried outwithin the General Assembly in order to prohibit human cloning. We hope that the text will be able to serve eventually as the basic document for discussion.

(*Signed*) Bruno Stagno
Permanent Representative

Annex I to the letter dated 2 April 2003 from the Permanent Representative of Costa Rica to the United Nations addressed to the Secretary-General

Preamble

The States Parties to this Convention,

Recalling the Universal Declaration on the Human Genome and Human Rights[1] adopted by the General Conference of the United

---

[1]   United Nations Educational, Scientific and Cultural Organization, Records of the General Conference, Twenty-ninth Session, Vol. I, Resolutions, resolution 16.

Nations Educational, Scientific and Cultural Organization on 11 November 1997, in particular article 11 thereof, in which the Conference specified that practices which are contrary to human dignity, such as reproductive cloning of human beings, shall not be permitted,

Recalling also General Assembly resolution 53/152 of 9 December 1998, by which the Assembly endorsed the Universal Declaration on the Human Genome and Human Rights,

Bearing in mind resolution 2001/71 of the Commission on Human Rights of 25 April 2001 entitled "Human rights and bioethics",[2] adopted by the Commission at its fifty-seventh session,

Recalling that, in accordance with the Universal Declaration of Human Rights, recognition of the inherent dignity and of the equal and inalienable rights of all members of the human family is the foundation of freedom, justice and peace in the world,

Convinced that the cloning of human beings, whether carried out on an experimental basis, in the context of fertility treatments or pre-implantation diagnosis, for tissue transplantation or for any other purpose whatsoever, is morally repugnant, unethical and contrary to respect for the person and constitutes a grave violation of fundamental human rights which cannot under any circumstances be justified or accepted,

Seeking to promote scientific and technical progress in the fields of biology and genetics in a manner respectful of fundamental human rights and for the benefit of all,

Concerned at recently disclosed information on research into and attempts at the creation of human beings through cloning processes,

Conscious of widespread preoccupations that the human body and its parts should not, as such, give rise to financial gain,

Determined to adopt permanent measures to avoid potential threats to human dignity,

Have agreed as follows:

---

[2]   See Official Records of the Economic and Social Council, 2001, Supplement No. 3 (E/2001/23), chap. II, sect. A.

Article 1
Definitions

For the purposes of this Convention:

1. "Somatic cell nuclear transfer" means introduction of nuclear material from a somatic cell into a fertilized or unfertilized oocyte whose nuclear material has been removed or inactivated;

2. "Somatic cell" means a cell containing a complete set of chromosomes;

3. "Genetically virtually identical organism" means an organism containing the same complete set of chromosomes as another organism;

4. "Victim" means both the person whose genetic material or oocyte is used without permission to commit an offence set forth in article 2, paragraph 1, and the living organism created by the commission of the offence set forth in article 2, paragraph 1.

Article 2
Scope of application (definition of the crime)

1. Any person commits an offence within the meaning of this Convention if that person intentionally engages in an action, such as somatic cell nuclear transfer or embryo-splitting, resulting in the creation of a living organism, at any stage of physical development, that is genetically virtually identical to an existing or previously existing human organism.

2. Any person also commits an offence if that person attempts to commit an offence set forth in paragraph 1 of this article.

3. Any person also commits an offence if that person:

    a) Participates as an accomplice in an offence set forth in paragraph 1 or 2 of this article;

    b) Organizes or directs others to commit an offence set forth in paragraph 1 or 2 of this article;

    c) Contributes to the commission of one or more of the offences set forth in paragraph 1 or 2 of this article by a group of persons acting with a common purpose. Such contribution shall be intentional and shall either:

(i) Be made with the aim of furthering the criminal activity or criminal purpose of the group, where such activity or purpose involves the commission of an offence as set forth in paragraph 1 of this article; or

(ii) Be made in the knowledge of the intention of the group to commit an offence set forth in paragraph 1 of this article.

Article 3
Obligation to criminalize

Each State Party shall adopt such measures as may be necessary:

a) To establish as criminal offences under its domestic law the offences set forth in article 2;

b) To make those offences punishable by appropriate penalties which take into account the grave nature of the offences.

Article 4
Liability of legal persons

1. Each State Party, in accordance with its domestic legal principles, shall take the necessary measures to enable a legal entity located in its territory or organized under its laws to be held liable when a person responsible for the management or control of that legal entity has, in that capacity, committed an offence set forth in article 2. Such liability may be criminal, civil or administrative.

2. Such liability is incurred without prejudice to the criminal liability of individuals who have committed the offences.

3. Each State Party shall ensure, in particular, that legal entities liable in accordance with paragraph 1 above are subject to effective, proportionate and dissuasive criminal, civil or administrative sanctions. Such sanctions may include monetary sanctions.

Article 5
Jurisdiction

1. Each State Party shall take such measures as may be necessary to establish its jurisdiction over the offences set forth in article 2 when:

a)   The offence is committed in the territory of that State;

b)   The offence is committed on board a vessel flying the flag of that State or an aircraft registered under the laws of that State at the time the offence is committed;

c)   The offence is committed by a national of that State.

2.   A State Party may also establish its jurisdiction over any such offence when:

a)   The offence was directed towards or resulted in the carrying out of an offence referred to in article 2, paragraph 1, in the territory of or against a national of that State;

b)   The victim of one of the offences set forth in article 2, paragraph 1, is a national of that State;

c)   The offence is committed by a stateless person who has his or her habitual residence in the territory of that State.

3.   Upon ratifying, accepting, approving or acceding to this Convention, each State Party shall notify the Secretary-General of the United Nations of the jurisdiction it has established in accordance with its domestic law in accordance with paragraph 2. Should any change take place, the State Party concerned shall immediately notify the Secretary-General.

4.   Each State Party shall likewise take such measures as may be necessary to establish its jurisdiction over the offences set forth in article 2 in cases where the alleged offender is present in its territory and it does not extradite that person to any of the States Parties that have established their jurisdiction in accordance with paragraph 1 or 2.

5.   When more than one State Party claims jurisdiction over one of the offences set forth in article 2, the relevant States Parties shall strive to coordinate their actions appropriately, in particular concerning the conditions for prosecution and the modalities for mutual legal assistance.

6.   Without prejudice to the norms of general international law, this Convention does not exclude he exercise of any criminal jurisdiction established by a State Party in accordance with its domestic law.

Article 6
Seizure of funds

1. Each State Party shall take appropriate measures, in accordance with its domestic legal principles, for the identification, detection and freezing or seizure of any funds used or allocated for the purpose of committing the offences set forth in article 2 as well as the proceeds derived from such offences, for purposes of possible forfeiture.

2. Each State Party shall take appropriate measures, in accordance with its domestic legal principles, for the forfeiture of funds used or allocated for the purpose of committing the offences set forth in article 2 and the proceeds derived from such offences.

3. Each State Party concerned may give consideration to concluding agreements on the sharing with other States Parties, on a regular or case-by-case basis, of the funds derived from the forfeitures referred to in this article.

4. Each State Party shall consider establishing mechanisms whereby the funds derived from the forfeitures referred to in this article are utilized to compensate the victims of offences referred to in article 2 or their families.

5. The provisions of this article shall be implemented without prejudice to the rights of third parties acting in good faith.

Article 7
Duty to investigate

1. Upon receiving information that a person who has committed or who is allegedto have committed an offence set forth in article 2 may be present in its territory, the State Party concerned shall immediately take such measures as may be necessary under its domestic law to investigate the facts contained in the information.

2. Upon being satisfied that the circumstances so warrant, the State Party in whose territory the offender or alleged offender is present shall take the appropriate measures under its domestic law so as to ensure that person's presence for the purpose of prosecution or extradition.

3.   Any person regarding whom the measures referred to in paragraph 2 are being taken shall be entitled to:

   a)   Communicate without delay with the nearest appropriate representative of the State of which that person is a national or which is otherwise entitled to protect that person's rights or, if that person is a stateless person, the State in the territory of which that person habitually resides;

   b)   Be visited by a representative of that State;

   c)   Be informed of that person's rights under subparagraphs (a) and (b).

4.   The rights referred to in paragraph 3 shall be exercised in conformity with the laws and regulations of the State in the territory of which the offender or alleged offender is present, subject to the provision that the said laws and regulations must enable full effect to be given to the purposes for which the rights accorded under paragraph 3 are intended.

Article 8
Obligation to prosecute or extradite

1.   The State Party in the territory of which the alleged offender is present shall, in cases to which article 5 applies, if it does not extradite that person, be obliged, without exception whatsoever and whether or not the offence was committed in its territory, to submit the case without undue delay to its competent authorities for the purpose of prosecution, through proceedings in accordance with the laws of that State. Those authorities shall take their decision in the same manner as in the case of any other offence of a grave nature under the law of that State.

2.   Whenever a State Party is permitted under its domestic law to extradite or otherwise surrender one of its nationals only upon the condition that the person will be returned to that State to serve the sentence imposed as a result of the trial or proceeding for which the extradition or surrender of the person was sought, and this State and the State seeking the extradition of the person agree with this option and any other terms they may deem appropriate, such a conditional extradition or surrender shall be sufficient to discharge the obligation set forth in paragraph 1.

Article 9
Existing extradition treaties

1. The offences set forth in article 2 shall be deemed to be included asextraditable offences in any extradition treaty existing between any of the. States Parties before the entry into force of this Convention. States Parties undertake to include such offences as extraditable offences in every extradition treaty to be subsequently concluded between them.

2. When a State Party which makes extradition conditional on the existence of a treaty receives a request for extradition from another State Party with which it has no extradition treaty, the requested State Party may, at its option, consider this Convention as a legal basis for extradition in respect of the offences set forth in article 2. Extradition shall be subject to the other conditions provided by the law of the requested State.

3. States Parties which do not make extradition conditional on the existence of a treaty shall recognize the offences set forth in article 2 as extraditable offences between themselves, subject to the conditions provided by the law of the requested State.

4. If necessary the offences set forth in article 2 shall be treated, for the purposes of extradition between States Parties, as if they had been committed not only in the place in which they occurred but also in the territory of the States that have established jurisdiction in accordance with article 7, paragraphs 1 and 2.

5. The provisions of all extradition treaties and arrangements in force between States Parties with regard to the offences set forth in article 2 shall be deemed to be modified as between States Parties to the extent that they are incompatible with this Convention.

Article 10
Judicial cooperation

1. States Parties shall afford one another the greatest measure of assistance in connection with criminal investigations or criminal or extradition proceedings in respect of the offences set forth in article 2, including assistance in obtaining evidence in their possession necessary for the proceedings.

2. The requesting State Party shall not use nor transmit information or evidence furnished by the requested State Party for investigations, prosecutions or proceedings other than those stated in the request without the prior consent of the requested State Party.

3. Each State Party may give consideration to establishing mechanisms to share with other States Parties information or evidence needed to establish criminal, civil or administrative liability pursuant to article 4.

4. States Parties shall carry out their obligations under paragraphs 1 and 2 in conformity with any treaties or other arrangements on mutual legal assistance or information exchange that may exist between them. In the absence of such treaties or arrangements, States Parties shall afford one another assistance in accordance with their domestic law.

Article 11
Rights of the accused

Any person who is taken into custody or regarding whom any other measures are taken or proceedings are carried out pursuant to this Convention shall be guaranteed fair treatment, including enjoyment of all rights and guarantees in conformity with the law of the State in the territory of which that person is present and applicable provisions of international law, including international human rights law.

Article 12
Preventive measures

1. States Parties shall cooperate in the prevention of the offences set forth in article 2 by taking all practicable measures, inter alia, by adapting their domestic legislation, if necessary, to prevent and counter preparations in their respective territories for the commission of those offences within or outside their territories, including:

    a) Measures to prohibit in their territories illegal activities of persons and organizations that knowingly encourage, instigate, organize or engage in the commission of offences set forth in article 2;

b) Measures requiring any research project involving human genetic material to be duly authorized by the competent authorities or, as appropriate, by a multidisciplinary national organ entrusted with that task;

c) Measures requiring centres and establishments where research or activities are conducted that use gene technology to be previously registered, approved and authorized for such purposes by the health or scientific authorities or, as appropriate, by a multidisciplinary national organ.

2. States Parties shall further cooperate in the prevention of offences set forth in article 2 by exchanging accurate and verified information in accordance with their domestic law and coordinating administrative and other measures taken, as appropriate, to prevent the commission of offences set forth in article 2, in particular by:

a) Establishing and maintaining channels of communication between their competent agencies and services to facilitate the secure and rapid exchange of information concerning all aspects of offences set forth in article 2;

b) Cooperating with one another in conducting inquiries, with respect to the offences set forth in article 2, concerning:

(i) The identity, whereabouts and activities of persons in respect of whom reasonable suspicion exists that they are involved in such offences;

(ii) The movement of funds relating to the commission of such offences.

3. States Parties may exchange information through the International Criminal Police Organization (Interpol).

Article 13
Safeguard clause

None of the provisions of this Convention shall be interpreted as limiting or otherwise affecting the possibility for each State Party to grant a wider measure of protection with regard to the applications of biology and medicine than is stipulated in this Convention.

Article 14
Settlement of disputes

1. Any disputes between two or more States Parties concerning the interpretation or application of this Convention which cannot be settled through negotiation within a reasonable time shall, at the request of one of them, be submitted to arbitration. If, within six months from the date of the request for arbitration, the parties are unable to agree on the organization of the arbitration, any one of those parties may refer the dispute to the International Court of Justice, by application, in conformity with the Statute of the Court.

2. Each State may at the time of signature, ratification, acceptance or approval of this Convention or accession thereto declare that it does not consider itself bound by paragraph 1 of this article. The other States Parties shall not be bound by paragraph 1 with respect to any State Party which has made such a reservation.

3. Any State which has made a reservation in accordance with paragraph 2 may at any time withdraw that reservation by notification to the Secretary-General of the United Nations.

Article 15
Signature and ratification

1. This Convention shall be open for signature by all States from ... to ... at United Nations Headquarters in New York.

2. This Convention is subject to ratification, acceptance or approval. The instruments of ratification, acceptance or approval shall be deposited with the Secretary-General of the United Nations.

3. This Convention shall be open to accession by any State. The instruments of accession shall be deposited with the Secretary-General of the United Nations.

Article 16
Reservations

No reservations shall be permitted to articles 1, 2 and 3 of this Convention.

Article 17
Entry into force

1. This Convention shall enter into force on the thirtieth day following the date of the deposit of the twenty-second instrument of ratification, acceptance, approval or accession with the Secretary-General of the United Nations.

2. For each State ratifying, accepting, approving or acceding to the Convention after the deposit of the twenty-second instrument of ratification, acceptance, approval or accession, the Convention shall enter into force on the thirtieth day after deposit by such State of its instrument of ratification, acceptance, approval or accession.

Article 18
Denunciation

1. Any State Party may denounce this Convention by written notification to the Secretary-General of the United Nations.

2. Denunciation shall take effect one year following the date on which notification is received by the Secretary-General of the United Nations.

Article 19
Authentic texts

The original of this Convention, of which the Arabic, Chinese, English, French, Russian and Spanish texts are equally authentic, shall be deposited with the Secretary-General of the United Nations, who shall send certified copies thereof to all States.

Annex II to the letter dated 2 April 2003 from the Permanent Representative of Costa Rica to the United Nations addressed to the Secretary-General Commentary to the Draft International Convention on the Prohibition of all Forms of Human Cloning

Introduction

The draft international convention on the prohibition of all forms of human cloning is intended as a contribution to the negotiation process currently being carried out within the United Nations General Assembly in order to prohibit human cloning. The text seeks to ensure respect for the dignity and basic rights of the human being in the broadest possible manner in view of the threat posed by experiments in the cloning of human beings.

The draft aims to prohibit both "reproductive" cloning of human beings, that is, cloning whereby human clones are "produced", implanted in a woman's uterus and culminate in the birth of a child that is genetically identical to another human being, as well as the ill-termed "therapeutic" cloning of humans, which is characterized by having experimental purposes and ending with the destruction and death of the cloned embryo.

During the fifty-eighth session of the General Assembly, the international community will have to decide whether it is to work on a broad prohibition of all forms of human cloning or whether it will elaborate only a prohibition limited to the reproductive cloning of human beings. The Government of Costa Rica, together with a number of friendly countries, has advocated the negotiation of a broad prohibition covering all forms of human cloning.

The Government of Costa Rica trusts that this draft will be an important contribution to the negotiation process by eventually becoming the basic document for discussion.

The draft includes four principal elements:

a) The definition of the crime of human cloning (article 2);

b) The obligation of States Parties to criminalize the offence, establish jurisdiction over its commission and punish or extradite the guilty parties (articles 3, 5, 7 and 8);

c) The obligation of States Parties to take measures to prevent such acts, including the regulation of experiments involving human genetic material (article 12);

d) A series of provisions to facilitate judicial and police cooperation
in the field (articles 9 and 10).

To the extent possible, the text is based on language used previously by
the General Assembly. The provisions on jurisdiction, cooperation and
the final clauses were inspired by the provisions of the recent
International Convention for the Suppression of the Financing of
Terrorism.

It should be noted that the draft does not seek to regulate abortion,
stem-cell research or *in vitro* fertilization. Similarly, the text does not
aim to define what a human being is and when the human person comes
about.

Title

The title of the draft convention contains the expression "human
cloning" not "cloning of human beings". This formulation is in keeping
with the decision to avoid discussing the definition of what constitutes
a human being.

Preamble

The preamble sets forth the general considerations that motivate States
to adopt the draft convention. The main paragraphs are: the fourth
preambular paragraph, which underscores the essential importance of
human dignity; the fifth preambular paragraph, which declares all forms
of human cloning immoral and a violation of human rights; and the
sixth preambular paragraph, which reaffirms the need to promote
scientific progress in accordance with respect for human rights.

Most of the preamble has been taken from draft resolution
A/C.6/57/L.3/Rev.1, sponsored by Antigua and Barbuda, Argentina,
Costa Rica, Dominica, Dominican Republic, El Salvador, Ethiopia, Fiji,
Georgia, Grenada, Honduras, Italy, Kenya, Kyrgyzstan, Marshall
Islands, Micronesia (Federated States of), Nicaragua, Nigeria, Panama,
Paraguay, Philippines, St. Vincent and the Grenadines, Spain, Suriname,
Tajikistan, Timor-Leste, Turkmenistan, Tuvalu, United States of
America and Uzbekistan on 18 October 2002. Preambular paragraphs
1, 2, 3, 7, 8 and 9 correspond respectively to preambular paragraphs 1,
2, 6, 8 and 10 of the draft resolution.

The fourth preambular paragraph has been taken from the third preambular paragraph of General Assembly resolution 53/152 on "the human genome and human rights", of 9 December 1998. The fifth preambular paragraph is based on preambular paragraph (c) of the resolution of the European Parliament on human cloning of 15 January 1998 *(Official Journal, 1998* (C 34) 164 (15 January 1998)). The sixth preambular paragraph is identical to the fifth preambular paragraph of General Assembly resolution 53/152.

Article 1
Definitions

This article defines some of the basic concepts used in the draft convention. Paragraphs 1, 2 and 3, which define concepts used in the description of the offence, should be read in the context of the commentary to article 2 (1): definition of the crime.

Paragraph 4, on the concept of the victim, should be considered within the context of articles 5 (2) (b) on jurisdiction, and 6 (2), dealing with compensation. The concept of victim as set forth is broad and includes not only the person who is "copied" by means of cloning — the donor of the genetic material — but also the woman whose oocyte is used and the human being who is created through cloning.

Article 2
Scope of application (definition of the crime)
Paragraph 1

This article contains the definition of the crime of the cloning of human beings.

The expression "commits ... intentionally" establishes the level of intentionality required for a penal norm. This phrase excludes the non-intentional commission of the offence as well as the spontaneous division of embryos that occurs in nature when twins are created.

The word "action" is a broad concept designed to include any technical, medical or scientific operation which may be used to create clones.

The list "such as somatic cell nuclear transfer or embryo-splitting" sets forth, by way of example, the two techniques which are currently used in cloning experiments. This list is not exhaustive, which makes the prohibition applicable to any other cloning technique that may be developed in the future.

The expression "a living organism ... that is genetically virtually identical" defines the prohibited object: the creation of living beings whose nuclear genetic material is identical. Article 1 (3) of the draft should be viewed in this context.

The words "at any stage of physical development" make this prohibition applicable to all forms of cloning since it prohibits the creation of a living organism from the first moment of its existence.

The reference to a "human organism" relates to the donor of the genetic material and limits this prohibition solely to the cloning of human beings, permitting, *a contrario sensu*, the cloning of vegetables and animals. This expression prohibits the use of nuclear material not only from adult donors but also from human embryos.

The words "existing or previously existing" prohibit cloning which uses as a donor of nuclear material living embryos either of persons currently alive or of historical figures who are deceased.

Paragraphs 2 and 3

The aim of these paragraphs is to prohibit attempts to commit and the various forms of criminal participation in the offence of human cloning. Paragraph 3 (c) covers criminal conspiracy and criminal activities organized in order to commit human cloning. The text is based on article 2, paragraphs 4 and 5, of the International Convention for the Suppression of the Financing of Terrorism of 9 December 1999.

Article 3
Obligation to criminalize

This article requires that States parties criminalize human cloning as an offence under their national legislation. It is identical to the text of article 4 of the International Convention for the Suppression of the Financing of Terrorism.

Article 4
Liability of legal persons

This article requires that States Parties punish, in accordance with their legal systems, legal persons that are used to commit the offence of human cloning. It is identical to the text of article 5 of the International Convention for the Suppression of the Financing of Terrorism.

Article 5
Jurisdiction

This article specifies the occasions on which States Parties will have jurisdiction to prosecute the offence. When an offence is committed by a national of the State Party or in its territory, that State will have to exercise its jurisdiction as a matter of obligation. Paragraph 4 stipulates that the State Party must exercise its jurisdiction in order to prosecute a person accused of committing the offence, if it is not willing to extradite him to a State which so requests.

The text of this article is based on article 7 of the International Convention for the Suppression of the Financing of Terrorism with the necessary changes made in paragraph 2. The reference to the victim in paragraph 2 (b) is based on article 6, paragraph 2, of the International Convention for the Suppression of Terrorist Bombings of 15 December 1997.

Article 6
Seizure of funds

This article sets forth the obligation to confiscate funds used to commit the crime of human cloning in order to compensate the victims. This text is identical to article 8 of the International Convention for the Suppression of the Financing of Terrorism.

Article 7
Duty to investigate

This norm lays down the obligation to investigate and detain preventively persons who commit the crime of human cloning. The article's wording is identical to that of article 9, paragraphs 1 to 4, of the

International Convention for the Suppression of the Financing of Terrorism.

Article 8
Obligation to prosecute or extradite

This article establishes the obligation to prosecute or extradite persons accused of this crime. Paragraph 2 sets forth a number of exceptions for States that permit the extradition of nationals under certain conditions. The text of this article was identical to that of article 10 of the International Convention for the Suppression of the Financing of Terrorism.

Article 9
Existing extradition treaties

This provision seeks to facilitate the extradition of accused persons by amending all existing bilateral extradition treaties between States Parties. Its wording is identical to that of article 11 of the International Convention for the Suppression of the Financing of Terrorism.

Article 10
Judicial cooperation

As its title indicates, this article, based on article 12, paragraphs 1, 3, 4 and 5, of the International Convention for the Suppression of the Financing of Terrorism, provides that the States bodies must lend one another the greatest possible judicial and police cooperation in the field.

Article 11
Rights of the accused

This article is a general safeguard clause guaranteeing respect for the basic rights of the accused and the principles of due process. It is identical to the text of article 17 of the International Convention for the Suppression of the Financing of Terrorism.

Article 12
Preventive measures

This article stipulates that States Parties must take all possible preventive measures in order to prevent the commission of the crime of human cloning. In particular, paragraph 1 (a) and (b) establishes the obligations of States Parties to regulate research involving human genetic material and to monitor research centres working in those fields. This article uses broad language allowing each State Party to design, in accordance with its own administrative organization, the best mechanism for carrying out this obligation.

The text of this article is based on article 18, paragraphs 1, 3 and 4, of the International Convention for the Suppression of the Financing of Terrorism. Paragraph 1 (b) and (c) was inspired by paragraphs 17 and 19 of Recommendation 1100 (1989) on the use of human embryos and foetuses in scientific research, of 2 February 1989, adopted by the Parliamentary Assembly of the Council of Europe at its fortieth ordinary session (third part), 30 January to 3 February 1989.

Article 13
Safeguard clause

This article protects the sovereign right of each State Party to adopt stricter measures when regulating research in the field of medicine and biology. Its text is based on article 27 of the Council of Europe Convention for the Protection of Human Rights and Dignity of the Human Being with regard to the Application of Biology and Medicine, of 4 April 1997 (Convention on Human Rights and Biomedicine) (Council of Europe, document DIR/JUR (96) 14, *European Treaty Series No. 164*).

Article 14
Settlement of disputes

This provision establishes a mechanism for the peaceful settlement of disputes. This article is identical to the text of article 24 of the International Convention for the Suppression of the Financing of Terrorism.

Article 15
Signature and ratification

This is the customary wording of clauses referring to the signature and ratification of an international treaty. The text is identical to the text of article 25 of the International Convention for the Suppression of the Financing of Terrorism.

Article 16
Reservations

This article prohibits reservations to the basic articles of the Convention in order to prevent the weakening of the judicial regime established under it through reservations and exceptions. This provision prevents the authorization of experimental cloning by making a reservation to the definition of the crime.

Article 17
Entry into force

This is the traditional wording of final clauses on the entry into force. The text is identical to that of article 26 of the International Convention for the Suppression of the Financing of Terrorism.

Article 18
Denunciation

This is the traditional wording referring to denunciation of the treaty. The text is identical to that of article 27 of the International Convention for the Suppression of the Financing of Terrorism.

Article 19
Authentic texts

This is the traditional wording on official languages included in all multilateral treaties of a universal nature adopted within the framework of the United Nations. Its text is identical to the language of article 28 of the International Convention for the Suppression of the Financing of Terrorism.

6. International Convention against the Reproductive Cloning of Human Beings (A/C.6/57/L.3/Rev.1)

United Nations, General Assembly
18 October 2002
Original: English

Antigua and Barbuda, Argentina, Costa Rica, Dominica, Dominican Republic, El Salvador, Eritrea, Ethiopia, Fiji, Georgia, Grenada, Honduras, Italy, Kazakhstan, Kenya, Kyrgyzstan, Lesotho, Marshall Islands, Micronesia, Nicaragua, Nigeria, Panama, Paraguay, Philippines, Saint Kitts and Nevis, Saint Lucia, Saint Vincent and the Grenadines, Spain, Suriname, Tajikistan, Timor-Leste, Tonga, Turkmenistan, Tuvalu, United States of America, Uzbekistan and Vanuatu: Draft Resolution

The General Assembly,

Recalling the Universal Declaration on the Human Genome and Human Rights,[1] adopted by the General Conference of the United Nations Educational, Scientific and Cultural Organization on 11 November 1997, and in particular article 11 thereof, which states that practices which are contrary to human dignity, such as the reproductive cloning of human beings, shall not be permitted,

Recalling also its resolution 53/152 of 9 December 1998, by which it endorsed the Universal Declaration on the Human Genome and Human Rights,

Bearing in mind Commission on Human Rights resolution 2001/71 of 25 April 2001, entitled "Human rights and bioethics",[2] adopted at the fifty-seventh session of the Commission,

---

[1] United Nations Educational, Scientific and Cultural Organization, Records of the General Conference, Twenty-ninth Session, Vol. 1, Resolutions, resolution 16.

[2] See Official Records of the Economic and Social Council, 2001, Supplement No. 3 (E/2001/23), chap. II, sect. A.

Mindful of the importance of the development of the life sciences for the benefit of mankind with full respect for the integrity and dignity of the human being,

Mindful also that certain practices pose potential dangers to the integrity and dignity of the individual,

Concerned at recently disclosed information on research into and attempts at the creation of human beings through cloning processes,

Determined to prevent as a matter of urgency such an attack on the human dignity of the individual,

Conscious of widespread preoccupations that the human body and its parts should not, as such, give rise to financial gain,

Recalling its resolution 56/93 of 12 December 2001, by which it decided to establish an Ad Hoc Committee, open to all States Members of the United Nations or members of specialized agencies or of the International Atomic Energy Agency, for the purpose of considering the elaboration of an international convention against the reproductive cloning of human beings,

Determined to adopt permanent and provisional measures, as appropriate, to prevent potential dangers to the human dignity of the individual,

1. *Welcomes* the report of the Ad Hoc Committee on an International Convention against the Reproductive Cloning of Human Beings on its work from 25 February to 1 March 2002;[3]

2. *Requests* the Ad Hoc Committee to be reconvened from 24 March to 4 April 2003 and prepare, as a matter of urgency, the draft text of an international convention against human cloning, bearing in mind that it will not prohibit the use of nuclear transfer or other cloning techniques to produce DNA molecules, organs, plants, tissues, cells other than human embryos or animals other than humans, and recommends that the work continue during the fifty-eighth session of the General Assembly from 29 September to 3 October 2003 within the framework of a working group of the Sixth Committee;

3. *Also requests* the Ad Hoc Committee, in developing the draft convention, to consider, inter alia, the following indicative elements:

   (a) Scope;

---

[3]   Official Records of the General Assembly, Fifty-seventh Session, Supplement No. 51 (A/57/51).

(b) Definitions;

(c) The objective;

(d) Implementation;

(e) Preventive measures;

(f) Jurisdiction;

(g) Promotion and strengthening of international cooperation;

(h) Exchange of information;

(i) Mechanisms for monitoring implementation;

4. *Solemnly declares* that, pending the adoption of an international convention against human cloning, States shall not permit any research, experiment, development or application in their territories or areas under their jurisdiction or control of any technique aimed at human cloning;

5. *Calls upon* States to adopt such measures as may be necessary to prohibit those techniques of genetic engineering that may have adverse consequences on the respect for human dignity;

6. *Requests* the Secretary-General to provide the Ad Hoc Committee with the necessary facilities for the performance of its work;

7. *Invites* the Ad Hoc Committee to take into consideration the contributions of United Nations agencies and competent international organizations, as well as other relevant bodies of international opinion in the process of negotiations;

8. *Requests* the Ad Hoc Committee to report on its work to the General Assembly at its fifty-eighth session;

9. *Decides* to include in the provisional agenda of its fifty-eighth session an item entitled "International convention against human cloning".

7. International Convention against the Reproductive Cloning of Human Beings (A/C.6/57/L.8)

United Nations, General Assembly

8 October 2002

Original: English and French

Belarus, Belgium, Brazil, Canada, China, Cuba, Czech Republic, Denmark, Finland, France, Germany, Greece, Hungary, Iceland, Japan, Latvia, Liechtenstein, Lithuania, Luxembourg, Norway, Slovenia and Switzerland: Draft Resolution

The General Assembly,

Recalling the Universal Declaration on the Human Genome and Human Rights,[1] adopted by the General Conference of the United Nations Educational, Scientific and Cultural Organization on 11 November 1997, and in particular article 11 thereof, which states that practices which are contrary to human dignity, such as reproductive cloning of human beings, shall not be permitted,

Recalling also its resolution 53/152 of 9 December 1998, by which it endorsed the Universal Declaration on the Human Genome and Human Rights,

Bearing in mind Commission on Human Rights resolution 2001/71 of 25 April 2001 entitled "Human rights and bioethics", adopted by the Commission at its fifty-seventh session,

Mindful of the importance of the development of the life sciences for the benefit of mankind, with full respect for the integrity and dignity of the human being,

Aware that the rapid development of the life sciences opens up tremendous prospects for the improvement of the health and the restoration of human dignity of individuals and mankind as a whole,

---

[1] United Nations Educational, Scientific and Cultural Organization, *Records of the General Conference, Twenty-ninth session*, Vol. I, Resolutions, resolution 16.

but also that certain practices pose potential dangers to the integrity and dignity of the individual,

Concerned by the seriousness of problems posed by the development of techniques of reproductive cloning of human beings applied to mankind, which may have consequences for respect for human dignity,

Particularly concerned, in the context of practices that are contrary to human dignity, at recently disclosed information on research into and attempts at the reproductive cloning of human beings,

Determined to prevent, as a matter of urgency, such an attack on the human dignity of the individual,

Recalling its resolution 56/93 of 12 December 2001, by which it decided to establish an Ad Hoc Committee, open to all States Members of the United Nations or members of specialized agencies or of the International Atomic Energy Agency, for the purpose of considering the elaboration of an international convention against the reproductive cloning of human beings,

Resolved to address issues related to other forms of human cloning, including through the elaboration of an appropriate separate international instrument, as soon as negotiations on a convention against the reproductive cloning of human beings have been concluded,

Bearing in mind that this purpose does not preclude the possibility of States parties adopting stricter national regulations,

Determined to adopt provisional measures at the national level to prevent potential dangers to the human dignity of the individual pending the adoption and entry into force of an international convention against the reproductive cloning of human beings and any other instrument in the field of cloning of human beings,

1. *Welcomes* the report of the Ad Hoc Committee on an International Convention against the Reproductive Cloning of Human Beings on its work from 25 February to 1 March 2002;[2]

2. *Decides* that the Ad Hoc Committee shall be reconvened from ___to ___ February and from ___ to ___ September 2003 in order to prepare, as a matter of urgency and if possible by the

---

[2] Official Records of the General Assembly, Fifty-seventh Session, Supplement No. 51 (A/57/51).

end of 2003, a draft international convention against the reproductive cloning of human beings;

3. Requests the Ad Hoc Committee, in developing the draft convention:

    a) To consider, inter alia, the following indicative elements: scope, definitions, prohibition of reproductive cloning of human beings, national implementation, including penalties and preventive measures, jurisdiction, promotion and strengthening of international cooperation and technical assistance, collection, exchange and analysis of information and mechanisms for monitoring implementation;

    b) To specify that the prohibition of reproductive cloning of human beings does not imply the endorsement of any other form of cloning of human beings for any purpose;

    c) To ensure that States parties shall not be prevented from adopting or maintaining stricter regulations on the prohibition of cloning of human beings than those contained in the draft convention;

4. *Requests* the Ad Hoc Committee to take into consideration the relevant existing international instruments;

5. *Decides* that it will consider, as a priority, proposals to address issues related to other forms of cloning of human beings, including one or more appropriate separate international instruments, as soon as negotiations on a draft international convention prohibiting the reproductive cloning of human beings have been concluded;

6. *Invites*, to that end, the World Health Organization and the United Nations Educational, Scientific and Cultural Organization to start elaborating, without delay, in close cooperation with the appropriate United Nations bodies, a joint preparatory document outlining from a scientific and ethical perspective the relevant issues to be considered, inter alia, the current state of the art of the human cloning technologies and the possible dual use of the existing non-human cloning techniques, and to submit this document no later than the end of 2003;

7. *Calls upon* those States which have not yet done so, pending the entry into force of an international convention against the reproductive cloning of human beings and their becoming

party thereto, to adopt at the national level a prohibition of reproductive cloning of human beings;

8. *Also calls upon* those States which have not yet done so to adopt at the national level a moratorium on or a prohibition of, other forms of cloning of human beings that are contrary to human dignity;

9. *Requests* the Secretary-General to provide the Ad Hoc Committee with the facilities necessary for the performance of its work;

10. *Invites* the Ad Hoc Committee to take into consideration the contributions of United Nations bodies and to closely involve the United Nations Educational, Scientific and Cultural Organization, the World Health Organization and the United Nations Conference on Trade and Development in the process of negotiations;

11. *Requests* the Ad Hoc Committee to report on its work to the General Assembly at its fifty-eighth session;

12. *Decides* to include in the provisional agenda of its fifty-eighth session the item entitled "International convention against the reproductive cloning of human beings".

8. International Convention against the Reproductive Cloning of Human Beings (A/RES/56/93)

United Nations, General Assembly
28 January 2002

Resolution adopted by the General Assembly
[on the report of the Sixth Committee (A/56/599)]

The General Assembly,

Recalling the Universal Declaration on the Human Genome and Human Rights,[1] adopted by the General Conference of the United Nations Educational, Scientific and Cultural Organization on 11 November 1997, in particular article 11 thereof, in which the Conference specified that practices which are contrary to human dignity, such as reproductive cloning of human beings, shall not be permitted and invited States and international organizations to cooperate in taking, at the national or international level, the measures necessary in that regard,

Recalling also its resolution 53/152 of 9 December 1998, by which it endorsed the Universal Declaration on the Human Genome and Human Rights,

Bearing in mind Commission on Human Rights resolution 2001/71 of 25 April 2001, entitled "Human rights and bioethics",[2] adopted at the fifty-seventh session of the Commission,

Noting the resolution on bioethics adopted by the General Conference of the United Nations Educational, Scientific and Cultural

---

[1]   United Nations Educational, Scientific and Cultural Organization, Records of the General Conference, Twenty-ninth Session, Vol. I, Resolutions, resolution 16.

[2]   See Official Records of the Economic and Social Council, 2001, Supplement No. 3 (E/2001/23), chap. II. sect. A.

Organization on 2 November 2001,[3] in which the Conference approved the recommendations by the Intergovernmental Bioethics Committee towards the possible elaboration, within the United Nations Educational, Scientific and Cultural Organization, of universal norms on bioethics,

Aware that the rapid development of the life sciences opens up tremendous prospects for the improvement of the health of individuals and mankind as a whole, but also that certain practices pose potential dangers to the integrity and dignity of the individual,

Particularly concerned, in the context of practices which are contrary to human dignity, at recently disclosed information on the research being conducted with a view to the reproductive cloning of human beings,

Determined to prevent such an attack on the human dignity of the individual,

Aware of the need for a multidisciplinary approach to the elaboration by the international community of an appropriate response to this problem,

1. *Decides* to establish an Ad Hoc Committee, open to all States Members of the United Nations or members of specialized agencies or of the International Atomic Energy Agency, for the purpose of considering the elaboration of an international convention against the reproductive cloning of human beings;

2. *Requests* the Secretary-General to invite the specialized agencies that work and have substantial interest in the field of bioethics, including, in particular, the United Nations Educational, Scientific and Cultural Organization and the World Health Organization, to participate as observers in the work of the Ad Hoc Committee;

3. *Decides* that the Ad Hoc Committee shall meet from 25 February to 1 March 2002 to consider the elaboration of a mandate for the negotiation of such an international convention, including a list of the existing international instruments to be taken into consideration and a list of legal issues to be addressed in the convention, with the understanding that the Ad Hoc Committee will open with an

---

[3] United Nations Educational, Scientific and Cultural Organization, *Records of the General Conference, Thirty-first Session*, Vol. I, Resolutions, resolution 22.

exchange of information and technical assessments provided by experts on genetics and bioethics, and recommends that the work continue during the fifty-seventh session of the General Assembly from 23 to 27 September 2002, within the framework of a working group of the Sixth Committee;

4. *Requests* the Secretary-General to provide the Ad Hoc Committee with the necessary facilities for the performance of its work;

5. *Requests* the Ad Hoc Committee to report on its work to the General Assembly at its fifty-seventh session;

6. *Recommends* that, upon the adoption of a negotiation mandate by the General Assembly, it may decide, taking into account the acute nature of the problem, to reconvene the Ad Hoc Committee, in order to open negotiations on the international convention referred to in paragraph 1 above;

7. *Decides* to include in the provisional agenda of its fifty-seventh session the item entitled "International convention against the reproductive cloning of human beings".

II. Other International Resolutions and Declarations

9. Resolution 2003/69: Human Rights and Bioethics (E/CN.4/2003/L.11/Add.7)

Commission on Human Rights
62nd meeting
25 April 2003
(Adopted without a vote.)

The Commission on Human Rights,

Recalling that, according to the Universal Declaration of Human Rights, the International Covenants on Human Rights and other human rights instruments, recognition of the inherent dignity and of the equal and inalienable rights of all members of the human family is the foundation of freedom, justice and peace in the world,

Seeking to preserve the dignity and integrity of the human being,

Recalling the right of everyone, as recognized in article 15 of the International Covenant on Economic, Social and Cultural Rights, to enjoy the benefits of scientific progress and its applications, and recalling article 7 of the International Covenant on Civil and Political Rights, which states that no one shall be subjected without his free consent to medical or scientific experimentation,

Aware that the rapid development of the life sciences opens up tremendous prospects for the improvement of the health of individuals and mankind as a whole, but also that certain practices may pose dangers to the integrity and dignity of the individual,

Seeking therefore to ensure that scientific progress benefits individuals and develops in a manner respectful of human rights,

Referring to the Universal Declaration on the Human Genome and Human Rights adopted on 11 November 1997 by the General Conference of the United Nations Educational, Scientific and Cultural Organization and to General Assembly resolution 53/152 of 9 December 1998 endorsing the Declaration,

Affirming the principle that the human genome underlies the fundamental unity of all members of the human family, as well as the recognition of their inherent dignity and diversity,

Recalling that article 10 of the Declaration affirms, inter alia, that no research or research applications concerning the human genome, in particular in the fields of biology, genetics and medicine, should prevail over respect for the human rights, fundamental freedoms and human dignity of individuals,

Welcoming resolution 22 adopted on 2 November 2001 at the 31st General Conference of the United Nations Educational, Scientific and Cultural Organization inviting the Director-General to submit to the General Conference at its 32nd session in 2003 the technical and legal studies undertaken regarding the possibility of elaborating universal norms on bioethics,

Recalling its resolutions 1991/45 of 5 March 1991, 1993/91 of 10 March 1993, 1997/71 of 16 April 1997, 1999/63 of 28 April 1999 and 2001/71 of 25 April 2001,

Referring to the United Nations Millennium Declaration in which Heads of State and Government resolved to ensure free access to information on the human genome sequence,

Referring also to resolution 1997/42 of 28 August 1997 of the Sub-Commission on the Promotion and Protection of Human Rights regarding this question,

Recalling the adoption by the Committee of Ministers of the Council of Europe, on 4 April 1997, of the Convention for the Protection of Human Rights and Dignity of the Human Being with regard to the Application of Biology and Medicine,

Convinced of the need to develop a life sciences ethic at the national and international levels, and recognizing the need to develop international rules and cooperation in order to ensure that mankind as a whole benefits from the use of the life sciences and to prevent any misuse of their applications,

Rejecting strongly any doctrine of racial superiority, along with theories which attempt to determine the existence of so-called distinct human races,

1. *Takes note* of the report of the Secretary-General (E/CN.4/2003/98 and Add.1);

2. *Expresses its appreciation* to the Governments that have responded to the request for information formulated by the Commission in its resolution 2001/71 of 25 April 2001 and invites the Governments which have not yet responded to do so;

3. *Invites* the United Nations High Commissioner for Human Rights to participate, within his area of competence, in the discussion on questions relating to human rights and bioethics;

4. *Welcomes* the initiative of the members of the United Nations Educational, Scientific and Cultural Organization to prepare an international declaration on human genetic data and calls upon Member States to cooperate fully in the finalization of a text;

5. *Urges* States to take measures for the protection and confidentiality of personal genetic data concerning persons living or dead; in order to protect human rights and fundamental freedoms, limitations to the principles of consent and confidentiality may only be prescribed by law, for compelling reasons within the bounds of public international law and international human rights law;

6. *Calls upon* States that have not yet done so to address the issue of discrimination arising from the application of genetics, in order to protect human rights, fundamental freedoms and dignity;

7. *Draws the attention* of Governments to the importance of research on the human genome and its applications for the improvement of the health of individuals and mankind as a whole, and to the need to safeguard the human rights, the dignity and the identity of the individual;

8. *Encourages* States to participate in the discussions of the working group of the Sixth Committee, to be held from 29 September to 3 October 2003 during the fifty-eighth session of the General Assembly under the agenda item "International convention against the reproductive cloning of human beings";

9. *Reaffirms* the importance of receiving information from the organizations and specialized agencies of the United Nations and invites the United Nations Educational, Scientific and Cultural

Organization, the World Health Organization, the Office of the United Nations High Commissioner for Human Rights and the other United Nations bodies and specialized agencies concerned to report to the Secretary-General on the activities conducted in their respective areas to ensure that the principles set forth in the Universal Declaration on the Human Genome and Human Rights are taken into account and to make these reports available to Governments;

10. *Invites* Governments that have not yet done so to consider establishing independent, multidisciplinary and pluralist committees of ethics to assess, notably in conjunction with the International Bioethics Committee of the United Nations Educational, Scientific and Cultural Organization, the ethical, social and human questions raised by the biomedical research undergone by human beings and, in particular, research relating to the human genome and its applications, and also invites them to inform the Secretary-General of the establishment of any such bodies, with a view to promoting exchanges of experience between such institutions;

11. *Requests again* the Sub-Commission on the Promotion and Protection of Human rights to consider what contribution it can make to the reflections of the International Bioethics Committee on the follow-up to the Universal Declaration on the Human Genome and Human Rights and to report on this matter to the Commission at its sixty-first session;

12. *Requests* the Secretary-General to submit a report based on these contributions for consideration by the Commission at its sixty-first session.

10. Declaration of Helsinki: Ethical Principles for Medical Research Involving Human Subjects

World Medical Association
Initiated: 1964 17.C
Original: English
Adopted by the 18th WMA General Assembly Helsinki, Finland, June 1964 and amended by the
29th WMA General Assembly, Tokyo, Japan, October 1975
35th WMA General Assembly, Venice, Italy, October 1983
41st WMA General Assembly, Hong Kong, September 1989
48th WMA General Assembly, Somerset West, Republic of South Africa, October 1996 and the
52nd WMA General Assembly, Edinburgh, Scotland, October 2000
Note of Clarification on Paragraph 29 added by the WMA General Assembly, Washington 2002

A. Introduction

1. The World Medical Association has developed the Declaration of Helsinki as a statement of ethical principles to provide guidance to physicians and other participants in medical research involving human subjects. Medical research involving human subjects includes research on identifiable human material or identifiable data.

2. It is the duty of the physician to promote and safeguard the health of the people. The physician's knowledge and conscience are dedicated to the fulfillment of this duty.

3. The Declaration of Geneva of the World Medical Association binds the physician with the words, "The health of my patient will be my first consideration," and the International Code of Medical Ethics declares that, "A physician shall act only in the patient's interest when providing medical care which might have the effect of weakening the physical and mental condition of the patient."

4. Medical progress is based on research which ultimately must rest in part on experimentation involving human subjects.

5.   In medical research on human subjects, considerations related to the well-being of the human subject should take precedence over the interests of science and society.

6.   The primary purpose of medical research involving human subjects is to improve prophylactic, diagnostic and therapeutic procedures and the understanding of the aetiology and pathogenesis of disease. Even the best proven prophylactic, diagnostic, and therapeutic methods must continuously be challenged through research for their effectiveness, efficiency, accessibility and quality.

7.   In current medical practice and in medical research, most prophylactic, diagnostic and therapeutic procedures involve risks and burdens.

8.   Medical research is subject to ethical standards that promote respect for all human beings and protect their health and rights. Some research populations are vulnerable and need special protection. The particular needs of the economically and medically disadvantaged must be recognized. Special attention is also required for those who cannot give or refuse consent for themselves, for those who may be subject to giving consent under duress, for those who will not benefit personally from the research and for those for whom the research is combined with care.

9.   Research Investigators should be aware of the ethical, legal and regulatory requirements for research on human subjects in their own countries as well as applicable international requirements. No national ethical, legal or regulatory requirement should be allowed to reduce or eliminate any of the protections for human subjects set forth in this Declaration.

B. Basic Principles for all Medical Research

10. It is the duty of the physician in medical research to protect the life, health, privacy, and dignity of the human subject.

11. Medical research involving human subjects must conform to generally accepted scientific principles, be based on a thorough knowledge of the scientific literature, other relevant sources of information, and on adequate laboratory and, where appropriate, animal experimentation.

12. Appropriate caution must be exercised in the conduct of research which may affect the environment, and the welfare of animals used for research must be respected.

13. The design and performance of each experimental procedure involving human subjects should be clearly formulated in an experimental protocol. This protocol should be submitted for consideration, comment, guidance, and where appropriate, approval to a specially appointed ethical review committee, which must be independent of the investigator, the sponsor or any other kind of undue influence. This independent committee should be in conformity with the laws and regulations of the country in which the research experiment is performed. The committee has the right to monitor ongoing trials. The researcher has the obligation to provide monitoring information to the committee, especially any serious adverse events. The researcher should also submit to the committee, for review, information regarding funding, sponsors, institutional affiliations, other potential conflicts of interest and incentives for subjects.

14. The research protocol should always contain a statement of the ethical considerations involved and should indicate that there is compliance with the principles enunciated in this Declaration.

15. Medical research involving human subjects should be conducted only by scientifically qualified persons and under the supervision of a clinically competent medical person. The responsibility for the human subject must always rest with a medically qualified person and never rest on the subject of the research, even though the subject has given consent.

16. Every medical research project involving human subjects should be preceded by careful assessment of predictable risks and burdens in comparison with foreseeable benefits to the subject or to others. This does not preclude the participation of healthy volunteers in medical research. The design of all studies should be publicly available.

17. Physicians should abstain from engaging in research projects involving human subjects unless they are confident that the risks involved have been adequately assessed and can be satisfactorily managed. Physicians should cease any investigation if the risks are found to outweigh the potential benefits or if there is conclusive proof of positive and beneficial results.

18. Medical research involving human subjects should only be conducted if the importance of the objective outweighs the inherent risks and burdens to the subject. This is especially important when the human subjects are healthy volunteers.

19. Medical research is only justified if there is a reasonable likelihood that the populations in which the research is carried out stand to benefit from the results of the research.

20. The subjects must be volunteers and informed participants in the research project.

21. The right of research subjects to safeguard their integrity must always be respected. Every precaution should be taken to respect the privacy of the subject, the confidentiality of the patient's information and to minimize the impact of the study on the subject's physical and mental integrity and on the personality of the subject.

22. In any research on human beings, each potential subject must be adequately informed of the aims, methods, sources of funding, any possible conflicts of interest, institutional affiliations of the researcher, the anticipated benefits and potential risks of the study and the discomfort it may entail. The subject should be informed of the right to abstain from participation in the study or to withdraw consent to participate at any time without reprisal. After ensuring that the subject has understood the information, the physician should then obtain the subject's freely-given informed consent, preferably in writing. If the consent cannot be obtained in writing, the non-written consent must be formally documented and witnessed.

23. When obtaining informed consent for the research project the physician should be particularly cautious if the subject is in a dependent relationship with the physician or may consent under duress. In that case the informed consent should be obtained by a well-informed physician who is not engaged in the investigation and who is completely independent of this relationship.

24. For a research subject who is legally incompetent, physically or mentally incapable of giving consent or is a legally incompetent minor, the investigator must obtain informed consent from the legally authorized representative in accordance with applicable law. These groups should not be included in research unless the research is necessary to promote the health of the population

represented and this research cannot instead be performed on legally competent persons.

25. When a subject deemed legally incompetent, such as a minor child, is able to give assent to decisions about participation in research, the investigator must obtain that assent in addition to the consent of the legally authorized representative.

26. Research on individuals from whom it is not possible to obtain consent, including proxy or advance consent, should be done only if the physical/mental condition that prevents obtaining informed consent is a necessary characteristic of the research population. The specific reasons for involving research subjects with a condition that renders them unable to give informed consent should be stated in the experimental protocol for consideration and approval of the review committee. The protocol should state that consent to remain in the research should be obtained as soon as possible from the individual or a legally authorized surrogate.

27. Both authors and publishers have ethical obligations. In publication of the results of research, the investigators are obliged to preserve the accuracy of the results. Negative as well as positive results should be published or otherwise publicly available. Sources of funding, institutional affiliations and any possible conflicts of interest should be declared in the publication. Reports of experimentation not in accordance with the principles laid down in this Declaration should not be accepted for publication.

C. Additional Principles for Medical Research Combined with Medical Care

28. The physician may combine medical research with medical care, only to the extent that the research is justified by its potential prophylactic, diagnostic or therapeutic value. When medical research is combined with medical care, additional standards apply to protect the patients who are research subjects.

29. The benefits, risks, burdens and effectiveness of a new method should be tested against those of the best current prophylactic, diagnostic, and therapeutic methods. This does not exclude the use of placebo, or no treatment, in studies where no proven prophylactic, diagnostic or therapeutic method exists. *(See footnote*)*

30. At the conclusion of the study, every patient entered into the study should be assured of access to the best proven prophylactic, diagnostic and therapeutic methods identified by the study.

31. The physician should fully inform the patient which aspects of the care are related to the research. The refusal of a patient to participate in a study must never interfere with the patient-physician relationship.

32. In the treatment of a patient, where proven prophylactic, diagnostic and therapeutic methods do not exist or have been ineffective, the physician, with informed consent from the patient, must be free to use unproven or new prophylactic, diagnostic and therapeutic measures, if in the physician's judgement it offers hope of saving life, re-establishing health or alleviating suffering. Where possible, these measures should be made the object of research, designed to evaluate their safety and efficacy. In all cases, new information should be recorded and, where appropriate, published. The other relevant guidelines of this Declaration should be followed.

*Footnote:

Note of Clarification on Paragraph 29 of the WMA Declaration of Helsinki

The WMA hereby reaffirms its position that extreme care must be taken in making use of a placebo-controlled trial and that in general this methodology should only be used in the absence of existing proven therapy. However, a placebo-controlled trial may be ethically acceptable, even if proven therapy is available, under the following circumstances:

- Where for compelling and scientifically sound methodological reasons its use is necessary to determine the efficacy or safety of a prophylactic, diagnostic or therapeutic method; or

- Where a prophylactic, diagnostic or therapeutic method is being investigated for a minor condition and the patients who receive placebo will not be subject to any additional risk of serious or irreversible harm.

All other provisions of the Declaration of Helsinki must be adhered to, especially the need for appropriate ethical and scientific review.

11. The Human Genome and Human Rights (A/RES/53/152)

United Nations, General Assembly
10 March 1999

Resolution Adopted by the General Assembly
[on the report of the Third Committee (A/53/625/Add.2)]

The General Assembly,

Guided by the purposes and principles set forth in the Charter of the United Nations, the Universal Declaration of Human Rights[1], the International Covenants on Human Rights[2] and the other relevant international human rights instruments,

Recalling Commission on Human Rights resolutions 1993/91 of 10 March 1993[3] and 1997/71 of 16 April 1997[4], on the question of human rights and bioethics,

Recalling also that, in accordance with the Universal Declaration of Human Rights, recognition of the inherent dignity and of the equal and inalienable rights of all members of the human family is the foundation of freedom, justice and peace in the world,

Aware of the rapid development of the life sciences and of ethical concerns raised by certain of their applications with regard to the dignity of the human race and the rights and freedoms of the individual,

Seeking to promote scientific and technical progress in the fields of biology and genetics in a manner respectful of fundamental rights and for the benefit of all,

---

[1] Resolution 217 A (III).

[2] Resolution 2200 A (XXI), annex.

[3] See Official Records of the Economic and Social Council, 1993, Supplement No. 3 and corrigenda (E/1993/23 and Corr.2, 4 and 5), chap. II, sect. A.

[4] Ibid., 1997, Supplement No. 3 (E/1997/23), chap. II, sect. A.

Emphasizing, in this regard, the importance of international cooperation in order to ensure that mankind as a whole benefits from the life sciences, while seeking to prevent them from being used for any purpose other than the good of mankind,

Recalling the Universal Declaration on the Human Genome and Human Rights[5] and the accompanying resolution on its implementation[6], both adopted on 11 November 1997 by the General Conference of the United Nations Educational, Scientific and Cultural Organization at its twenty-ninth session,

Recognizing the importance of the process of follow-up to the Universal Declaration on the Human Genome and Human Rights within the framework of the United Nations Educational, Scientific and Cultural Organization,

Convinced of the need to develop a life-sciences ethic at the national and international levels,

Endorses the Universal Declaration on the Human Genome and Human Rights adopted by the General Conference of the United Nations Educational, Scientific and Cultural Organization on 11 November 1997.

85th plenary meeting
9 December 1998

---

[5] United Nations Educational, Scientific and Cultural Organization, Records of the General Conference, Twenty-ninth Session, vol. I, Resolutions, resolution 16.

[6] Ibid., resolution 17.

12. Resolution on Ethical, Scientific and Social Implications of Cloning in Human Health (WHA 51.10)

World Health Organisation
16 May 1998

The Fifty-first World Health Assembly,

Recalling resolution WHA50.37 and its condemnation of human cloning for reproductive purposes as contrary to human dignity;

Noting the general consensus reached at the national and international levels since the Fiftieth World Health Assembly regarding human cloning for reproductive purposes;

Noting in particular UNESCO's Universal Declaration on the Human Genome and Human Rights and the Council of Europe's Additional Protocol to the Convention on Human Rights and Dignity of the Human Being with regard to the Application of Biology and Medicine, which deal with the prohibition of cloning of human beings;

Considering that the currently available information from animal studies involving cloning by somatic cell nuclear transfer indicates that this would be an unsafe procedure for reproductive purposes in the human;

Recognizing that developments in cloning have unprecedented ethical implications and raise serious matters for concern in terms of safety of the individual and subsequent generations of human beings,

1. REAFFIRMS that cloning for the replication of human individuals is ethically unacceptable and contrary to human dignity and integrity;

2. URGES Member States to foster continued and informed debate on these issues and to take appropriate steps, including legal and juridical measures, to prohibit cloning for the purpose of replicating human individuals;

3. REQUESTS the Director-General:

    a) to establish a group, involving also government experts, with the aim of clarifying concepts and developing guidelines relating to the use of cloning procedures for non-reproductive purposes;

b) to continue to monitor, assess and clarify, in consultation with other international organizations, national governments and professional and scientific bodies, the ethical, scientific, social and legal implications of the use of cloning for human health;

c) to ensure that Member States are kept informed of developments in this area in order to facilitate decisions on national regulatory frameworks;

4. to report to the Executive Board at its 103rd session and to the Fifty-second World Health Assembly on action taken by the Organization in this field.

Tenth plenary meeting, 16 May 1998

13. Universal Declaration on the Human Genome and Human Rights

United Nations Educational, Scientific and Cultural Organization
11 November 1997

The General Conference,

Recalling that the Preamble of UNESCO's Constitution refers to "the democratic principles of the dignity, equality and mutual respect of men", rejects any "doctrine of the inequality of men and races", stipulates "that the wide diffusion of culture, and the education of humanity for justice and liberty and peace are indispensable to the dignity of men and constitute a sacred duty which all the nations must fulfil in a spirit of mutual assistance and concern", proclaims that "peace must be founded upon the intellectual and moral solidarity of mankind", and states that the Organization seeks to advance "through the educational and scientific and cultural relations of the peoples of the world, the objectives of international peace and of the common welfare of mankind for which the United Nations Organization was established and which its Charter proclaims",

Solemnly recalling its attachment to the universal principles of human rights, affirmed in particular in the Universal Declaration of Human Rights of 10 December 1948 and in the two International United Nations Covenants on Economic, Social and Cultural Rights and on Civil and Political Rights of 16 December 1966, in the United Nations Convention on the Prevention and Punishment of the Crime of Genocide of 9 December 1948, the International United Nations Convention on the Elimination of All Forms of Racial Discrimination of 21 December 1965, the United Nations Declaration on the Rights of Mentally Retarded Persons of 20 December 1971, the United Nations Declaration on the Rights of Disabled Persons of 9 December 1975, the United Nations Convention on the Elimination of All Forms of Discrimination Against Women of 18 December 1979, the United Nations Declaration of Basic Principles of Justice for Victims of Crime and Abuse of Power of 29 November 1985, the United Nations Convention on the Rights of the Child of 20 November 1989, the United Nations Standard Rules on the Equalization of Opportunities

for Persons with Disabilities of 20 December 1993, the Convention on
the Prohibition of the Development, Production and Stockpiling of
Bacteriological (Biological) and Toxin Weapons and on their
Destruction of 16 December 1971, the UNESCO Convention against
Discrimination in Education of 14 December 1960, the UNESCO
Declaration of the Principles of International Cultural Co-operation of
4 November 1966, the UNESCO Recommendation on the Status of
Scientific Researchers of 20 November 1974, the UNESCO Declaration
on Race and Racial Prejudice of 27 November 1978, the ILO
Convention (N° 111) concerning Discrimination in Respect of
Employment and Occupation of 25 June 1958 and the ILO Convention
(N° 169) concerning Indigenous and Tribal Peoples in Independent
Countries of 27 June 1989,

Bearing in mind, and without prejudice to, the international
instruments which could have a bearing on the applications of genetics
in the field of intellectual property, inter alia, the Bern Convention for
the Protection of Literary and Artistic Works of 9 September 1886 and
the UNESCO Universal Copyright Convention of 6 September 1952,
as last revised in Paris on 24 July 1971, the Paris Convention for the
Protection of Industrial Property of 20 March 1883, as last revised at
Stockholm on 14 July 1967, the Budapest Treaty of the WIPO on
International Recognition of the Deposit of Micro-organisms for the
Purposes of Patent Procedures of 28 April 1977, and the Trade Related
Aspects of Intellectual Property Rights Agreement (TRIPs) annexed to
the Agreement establishing the World Trade Organization, which
entered into force on 1st January 1995,

Bearing in mind also the United Nations Convention on Biological
Diversity of 5 June 1992 and emphasizing in that connection that the
recognition of the genetic diversity of humanity, must not give rise to
any interpretation of a social or political nature which could call into
question "the inherent dignity and (...) the equal and inalienable rights
of all members of the human family", in accordance with the Preamble
to the Universal Declaration of Human Rights,

Recalling 22 C/Resolution 13.1, 23 C/Resolution 13.1, 24 C/Resolution
13.1, 25 C/Resolutions 5.2 and 7.3, 27 C/Resolution 5.15 and 28
C/Resolutions 0.12, 2.1 and 2.2, urging UNESCO to promote and
develop ethical studies, and the actions arising out of them, on the
consequences of scientific and technological progress in the fields of
biology and genetics, within the framework of respect for human rights
and fundamental freedoms,

Recognizing that research on the human genome and the resulting applications open up vast prospects for progress in improving the health of individuals and of humankind as a whole, but emphasizing that such research should fully respect human dignity, freedom and human rights, as well as the prohibition of all forms of discrimination based on genetic characteristics,

Proclaims the principles that follow and adopts the present Declaration.

A. Human Dignity and the Human Genome

Article 1

The human genome underlies the fundamental unity of all members of the human family, as well as the recognition of their inherent dignity and diversity. In a symbolic sense, it is the heritage of humanity.

Article 2

a) Everyone has a right to respect for their dignity and for their rights regardless of their genetic characteristics.

b) That dignity makes it imperative not to reduce individuals to their genetic characteristics and to respect their uniqueness and diversity.

Article 3

The human genome, which by its nature evolves, is subject to mutations. It contains potentialities that are expressed differently according to each individual's natural and social environment including the individual's state of health, living conditions, nutrition and education.

Article 4

The human genome in its natural state shall not give rise to financial gains.

B. Rights of the Persons Concerned

Article 5

a) Research, treatment or diagnosis affecting an individual's genome shall be undertaken only after rigorous and prior assessment of the potential risks and benefits pertaining thereto and in accordance with any other requirement of national law.

b) In all cases , the prior, free and informed consent of the person concerned shall be obtained. If the latter is not in a position to consent, consent or authorization shall be obtained in the manner prescribed by law, guided by the person's best interest.

c) The right of each individual to decide whether or not to be informed of the results of genetic examination and the resulting consequences should be respected.

d) In the case of research, protocols shall, in addition, be submitted for prior review in accordance with relevant national and international research standards or guidelines.

e) If according to the law a person does not have the capacity to consent, research affecting his or her genome may only be carried out for his or her direct health benefit, subject to the authorization and the protective conditions prescribed by law. Research which does not have an expected direct health benefit may only be undertaken by way of exception, with the utmost restraint, exposing the person only to a minimal risk and minimal burden and if the research is intended to contribute to the health benefit of other persons in the same age category or with the same genetic condition, subject to the conditions prescribed by law, and provided such research is compatible with the protection of the individual's human rights.

Article 6

No one shall be subjected to discrimination based on genetic characteristics that is intended to infringe or has the effect of infringing human rights, fundamental freedoms and human dignity.

Article 7

Genetic data associated with an identifiable person and stored or processed for the purposes of research or any other purpose must be held confidential in the conditions foreseen set by law.

Article 8

Every individual shall have the right, according to international and national law, to just reparation for any damage sustained as a direct and determining result of an intervention affecting his or her genome.

Article 9

In order to protect human rights and fundamental freedoms, limitations to the principles of consent and confidentiality may only be prescribed by law, for compelling reasons within the bounds of public international law and the international law of human rights.

C. Research on the Human Genome

Article 10

No research or research its applications concerning the human genome, in particular in the fields of biology, genetics and medicine, should prevail over respect for the human rights, fundamental freedoms and human dignity of individuals or, where applicable, of groups of people.

Article 11

Practices which are contrary to human dignity, such as reproductive cloning of human beings, shall not be permitted. States and competent international organizations are invited to co-operate in identifying such practices and in taking, at national or international level, the measures necessary to ensure that the principles set out in this Declaration are respected.

Article 12

a) Benefits from advances in biology, genetics and medicine, concerning the human genome, shall be made available to all, with due regard to the dignity and human rights of each individual.

b) Freedom of research, which is necessary for the progress of knowledge, is part of freedom of thought. The applications of research, including applications in biology, genetics and medicine, concerning the human genome, shall seek to offer relief from suffering and improve the health of individuals and humankind as a whole.

D. Conditions for the Exercise of Scientific Activity

Article 13

The responsibilities inherent in the activities of researchers, including meticulousness, caution, intellectual honesty and integrity in carrying out their research as well as in the presentation and utilization of their findings, should be the subject of particular attention in the framework of research on the human genome, because of its ethical and social implications. Public and private science policy-makers also have particular responsibilities in this respect.

Article 14

States should take appropriate measures to foster the intellectual and material conditions favourable to freedom in the conduct of research on the human genome and to consider the ethical, legal, social and economic implications of such research, on the basis of the principles set out in this Declaration.

Article 15

States should take appropriate steps to provide the framework for the free exercise of research on the human genome with due regard for the principles set out in this Declaration, in order to safeguard respect for human rights, fundamental freedoms and human dignity and to protect public health. They should seek to ensure that research results are not used for non-peaceful purposes.

Article 16

States should recognize the value of promoting, at various levels as appropriate, the establishment of independent, multidisciplinary and pluralist ethics committees to assess the ethical, legal and social issues raised by research on the human genome and its applications.

E. Solidarity and International Co-operation

Article 17

States should respect and promote the practice of solidarity towards individuals, families and population groups who are particularly vulnerable to or affected by disease or disability of a genetic character. They should foster, inter alia, research on the identification, prevention and treatment of genetically-based and genetically-influenced diseases, in particular rare as well as endemic diseases which affect large numbers of the world's population.

Article 18

States should make every effort, with due and appropriate regard for the principles set out in this Declaration, to continue fostering the international dissemination of scientific knowledge concerning the human genome, human diversity and genetic research and, in that regard, to foster scientific and cultural co-operation, particularly between industrialized and developing countries.

Article 19

a) In the framework of international co-operation with developing countries, States should seek to encourage measures enabling:

   (i)   1.assessment of the risks and benefits pertaining to research on the human genome to be carried out and abuse to be prevented;

(ii) the capacity of developing countries to carry out research on human biology and genetics, taking into consideration their specific problems, to be developed and strengthened;

(iii) developing countries to benefit from the achievements of scientific and technological research so that their use in favour of economic and social progress can be to the benefit of all;

(iv) the free exchange of scientific knowledge and information in the areas of biology, genetics and medicine to be promoted.

b) Relevant international organizations should support and promote the initiatives taken by States for the above mentioned purposes.

F. Promotion of the Principles Set out in the Declaration

Article 20

States should take appropriate measures to promote the principles set out in the Declaration, through education and relevant means, inter alia through the conduct of research and training in interdisciplinary fields and through the promotion of education in bioethics, at all levels, in particular for those responsible for science policies.

Article 21

States should take appropriate measures to encourage other forms of research, training and information dissemination conducive to raising the awareness of society and all of its members of their responsibilities regarding the fundamental issues relating to the defence of human dignity which may be raised by research in biology, in genetics and in medicine, and its applications. They should also undertake to facilitate on this subject an open international discussion, ensuring the free expression of various socio-cultural, religious and philosophical opinions.

G. Implementation of the Declaration

Article 22

States should make every effort to promote the principles set out in this Declaration and should, by means of all appropriate measures, promote their implementation.

Article 23

States should take appropriate measures to promote, through education, training and information dissemination, respect for the above mentioned principles and to foster their recognition and effective application. States should also encourage exchanges and networks among independent ethics committees, as they are established, to foster full collaboration.

Article 24

The International Bioethics Committee of UNESCO should contribute to the dissemination of the principles set out in this Declaration and to the further examination of issues raised by their applications and by the evolution of the technologies in question. It should organize appropriate consultations with parties concerned, such as vulnerable groups. It should make recommendations, in accordance with UNESCO's statutory procedures, addressed to the General Conference and give advice concerning the follow-up of this Declaration, in particular regarding the identification of practices that could be contrary to human dignity, such as germ-line interventions.

Article 25

Nothing in this Declaration may be interpreted as implying for any State, group or person any claim to engage in any activity or to perform any act contrary to human rights and fundamental freedoms, including the principles set out in this Declaration.

III. Council of Europe

14. Additional Protocol to the Convention for the Protection of Human Rights and Dignity of the Human Being with regard to the Application of Biology and Medicine, on the Prohibition of Cloning Human Beings

European Treaty Series - No. 168
Paris, 12 January 1998

The member States of the Council of Europe, the other States and the European Community Signatories to this Additional Protocol to the Convention for the Protection of Human Rights and Dignity of the Human Being with regard to the Application of Biology and Medicine,

Noting scientific developments in the field of mammal cloning, particularly through embryo splitting and nuclear transfer;

Mindful of the progress that some cloning techniques themselves may bring to scientific knowledge and its medical application;

Considering that the cloning of human beings may become a technical possibility;

Having noted that embryo splitting may occur naturally and sometimes result in the birth of genetically identical twins;

Considering however that the instrumentalisation of human beings through the deliberate creation of genetically identical human beings is contrary to human dignity and thus constitutes a misuse of biology and medicine;

Considering also the serious difficulties of a medical, psychological and social nature that such a deliberate biomedical practice might imply for all the individuals involved;

Considering the purpose of the Convention on Human Rights and Biomedicine, in particular the principle mentioned in Article 1 aiming to protect the dignity and identity of all human beings,

Have agreed as follows:

Article 1

(1) Any intervention seeking to create a human being genetically identical to another human being, whether living or dead, is prohibited.

(2) For the purpose of this article, the term human being "genetically identical" to another human being means a human being sharing with another the same nuclear gene set.

Article 2

No derogation from the provisions of this Protocol shall be made under Article 26, paragraph 1, of the Convention.

Article 3

As between the Parties, the provisions of Articles 1 and 2 of this Protocol shall be regarded as additional articles to the Convention and all the provisions of the Convention shall apply accordingly.

Article 4

This Protocol shall be open for signature by Signatories to the Convention. It is subject to ratification, acceptance or approval. A Signatory may not ratify, accept or approve this Protocol unless it has previously or simultaneously ratified, accepted or approved the Convention. Instruments of ratification, acceptance or approval shall be deposited with the Secretary General of the Council of Europe.

Article 5

(1) This Protocol shall enter into force on the first day of the month following the expiration of a period of three months after the date on which five States, including at least four member States of the Council

of Europe, have expressed their consent to be bound by the Protocol in accordance with the provisions of Article 4.

(2) In respect of any Signatory which subsequently expresses its consent to be bound by it, the Protocol shall enter into force on the first day of the month following the expiration of a period of three months after the date of the deposit of the instrument of ratification, acceptance or approval.

Article 6

(1) After the entry into force of this Protocol, any State which has acceded to the Convention may also accede to this Protocol.

(2) Accession shall be effected by the deposit with the Secretary General of the Council of Europe of an instrument of accession which shall take effect on the first day of the month following the expiration of a period of three months after the date of its deposit.

Article 7

(1) Any Party may at any time denounce this Protocol by means of a notification addressed to the Secretary General of the Council of Europe.

(2) Such denunciation shall become effective on the first day of the month following the expiration of a period of three months after the date of receipt of such notification by the Secretary General.

Article 8

The Secretary General of the Council of Europe shall notify the member States of the Council of Europe, the European Community, any Signatory, any Party and any other State which has been invited to accede to the Convention of:

a)   any signature;

b)   the deposit of any instrument of ratification, acceptance, approval or accession;

c)   any date of entry into force of this Protocol in accordance with Articles 5 and 6;

  d) any other act, notification or communication relating to this
      Protocol.

In witness whereof the undersigned, being duly authorised thereto,
have signed this Protocol.

Done at Paris, this twelfth day of January 1998, in English and in
French, both texts being equally authentic, in a single copy which shall
be deposited in the archives of the Council of Europe. The Secretary
General of the Council of Europe shall transmit certified copies to each
member State of the Council of Europe, to the non-member States
which have participated in the elaboration of this Protocol, to any State
invited to accede to the Convention and to the European Community.

15. Convention for the Protection of Human Rights and Dignity of the Human Being with regard to the Application of Biology and Medicine (Convention on Human Rights and Biomedicine)

European Treaty Series – No. 164
Oviedo, 4 April 1997

The member States of the Council of Europe, the other States and the European Community, signatories hereto,

Bearing in mind the Universal Declaration of Human Rights proclaimed by the General Assembly of the United Nations on 10 December 1948;

Bearing in mind the Convention for the Protection of Human Rights and Fundamental Freedoms of 4 November 1950;

Bearing in mind the European Social Charter of 18 October 1961;

Bearing in mind the International Covenant on Civil and Political Rights and the International Covenant on Economic, Social and Cultural Rights of 16 December 1966;

Bearing in mind the Convention for the Protection of Individuals with regard to Automatic Processing of Personal Data of 28 January 1981;

Bearing also in mind the Convention on the Rights of the Child of 20 November 1989;

Considering that the aim of the Council of Europe is the achievement of a greater unity between its members and that one of the methods by which that aim is to be pursued is the maintenance and further realisation of human rights and fundamental freedoms;

Conscious of the accelerating developments in biology and medicine;

Convinced of the need to respect the human being both as an individual and as a member of the human species and recognising the importance of ensuring the dignity of the human being;

Conscious that the misuse of biology and medicine may lead to acts endangering human dignity;

Affirming that progress in biology and medicine should be used for the benefit of present and future generations;

Stressing the need for international co-operation so that all humanity may enjoy the benefits of biology and medicine;

Recognising the importance of promoting a public debate on the questions posed by the application of biology and medicine and the responses to be given thereto;

Wishing to remind all members of society of their rights and responsibilities;

Taking account of the work of the Parliamentary Assembly in this field, including Recommendation 1160 (1991) on the preparation of a convention on bioethics;

Resolving to take such measures as are necessary to safeguard human dignity and the fundamental rights and freedoms of the individual with regard to the application of biology and medicine,

Have agreed as follows:

Chapter I – General provisions

Article 1
Purpose and object

Parties to this Convention shall protect the dignity and identity of all human beings and guarantee everyone, without discrimination, respect for their integrity and other rights and fundamental freedoms with regard to the application of biology and medicine.

Each Party shall take in its internal law the necessary measures to give effect to the provisions of this Convention.

Article 2
Primacy of the human being

The interests and welfare of the human being shall prevail over the sole interest of society or science.

Article 3
Equitable access to health care

Parties, taking into account health needs and available resources, shall take appropriate measures with a view to providing, within their jurisdiction, equitable access to health care of appropriate quality.

Article 4
Professional standards

Any intervention in the health field, including research, must be carried out in accordance with relevant professional obligations and standards.

Chapter II – Consent

Article 5
General rule

An intervention in the health field may only be carried out after the person concerned has given free and informed consent to it.

This person shall beforehand be given appropriate information as to the purpose and nature of the intervention as well as on its consequences and risks.

The person concerned may freely withdraw consent at any time.

Article 6
Protection of persons not able to consent

(1) Subject to Articles 17 and 20 below, an intervention may only be carried out on a person who does not have the capacity to consent, for his or her direct benefit.

(2) Where, according to law, a minor does not have the capacity to consent to an intervention, the intervention may only be carried out with the authorisation of his or her representative or an authority or a person or body provided for by law. The opinion of the minor shall be

taken into consideration as an increasingly determining factor in proportion to his or her age and degree of maturity.

(3) Where, according to law, an adult does not have the capacity to consent to an intervention because of a mental disability, a disease or for similar reasons, the intervention may only be carried out with the authorisation of his or her representative or an authority or a person or body provided for by law. The individual concerned shall as far as possible take part in the authorisation procedure.

(4) The representative, the authority, the person or the body mentioned in paragraphs 2 and 3 above shall be given, under the same conditions, the information referred to in Article.

(5) The authorisation referred to in paragraphs 2 and 3 above may be withdrawn at any time in the best interests of the person concerned.

Article 7
Protection of persons who have a mental disorder

Subject to protective conditions prescribed by law, including supervisory, control and appeal procedures, a person who has a mental disorder of a serious nature may be subjected, without his or her consent, to an intervention aimed at treating his or her mental disorder only where, without such treatment, serious harm is likely to result to his or her health.

Article 8
Emergency situation

When because of an emergency situation the appropriate consent cannot be obtained, any medically necessary intervention may be carried out immediately for the benefit of the health of the individual concerned.

Article 9
Previously expressed wishes

The previously expressed wishes relating to a medical intervention by a patient who is not, at the time of the intervention, in a state to express his or her wishes shall be taken into account.

Chapter III – Private life and right to information

Article 10
Private life and right to information

(1) Everyone has the right to respect for private life in relation to information about his or her health.

(2) Everyone is entitled to know any information collected about his or her health. However, the wishes of individuals not to be so informed shall be observed.

(3) In exceptional cases, restrictions may be placed by law on the exercise of the rights contained in paragraph 2 in the interests of the patient.

Chapter IV – Human genome

Article 11
Non-discrimination

Any form of discrimination against a person on grounds of his or her genetic heritage is prohibited.

Article 12
Predictive genetic tests

Tests which are predictive of genetic diseases or which serve either to identify the subject as a carrier of a gene responsible for a disease or to detect a genetic predisposition or susceptibility to a disease may be performed only for health purposes or for scientific research linked to health purposes, and subject to appropriate genetic counselling.

Article 13
Interventions on the human genome

An intervention seeking to modify the human genome may only be undertaken for preventive, diagnostic or therapeutic purposes and only if its aim is not to introduce any modification in the genome of any descendants.

Article 14
Non-selection of sex

The use of techniques of medically assisted procreation shall not be allowed for the purpose of choosing a future child's sex, except where serious hereditary sex-related disease is to be avoided.

Chapter V – Scientific research

Article 15
General rule

Scientific research in the field of biology and medicine shall be carried out freely, subject to the provisions of this Convention and the other legal provisions ensuring the protection of the human being.

Article 16
Protection of persons undergoing research

Research on a person may only be undertaken if all the following conditions are met:

(i)   there is no alternative of comparable effectiveness to research on humans;

(ii)   the risks which may be incurred by that person are not disproportionate to the potential benefits of the research;

(iii)   the research project has been approved by the competent body after independent examination of its scientific merit, including assessment of the importance of the aim of the research, and multidisciplinary review of its ethical acceptability;

(iv)   the persons undergoing research have been informed of their rights and the safeguards prescribed by law for their protection;

(v)   the necessary consent as provided for under Article 5 has been given expressly, specifically and is documented. Such consent may be freely withdrawn at any time.

Article 17
Protection of persons not able to consent to research

(1) Research on a person without the capacity to consent as stipulated in Article 5 may be undertaken only if all the following conditions are met:

(i)   the conditions laid down in Article 16, sub-paragraphs i to iv, are fulfilled;

(ii)   the results of the research have the potential to produce real and direct benefit to his or her health;

(iii)   research of comparable effectiveness cannot be carried out on individuals capable of giving consent;

(iv)   the necessary authorisation provided for under Article 6 has been given specifically and in writing; and

(v)   the person concerned does not object.

(2) Exceptionally and under the protective conditions prescribed by law, where the research has not the potential to produce results of direct benefit to the health of the person concerned, such research may be authorised subject to the conditions laid down in paragraph 1, sub-paragraphs i, iii, iv and v above, and to the following additional conditions:

(i)   the research has the aim of contributing, through significant improvement in the scientific understanding of the individual's condition, disease or disorder, to the ultimate attainment of results capable of conferring benefit to the person concerned or to other persons in the same age category or afflicted with the same disease or disorder or having the same condition;

(ii)   the research entails only minimal risk and minimal burden for the individual concerned.

Article 18
Research on embryos *in vitro*

(1) Where the law allows research on embryos *in vitro*, it shall ensure adequate protection of the embryo.

(2) The creation of human embryos for research purposes is prohibited.

Chapter VI – Organ and tissue removal from living donors for transplantation purposes

Article 19
General rule

(1) Removal of organs or tissue from a living person for transplantation purposes may be carried out solely for the therapeutic benefit of the recipient and where there is no suitable organ or tissue available from a deceased person and no other alternative therapeutic method of comparable effectiveness.

(2) The necessary consent as provided for under Article 5 must have been given expressly and specifically either in written form or before an official body.

Article 20
Protection of persons not able to consent to organ removal

(1) No organ or tissue removal may be carried out on a person who does not have the capacity to consent under Article 5.

(2) Exceptionally and under the protective conditions prescribed by law, the removal of regenerative tissue from a person who does not have the capacity to consent may be authorised provided the following conditions are met:

    (i)   there is no compatible donor available who has the capacity to consent;

    (ii) the recipient is a brother or sister of the donor;

    (iii) the donation must have the potential to be life-saving for the recipient;

(iv) the authorisation provided for under paragraphs 2 and 3 of Article 6 has been given specifically and in writing, in accordance with the law and with the approval of the competent body;

(v) the potential donor concerned does not object.

Chapter VII – Prohibition of financial gain and disposal of a part of the human body

Article 21
Prohibition of financial gain

The human body and its parts shall not, as such, give rise to financial gain.

Article 22
Disposal of a removed part of the human body

When in the course of an intervention any part of a human body is removed, it may be stored and used for a purpose other than that for which it was removed, only if this is done in conformity with appropriate information and consent procedures.

Chapter VIII – Infringements of the provisions of the Convention

Article 23
Infringement of the rights or principles

The Parties shall provide appropriate judicial protection to prevent or to put a stop to an unlawful infringement of the rights and principles set forth in this Convention at short notice.

Article 24
Compensation for undue damage.

The person who has suffered undue damage resulting from an intervention is entitled to fair compensation according to the conditions and procedures prescribed by law.

Article 25
Sanctions

Parties shall provide for appropriate sanctions to be applied in the event of infringement of the provisions contained in this Convention.

Chapter IX – Relation between this Convention and other provisions

Article 26
Restrictions on the exercise of the rights

(1) No restrictions shall be placed on the exercise of the rights and protective provisions contained in this Convention other than such as are prescribed by law and are necessary in a democratic society in the interest of public safety, for the prevention of crime, for the protection of public health or for the protection of the rights and freedoms of others.

(2) The restrictions contemplated in the preceding paragraph may not be placed on Articles 11, 13, 14, 16, 17, 19, 20 and 21.

Article 27
Wider protection

None of the provisions of this Convention shall be interpreted as limiting or otherwise affecting the possibility for a Party to grant a wider measure of protection with regard to the application of biology and medicine than is stipulated in this Convention.

Chapter X – Public debate

Article 28
Public debate

Parties to this Convention shall see to it that the fundamental questions raised by the developments of biology and medicine are the subject of appropriate public discussion in the light, in particular, of relevant medical, social, economic, ethical and legal implications, and that their possible application is made the subject of appropriate consultation.

Chapter XI – Interpretation and follow-up of the Convention

Article 29
Interpretation of the Convention

The European Court of Human Rights may give, without direct reference to any specific proceedings pending in a court, advisory opinions on legal questions concerning the interpretation of the present Convention at the request of:

- the Government of a Party, after having informed the other Parties;
- the Committee set up by Article 32, with membership restricted to the Representatives of the Parties to this Convention, by a decision adopted by a two-thirds majority of votes cast.

Article 30
Reports on the application of the Convention

On receipt of a request from the Secretary General of the Council of Europe any Party shall furnish an explanation of the manner in which its internal law ensures the effective implementation of any of the provisions of the Convention.

Chapter XII – Protocols

Article 31
Protocols

Protocols may be concluded in pursuance of Article 32, with a view to developing, in specific fields, the principles contained in this Convention.

The Protocols shall be open for signature by Signatories of the Convention. They shall be subject to ratification, acceptance or approval. A Signatory may not ratify, accept or approve Protocols without previously or simultaneously ratifying accepting or approving the Convention.

Chapter XIII – Amendments to the Convention

Article 32
Amendments to the Convention

(1) The tasks assigned to "the Committee" in the present article and in Article 29 shall be carried out by the Steering Committee on Bioethics (CDBI), or by any other committee designated to do so by the Committee of Ministers.

(2) Without prejudice to the specific provisions of Article 29, each member State of the Council of Europe, as well as each Party to the present Convention which is not a member of the Council of Europe, may be represented and have one vote in the Committee when the Committee carries out the tasks assigned to it by the present Convention.

(3) Any State referred to in Article 33 or invited to accede to the Convention in accordance with the provisions of Article 34 which is not Party to this Convention may be represented on the Committee by an observer. If the European Community is not a Party it may be represented on the Committee by an observer.

(4) In order to monitor scientific developments, the present Convention shall be examined within the Committee no later than five years from its entry into force and thereafter at such intervals as the Committee may determine.

(5) Any proposal for an amendment to this Convention, and any proposal for a Protocol or for an amendment to a Protocol, presented by a Party, the Committee or the Committee of Ministers shall be communicated to the Secretary General of the Council of Europe and forwarded by him to the member States of the Council of Europe, to the European Community, to any Signatory, to any Party, to any State invited to sign this Convention in accordance with the provisions of Article 33 and to any State invited to accede to it in accordance with the provisions of Article 34.

(6) The Committee shall examine the proposal not earlier than two months after it has been forwarded by the Secretary General in accordance with paragraph 5. The Committee shall submit the text adopted by a two-thirds majority of the votes cast to the Committee of Ministers for approval. After its approval, this text shall be forwarded to the Parties for ratification, acceptance or approval.

(7) Any amendment shall enter into force, in respect of those Parties which have accepted it, on the first day of the month following the expiration of a period of one month after the date on which five Parties, including at least four member States of the Council of Europe, have informed the Secretary General that they have accepted it. In respect of any Party which subsequently accepts it, the amendment shall enter into force on the first day of the month following the expiration of a period of one month after the date on which that Party has informed the Secretary General of its acceptance.

Chapter XIV – Final clauses

Article 33
Signature, ratification and entry into force

(1) This Convention shall be open for signature by the member States of the Council of.Europe, the non-member States which have participated in its elaboration and by the European Community.

(2) This Convention is subject to ratification, acceptance or approval. Instruments of ratification, acceptance or approval shall be deposited with the Secretary General of the Council of Europe.

(3) This Convention shall enter into force on the first day of the month following the expiration of a period of three months after the date on which five States, including at least four member States of the Council

of Europe, have expressed their consent to be bound by the Convention in accordance with the provisions of paragraph 2 of the present article.

(4) In respect of any Signatory which subsequently expresses its consent to be bound by it, the Convention shall enter into force on the first day of the month following the expiration of a period of three months after the date of the deposit of its instrument of ratification, acceptance or approval.

Article 34
Non-member States

(1) After the entry into force of this Convention, the Committee of Ministers of the Council of Europe may, after consultation of the Parties, invite any non-member State of the Council of Europe to accede to this Convention by a decision taken by the majority provided for in Article 20, paragraph d, of the Statute of the Council of Europe, and by the unanimous vote of the representatives of the Contracting States entitled to sit on the Committee of Ministers.

(2) In respect of any acceding State, the Convention shall enter into force on the first day of the month following the expiration of a period of three months after the date of deposit of the instrument of accession with the Secretary General of the Council of Europe.

Article 35
Territories

(1) Any Signatory may, at the time of signature or when depositing its instrument of ratification, acceptance or approval, specify the territory or territories to which this Convention shall apply. Any other State may formulate the same declaration when depositing its instrument of accession.

(2) Any Party may, at any later date, by a declaration addressed to the Secretary General of the Council of Europe, extend the application of this Convention to any other territory specified in the declaration and for whose international relations it is responsible or on whose behalf it is authorised to give undertakings. In respect of such territory the Convention shall enter into force on the first day of the month

following the expiration of a period of three months after the date of receipt of such declaration by the Secretary General.

(3) Any declaration made under the two preceding paragraphs may, in respect of any territory specified in such declaration, be withdrawn by a notification addressed to the Secretary General. The withdrawal shall become effective on the first day of the month following the expiration of a period of three months after the date of receipt of such notification by the Secretary General.

Article 36
Reservations

(1) Any State and the European Community may, when signing this Convention or when depositing the instrument of ratification, acceptance, approval or accession, make a reservation in respect of any particular provision of the Convention to the extent that any law then in force in its territory is not in conformity with the provision. Reservations of a general character shall not be permitted under this article.

(2) Any reservation made under this article shall contain a brief statement of the relevant law.

(3) Any Party which extends the application of this Convention to a territory mentioned in the declaration referred to in Article 35, paragraph 2, may, in respect of the territory concerned, make a reservation in accordance with the provisions of the preceding paragraphs.

(4) Any Party which has made the reservation mentioned in this article may withdraw it by means of a declaration addressed to the Secretary General of the Council of Europe. The withdrawal shall become effective on the first day of the month following the expiration of a period of one month after the date of its receipt by the Secretary General.

Article 37
Denunciation

(1) Any Party may at any time denounce this Convention by means of a notification addressed to the Secretary General of the Council of Europe.

(2) Such denunciation shall become effective on the first day of the month following the expiration of a period of three months after the date of receipt of the notification by the Secretary General.

Article 38
Notifications

The Secretary General of the Council of Europe shall notify the member States of the Council, the European Community, any Signatory, any Party and any other State which has been invited to accede to this Convention of:

a) any signature;

b) the deposit of any instrument of ratification, acceptance, approval or accession;

c) any date of entry into force of this Convention in accordance with Articles 33 or 34;

d) any amendment or Protocol adopted in accordance with Article 32, and the date on which such an amendment or Protocol enters into force;

e) any declaration made under the provisions of Article 35;

f) any reservation and withdrawal of reservation made in pursuance of the provisions of Article 36;

g) any other act, notification or communication relating to this Convention.

In witness whereof the undersigned, being duly authorised thereto, have signed this Convention.

Done at Oviedo (Asturias), this 4th day of April 1997, in English and French, both texts being equally authentic, in a single copy which shall be deposited in the archives of the Council of Europe. The Secretary General of the Council of Europe shall transmit certified copies to each member State of the Council of Europe, to the European Community, to the non-member States which have participated in the elaboration of this Convention, and to any State invited to accede to this Convention.

IV. European Union

16. Charter of Fundamental Rights of the European Union (excerpts)

O.J. C 364/01, p. 1
18 December 2000

Preamble

The peoples of Europe, in creating an ever closer union among them, are resolved to share a peaceful future based on common values.

Conscious of its spiritual and moral heritage, the Union is founded on the indivisible, universal values of human dignity, freedom, equality and solidarity; it is based on the principles of democracy and the rule of law. It places the individual at the heart of its activities, by establishing the citizenship of the Union and by creating an area of freedom, security and justice.

The Union contributes to the preservation and to the development of these common values while respecting the diversity of the cultures and traditions of the peoples of Europe as well as the national identities of the Member States and the organisation of their public authorities at national, regional and local levels; it seeks to promote balanced and sustainable development and ensures free movement of persons, goods, services and capital, and the freedom of establishment.

To this end, it is necessary to strengthen the protection of fundamental rights in the light of changes in society, social progress and scientific and technological developments by making those rights more visible in a Charter.

This Charter reaffirms, with due regard for the powers and tasks of the Community and the Union and the principle of subsidiarity, the rights as they result, in particular, from the constitutional traditions and international obligations common to the Member States, the Treaty on European Union, the Community Treaties, the European Convention for the Protection of Human Rights and Fundamental Freedoms, the Social Charters adopted by the Community and by the Council of Europe and the case-law of the Court of Justice of the European Communities and of the European Court of Human Rights.

Enjoyment of these rights entails responsibilities and duties with regard to other persons, to the human community and to future generations.

The Union therefore recognises the rights, freedoms and principles set out hereafter.

Chapter I – Dignity

Article 1
Human dignity

Human dignity is inviolable. It must be respected and protected.

Article 2
Right to life

1. Everyone has the right to life.
2. No one shall be condemned to the death penalty, or executed.

Article 3
Right to the integrity of the person

1. Everyone has the right to respect for his or her physical and mental integrity.
2. In the fields of medicine and biology, the following must be respected in particular:
    - the free and informed consent of the person concerned, according to the procedures laid down by law,

- the prohibition of eugenic practices, in particular those aiming at the selection of persons,
- the prohibition on making the human body and its parts as such a source of financial gain,
- the prohibition of the reproductive cloning of human beings.

Article 4
Prohibition of torture and inhuman or degrading treatment or punishment

No one shall be subjected to torture or to inhuman or degrading treatment or punishment.

Article 5
Prohibition of slavery and forced labour

1. No one shall be held in slavery or servitude.
2. No one shall be required to perform forced or compulsory labour.
3. Trafficking in human beings is prohibited.

Chapter II – Freedoms

Article 6
Right to liberty and security

Everyone has the right to liberty and security of person.

Article 7
Respect for private and family life

Everyone has the right to respect for his or her private and family life, home and communications.

Article 8
Protection of personal data

1. Everyone has the right to the protection of personal data concerning him or her.

2. Such data must be processed fairly for specified purposes and on the basis of the consent of the person concerned or some other legitimate basis laid down by law. Everyone has the right of access to data which has been collected concerning him or her, and the right to have it rectified.

3. Compliance with these rules shall be subject to control by an independent authority.

Article 9
Right to marry and right to found a family

The right to marry and the right to found a family shall be guaranteed in accordance with the national laws governing the exercise of these rights.

Article 10
Freedom of thought, conscience and religion

1. Everyone has the right to freedom of thought, conscience and religion. This right includes freedom to change religion or belief and freedom, either alone or in community with others and in public or in private, to manifest religion or belief, in worship, teaching, practice and observance.

2. The right to conscientious objection is recognised, in accordance with the national laws governing the exercise of this right.

Article 11
Freedom of expression and information

1. Everyone has the right to freedom of expression. This right shall include freedom to hold opinions and to receive and impart information and ideas without interference by public authority and regardless of frontiers.

2. The freedom and pluralism of the media shall be respected.

Article 12
Freedom of assembly and of association

1. Everyone has the right to freedom of peaceful assembly and to freedom of association at all levels, in particular in political, trade union and civic matters, which implies the right of everyone to form and to join trade unions for the protection of his or her interests.

2. Political parties at Union level contribute to expressing the political will of the citizens of the Union.

Article 13
Freedom of the arts and sciences

The arts and scientific research shall be free of constraint. Academic freedom shall be respected.

Article 14
Right to education

1. Everyone has the right to education and to have access to vocational and continuing training.

2. This right includes the possibility to receive free compulsory education.

3. The freedom to found educational establishments with due respect for democratic principles and the right of parents to ensure the education and teaching of their children in conformity with their religious, philosophical and pedagogical convictions shall be respected, in accordance with the national laws governing the exercise of such freedom and right.

17. European Parliament Resolution on Human Cloning

B5-0710, 0751, 0753 and 0764/2000
7 September 2000

The European Parliament,

- having regard to the proposal by the United Kingdom Government to permit medical research using embryos created by cell nuclear replacement (so-called 'therapeutic cloning'),
- having regard to its resolutions of 16 March 1989 on the ethical and legal problems of genetic engineering[1] and on artificial insemination 'in vivo' and 'in vitro'[2], of 28 October 1993 on the cloning of the human embryo[3], of 12 March 1997 on cloning[4], of 15 January 1998 on human cloning[5], and of 30 March 2000[6],
- having regard to the Council of Europe's Convention for the protection of human rights and dignity of the human being with regard to the application of biology and medicine – the Convention on human rights and biomedicine – and its own resolution of 20 September 1996 on this subject[7], and the additional protocol which forbids the cloning of human beings,
- having regard to Recommendation 1046 of the Parliamentary Assembly of the Council of Europe on the use of human embryos,
- having regard to the Community's Fifth Framework Research Programme and specific programmes thereunder,

---

[1] OJ C 96, 17.4.1989, p. 165.

[2] OJ C 96, 17.4.1989, p. 171.

[3] OJ C 315, 22.11.1993, p. 224.

[4] OJ C 115, 14.4.1997, p. 92.

[5] OJ C 34, 2.2.1998, p. 164.

[6] Texts Adopted, Item 9.

[7] OJ C 320, 20.9.1996, p. 268.

- having regard to Directive 98/44/EC of the European Parliament and of the Council of 6 July 1998 on the legal protection of biotechnological inventions[8],

A.   whereas human dignity and the consequent value of each human being are the main aims of Member States, as stated in many modern constitutions,

B.   whereas the undoubted need for medical research resulting from advances in knowledge of human genetics must be balanced against strict ethical and social constraints,

C.   whereas there are other ways than embryonic cloning of curing serious illnesses, such as those that involve taking stem cells from adults or from the umbilical cords of new-born babies, and other external causes of disease which require research,

D.   whereas the Fifth Framework programme and Council Decision 1999/167/EC of 25 January 1999 adopting a specific programme for research, technological development and demonstration on quality of life and management of living resources (1998 to 2002) state 'In the same way, no research activity understood in the sense of the term "cloning", with the aim of replacing a germ or embryo cell nucleus with that of the cell of any individual, a cell from an embryo or a cell coming from a later stage of development to the human embryo, will be supported',

E.   whereas therefore there is a prohibition on the use of Community funds, either directly or indirectly, for any such research,

F.   whereas aforementioned Directive 98/44/EC states that there is a consensus within the Community that interventions in the human germ line and the cloning of human beings offends against ordre public and morality,

G.   whereas an attempt is being made to use linguistic sleight of hand to erode the moral significance of human cloning,

H.   whereas there is no difference between cloning for therapeutic purposes and cloning for the purposes of reproduction, and whereas any relaxation of the present ban will lead to pressure for further developments in embryo production and usage,

I.   whereas Parliament defines human cloning as the creation of human embryos having the same genetic make-up as another

---

[8]   OJ L 213, 30.7.1998, p. 13.

human being, dead or alive, at any stage of their development, without any possible distinction as regards the method used,

J. whereas the proposals of the United Kingdom Government require the assent of the Members of both Houses of the United Kingdom Parliament, who are to be permitted a free vote of conscience on the issue,

1. Believes that human rights and respect for human dignity and human life must be the constant aim of political legislative activity;

2. Considers that 'therapeutic cloning', which involves the creation of human embryos solely for research purposes, poses a profound ethical dilemma, irreversibly crosses a boundary in research norms and is contrary to public policy as adopted by the European Union;

3. Calls on the UK Government to review its position on human embryo cloning and calls on its honourable colleagues, the Members of the United Kingdom Parliament, to exercise their votes of conscience and reject the proposal to permit research using embryos created by cell nuclear transfer when it is laid before them;

4. Repeats its call to each Member State to enact binding legislation prohibiting all research into any kind of human cloning within its territory and providing for criminal penalties for any breach;

5. Urges maximum political, legislative, scientific and economic efforts to be aimed at therapies that use stem cells taken from adult subjects;

6. Reaffirms its support for biotechnological scientific research in medicine, provided that is balanced against strict ethical and social constraints;

7. Renews its call for human artificial insemination techniques that do not produce an excess number of embryos in order to avoid generating superfluous embryos;

8. Calls on the appropriate national and Community authorities to ensure that the ban on patenting or cloning human beings is reaffirmed and to adopt rules to this end;

9. Calls on the Commission to guarantee full respect for the terms of the Fifth Framework Programme and all specific

programmes thereunder, and points out that the best way to implement this decision is to ensure that no research institution that is in any way involved in the cloning of human embryos gets money from the EU budget for any of their work;

10. Repeats its insistence that there should be a universal and specific ban at the level of the United Nations on the cloning of human beings at all stages of formation and development;

11. Considers that any temporary committee set up by this Parliament to examine the ethical and legal issues raised by new developments in the field of human genetics should take as a starting point the views already expressed in resolutions of this House. The committee should examine questions for which Parliament has not yet expressed a clear position. Its powers, composition and term of office shall be defined on a proposal from the Conference of Presidents, without any limitation of the powers of the permanent committee responsible for matters relating to the monitoring and the application of Community law on these issues;

12. Instructs its President to forward this resolution to the Commission, the Council, the governments of the Member States, the Members of the UK Parliament, and the Secretary-General of the United Nations.

18. European Parliament Resolution on Cloning

O.J. C 115/97, p. 92
12 March 1997

The European Parliament,

- having regard to the alarm caused by the announcement on 24 February 1997 from the Roslin Institute and Pharmaceutical Proteins Ltd of Scotland of the production of a sheep cloned from an adult cell and the possibility of such reproductive techniques being used to produce human embryos,

- having regard to its resolutions of 16 March 1989 on the ethical and legal problems of genetic engineering[1] and artificial insemination 'in vivo' and 'in vitro'[2] and 28 October 1993 on the cloning of human embryos[3],

- having regard to the Council of Europe's Convention for the Protection of Human Rights and Dignity of the Human Being with regard to the Application of Biology and Medicine ('Bioethics Convention')[4], and Parliament's resolution of 20 September 1996 thereon[5],

- having regard to the reports of the Commission's ethical advisory group on biotechnology,

- having regard to recommendation 1046 of the Parliamentary Assembly of the Council of Europe on the use of human embryos[6],

---

[1] OJ C 96, 17.4.1989, p. 165.

[2] OJ C 96, 17.4.1989, p. 171.

[3] OJ C 315, 22.11.1993, p. 224.

[4] Adopted by the Committee of Ministers on 19 November 1996, document DIR/JUR(96)14 of the Directorate of Legal Affairs of the Council of Europe.

[5] OJ C 320, 28.11.1996, p. 268.

[6] Recommendation 1046 (1986) adopted on 24 September 1986 (18th sitting).

- confirming its opposition to the cloning of human embryos, the position it adopted in its resolutions of 1989 and 1993 referred to above,

A. whereas cloning breaks new ethical ground and has led to great public concern,

B. in the clear conviction that the cloning of human beings, whether experimentally, in the context of fertility treatment, preimplantation diagnosis, tissue transplantation or for any other purpose whatsoever, cannot under any circumstances be justified or tolerated by any society, because it is a serious violation of fundamental human rights and is contrary to the principle of equality of human beings as it permits a eugenic and racist selection of the human race, it offends against human dignity and it requires experimentation on humans,

C. whereas there is a need to ensure that the benefits of biotechnology are not lost as a result of sensationalist and alarmist information,

D. whereas adequate methods of regulating and policing developments in the field of genetics must be established,

E. whereas all necessary information must be made available to the public, and the EU must now take the lead in promoting full public consideration of these questions,

F. whereas the Convention on Human Rights and Biomedicine does not expressly ban the cloning of human beings, and in any event is not yet in force in any EU Member State,

G. whereas some Member States have no national legislation prohibiting the cloning of human beings,

H. whereas cloning of humans for all purposes should be banned in the EU,

I. whereas international action is required,

1. Stresses that each individual has a right to his or her own genetic identity and that human cloning is, and must continue to be, prohibited;

2. Calls for an explicit worldwide ban on the cloning of human beings;

3. Urges the Member States to ban the cloning of human beings at all stages of formation and development, regardless of the method used, and to provide for penal sanctions to deal with any violation;

4. Calls on the Commission to report to it on any research carried out in this field on Community territory and on the legal framework existing in the Member States;

5. Calls on the Commission to check whether human cloning could form part of research programmes financed by the Community and, if so, to block the appropriations for them;

6. Believes it is essential to establish ethical standards, based on respect for human dignity, in the areas of biology, biotechnology and medicine;

7. Believes that it is desirable for such standards to apply globally and that they should conform to a high level of protection;

8. Considers that the direct protection of the dignity and rights of individuals is of absolute priority as compared with any social or third- party interest;

9. Calls for the establishment of a European Union Ethics Committee to assess ethical aspects of applications of gene technology and to monitor developments in this field; calls on the Commission to submit proposals for the composition and terms of reference of the committee under the procedure set out in Article 189b of the EC Treaty, while ensuring that it is constituted with full respect for transparency and democratic principles, and that all appropriate interested groups are represented;

10. Considers that, in view of the universality of the principles relating to the dignity of the human being, efforts must be made by the European Union, its Member States and the United Nations to promote worldwide governance on this issue and to promote and put into effect binding international agreements in order to ensure that such principles are applied worldwide;

11. Calls on researchers and doctors engaged in research on the human genome to abstain spontaneously from participating in the cloning of human beings until the entry into force of a legally binding ban;

12. Aknowledges that research in the field of biotechnology, in particular the manufacture of proteins, medicines and vaccines for human use, could help to combat certain diseases;

13. Considers that the international scientific community and governments should provide the public with complete and up-

to-date information on current research relating to gene technology;

14. Calls on the Commission, in connection with its research programmes, to prepare a recommendation concerning bioethics laying down strict limits on its research in accordance with respect for human life and to consider, if necessary, whether action at Community level is necessary;

15. Calls on the Commission to propose Community legislation on animal cloning and in particular on the new scientific developments, with strict controls to guarantee human health and the continuation of animal species and races and to safeguard biological diversity;

16. Instructs its President to forward this resolution to the Commission, the Council, the governments of the Member States, the Secretary-General and Parliamentary Assembly of the Council of Europe and the Secretary- General of the United Nations.

V. German Law

19. Act Ensuring Protection of Embryos in Connection with the Importation and Utilization of Human Embryonic Stem Cells (Stammzellgesetz)

28 June 2002
(Inofficial translation of the German Federal Ministry of Justice)

The Bundestag has adopted the following Act:

Section 1
Purpose of the Act

In consideration of the State's obligation to respect and protect human dignity and the right to life and to guarantee the freedom of research, the purpose of the present Act is

1. to ban, as a matter of principle, the importation and utilization of embryonic stem cells,

2. to prevent demand in Germany from causing the derivation of embryonic stem cells or the production of embryos with the aim of deriving embryonic stem cells, and

3. to determine the requirements for permitting, as an exception, the importation and utilization of embryonic stem cells for research purposes.

Section 2
Scope

The present Act shall apply to the importation and utilization of embryonic stem cells.

Section 3
Definitions

For the purpose of the present Act

1. stem cells mean all human cells which have the potential to multiply by cell division if in a suitable environment and which by themselves or through their daughter cells are capable, under favourable conditions, of developing into specialized cells, not, however, into a human being (pluripotent stem cells),

2. embryonic stem cells mean all pluripotent stem cells derived from embryos which have been produced in vitro and have not been used to induce pregnancy or which have been taken from a woman before completion of nidation,

3. embryonic stem cell lines mean all embryonic stem cells which are kept in culture or those which are subsequently stored using cryopreservation methods,

4. embryo means any human totipotent cell which has the potential to divide and to develop into a human being if the necessary conditions prevail,

5. importation means the introduction of embryonic stem cells into the territorial scope of the present Act.

Section 4
Importation and utilization of embryonic stem cells

(1) The importation and utilization of embryonic stem cells shall be prohibited.

(2) Notwithstanding para 1, the importation and utilization of embryonic stem cells for research purposes shall be permissible under the conditions stipulated in section 6 if

1. the competent agency has satisfied itself that

   a) the embryonic stem cells were derived before 1 January 2002 in the country of origin in accordance with relevant national legislation there and are kept in culture or are subsequently stored using cryopreservation methods (embryonic stem cell line),

   b) the embryos from which they were derived have been produced by medically-assisted in vitro fertilization in order to induce pregnancy and were definitely no longer used for this purpose and that there is no evidence that this was due to reasons inherent in the embryos themselves,

   c) no compensation or other benefit in money's worth has been granted or promised for the donation of embryos for the purpose of stem cell derivation and if

2. other legal provisions, in particular those of the German Embryo Protection Act , do not conflict with the importation or utilization of embryonic stem cells.

(3) Approval shall be refused if the embryonic stem cells have obviously been derived in contradiction to major principles of the German legal system. Approval may not be refused by arguing that the stem cells have been derived from human embryos.

Section 5
Research using embryonic stem cells

Research involving embryonic stem cells shall not be conducted unless it has been shown by giving scientific reasons that

1. such research serves eminent research aims to generate scientific knowledge in basic research or to increase medical knowledge for the development of diagnostic, preventive or therapeutic methods to be applied to humans and that,

2. according to the state-of-the-art of science and technology,

   a) the questions to be studied in the research project concerned have been clarified as far as possible through in vitro models using animal cells or through animal experiments and

   b) the scientific knowledge to be obtained from the research project concerned cannot be expected to be gained by using cells other than embryonic stem cells.

Section 6
Approval

(1) Any importation and any utilization of embryonic stem cells shall be subject to approval by the competent agency.

(2) Applications for approval must be submitted in writing. In the documents accompanying the application, the applicant shall provide the following information in particular:

1. Name and official address of the person responsible for the research project concerned,

2. a description of the research project including scientific reasons showing that the research project meets the requirements set forth in section 5 above,

3. a documentation concerning the embryonic stem cells to be imported or used showing that the requirements set forth in no. 1 of para 2 of section 4 above have been complied with or equivalent evidence that

   a) the embryonic stem cells to be imported or used are identical with those registered in a scientifically recognized, publicly accessible registry maintained by government agencies or agencies authorized by the government and that,

   b) by way of such registration, the requirements set forth in no. 1 of para 2 of section 4 above have been complied with.

(3) The competent agency shall immediately acknowledge in writing receipt of the application and the attached documents. At the same time, the agency shall request the opinion of the Central Ethics Commission on Stem Cell Research. On receipt of the opinion, the agency shall notify the applicant of the content and the date of the opinion adopted by the Central Ethics Commission on Stem Cell Research.

(4) Approval shall be given if

1. the requirements set forth in para 2 of section 4 above have been complied with,

2. the requirements set forth in section 5 above have been complied with and, accordingly, the research project is ethically acceptable, and if

3. an opinion by the Central Ethics Commission on Stem Cell Research has been submitted following a request by the competent agency to this effect.

(5) If the application, complete with documentation, and the opinion of the Central Ethics Commission on Stem Cell Research have been received, the agency shall decide in writing on the application within a period of two months. In doing so, the agency shall consider the opinion adopted by the Central Ethics Commission on Stem Cell Research. If the competent agency's decision differs from the opinion adopted by the Central Ethics Commission on Stem Cell Research, the agency shall give its reasons in writing.

(6) Approval can be limited in time or by imposing obligations to the extent necessary for complying with or continuing to meet the approval requirements pursuant to para 4 above. If, following approval, events occur which conflict with the granting of approval, approval can be withdrawn wholly or in part with effect in the future or be limited in time or be made dependent on the fulfilment of conditions to the extent necessary for complying with or continuing to meet the approval requirements set forth in para 4 above. Any objection to or action for rescission of withdrawal or revocation of approval shall not suspend the effect of the decision.

Section 7
Competent agency

(1) The Federal Ministry for Health shall determine by ordinance which authority in its portfolio shall be the competent agency. The agency shall discharge – as federal administrative tasks – the duties assigned to it by virtue of the present Act and shall be supervised by the Federal Ministry for Health.

(2) Costs (fees and expenses) shall be charged for official acts performed by virtue of the present Act. The law on administrative costs shall apply. In addition to the exemption of the legal entities mentioned in para 1 of section 8 of the law on administrative costs, non-profit research organizations shall be exempt from paying any fees.

(3) The Federal Ministry for Health shall be authorized to determine, by ordinance and in agreement with the Federal Ministry of Education and Research, the acts which shall be subject to a fee, providing for fixed rates or tiered rates. In fixing such rates, the importance, the commercial value or any other benefit arising from approval for those having to pay fees shall be taken into account. The ordinance can

provide for a fee to be charged for an uncompleted official act if the person who requested the official act is responsible for noncompletion.

(4) The applicants' own expenses incurred in the course of providing the information the agency requires to decide on approval shall not be reimbursed.

Section 8
The Central Ethics Commission on Stem Cell Research

(1) An independent, interdisciplinary Central Ethics Commission on Stem Cell Research shall be established at the competent agency; it shall be composed of nine experts from the disciplines of biology, ethics, medicine and theology. The experts to be nominated shall include four members from the disciplines of ethics and theology and five scientists from the fields of biology and medicine. The Commission shall elect a chair and a deputy chair from among ist members.

(2) The members of the Central Ethics Commission on Stem Cell Research shall be appointed by the Federal Government for a three years' term. Reappointment is possible. As a rule, a deputy shall be appointed for each member.

(3) The members and their deputies shall be independent and not bound by instructions. They shall be obliged to observe secrecy. Sections 20 and 21 of the Law on Administrative Procedures shall apply mutatis mutandis.

(4) The Federal Government shall be authorized to enact an ordinance specifying the details concerning the appointment of, and the procedure to be followed by, the Central Ethics Commission on Stem Cell Research, the invitation of external experts, and cooperation with the competent agency including deadlines.

Section 9
Duties of the Central Ethics Commission on Stem Cell Research

The Central Ethics Commission on Stem Cell Research shall examine and evaluate applications and accompanying documents in order to determine whether the requirements set forth in section 5 above have been complied with and, accordingly, the research project is ethically acceptable.

Section 10
Confidentiality

(1) The application documents referred to in section 6 above shall be treated as confidential.

(2) Notwithstanding para 1 above, the following data may be entered into the registry referred to in section 11 below:

1. the information to be provided on the embryonic stem cells in accordance with no. 1 of para 2 of section 4 above,

2. the name and official address of the person responsible for the research project,

3. basic data concerning the research project, in particular a brief description of the planned research specifying the reasons for ist eminence, naming the institution where the research will be conducted and indicating ist expected duration.

(3) If an application is withdrawn before a decision on approval has been made, the competent agency shall delete the data stored in connection with the application and return such application and accompanying documents.

Section 11
Registry

Information on the embryonic stem cells and basic data concerning approved research projects shall be registered by the competent agency in a publicly accessible registry.

Section 12
Obligation to notify

The person responsible for the research project has to notify the competent agency without delay of any major changes occurring after application which affect the permissibility of the importation or utilization of the embryonic stem cells in question. Section 6 shall remain unaffected.

Section 13
Penal provisions

(1) Any person who imports or uses embryonic stem cells without having obtained approval pursuant to para 1 of section 6 above shall be punished with imprisonment of up to three years or shall be fined. Any person who obtains approval by deliberately giving false information shall be deemed to have acted without approval within the meaning of the preceding sentence. The attempt shall be punishable.

(2) Any person who fails to meet a binding requirement imposed pursuant to the first or second sentence of para 6 of section 6 above shall be punished with imprisonment of up to one year or shall be fined.

Section 14
Provisions on administrative fines

(1) An administrative offence shall be deemed to be committed by any person who,

1. contrary to the second sentence of para 2 of section 6 above, provides incorrect or incomplete information or,

2. contrary to the first sentence of section 12 above, does not notify changes or gives an incorrect, incomplete or belated notification.

(2) The administrative offence can be punished with an administrative fine of up to fifty thousand Euro.

Section 15
Report

The Federal Government shall submit to the Deutscher Bundestag a report presenting the experience gained with the implementation of the present Act every two years, beginning at the end of 2003. The report shall also describe the results of research using other types of human stem cells.

Section 16
Entry into force

The present Act shall enter into force on the first day of the month following promulgation.

20. Act for Protection of Embryos (Embryonenschutzgesetz)

13 December 1990
(Inofficial translation of the German Federal Ministry of Justice)

The following Act has been adopted by the Bundestag:

Section 1
Improper use of reproduction technology

(1) Anyone will be punished with up to three years imprisonment or a fine, who

1. transfers into a woman an unfertilised egg cell produced by another woman,

2. attempts to fertilise artificially an egg cell for any purpose other than bringing about a pregnancy of the woman from whom the egg cell originated,

3. attempts, within one treatment cycle, to transfer more than three embryos into an woman,

4. attempts, by gamete intrafallopian transfer, to fertilise more than three egg cells within one treatment cycle,

5. attempts to fertilise more egg cells from a woman than may be transferred to her within one treatment cycle,

6. removes an embryo from a woman before completion of implantation in the uterus, in order to transfer it to another woman or to use it for another purpose not serving its preservation, or

7. attempts to carry out an artificial fertilisation of a woman who is prepared to give up her child permanently after birth (surrogate mother) or to transfer a human embryo into her.

(2) Likewise anyone will be punished who

1. brings about artificially the penetration of a human egg cell by a human sperm cell, or

2. transfers a human sperm cell into a human egg cell artificially,

without intending to bring about a pregnancy in the woman from whom the egg cell originated.

(3)

1. In the case of paragraph 1, number 1, 2 and 6, the woman from whom the egg cell or embryo originated, and likewise the woman into whom the egg cell or embryo will be transferred, and

2. in the case of paragraph 1, number 7, the surrogate mother and likewise the person who wishes to take long-term care of the child, will not be punished.

(4) In the case of paragraph 1, number 6, and paragraph 2, any attempt is punishable.

Section 2
Improper use of human embryos

(1) Anyone who disposes of, or hands over or acquires or uses for a purpose not serving ist preservation, a human embryo produced outside the body, or removed from a woman before the completion of implantation in the uterus, will be punished with imprisonment up to three years or a fine.

(2) Likewise anyone will be punished who causes a human embryo to develop further outside the body for any purpose other than the bringing about of a pregnancy.

(3) Any attempt is punishable.

Section 3
Forbidden sex selection

Anyone who attempts to fertilise artificially a human egg cell with a sperm cell, that is selected for the sex chromosome contained in it, will be punished with up to one years's imprisonment or a fine. This does not apply when the selection of an sperm cell is made by a doctor in order to preserve the child from falling ill with Duchenne-type muscular dystrophy or a similarly severe sex-linked genetic illness, and the illness threatening the child is recognised as being of appropriate severity by the body responsible according to Land legislation.

Section 4
Unauthorised fertilisation, unauthorised embryo transfer and artificial fertilisation after death

(1) Anyone will be punished with up to three years imprisonment or a fine, who

1. attempts artificially to fertilise an egg cell without the woman, whose egg cell is to be fertilised, and the man, whose sperm cell will be used for fertilisation, having given consent,

2. attempts to transfer an embryo into an woman without her consent, or

3. knowingly fertilises artificially an egg cell with the sperm of a man after his death.

(2) In the case of paragraph 1 number 3, the woman by whom the artificial fertilisation was taken on will not be punished.

Section 5
Artificial alteration of human germ line cells

(1) Anyone who artificially alters the genetic information of a human germ line cell will be punished with imprisonment up to five years or a fine.

(2) Likewise anyone will be punished who uses a human germ cell with artificially altered genetic information for fertilisation.

(3) Any attempt is punishable.

(4) Paragraph 1 does not apply to

1. an artificial alteration of the genetic information of a germ cell situated outside the body, if any use of it for fertilisation has been ruled out,

2. an artificial alteration of the genetic information of a different body's germ line cell, that has been removed from a dead embryo, from a human being or from a deceased person, if it has ruled out that

    a) they will be transferred to an embryo, fetus or human being or

    b) a germ cell will originate from them,

    and likewise

3. inoculation, radiation, chemotherapeutic or other treatment by which an alteration of the genetic information of germ line cells is not intended.

Section 6
Cloning

(1) Anyone who causes artificially a human embryo to develop with the same genetic information as another embryo, fetus, human being or deceased person will be punished with imprisonment up to five years or a fine.

(2) Likewise anyone will be punished who transfers into a woman an embryo designated in paragraph 1.

(3) Any attempt is punishable.

Section 7
Formation of chimaerae and hybrids

(1) Anyone who attempts

1. to unite embryos with different genetic material to a cell conglomerate using at least one human embryo,

2. to join a human embryo with a cell that contains genetic information different from the embryo cells and induces them further to develop, or

3. by fertilisation of a human egg cell with the sperm of an animal or by fertilisation of an animal's egg cell with the sperm of a man to generate an embryo capable of development,

will be punished with imprisonment up to five years or a fine.

(2) Likewise anyone will be punished who attempts

1. to transfer an embryo arising out of a procedure defined in paragraph 1 to

   a) a woman or
   b) an animal

      or

2. to transfer an human embryo into an animal.

Section 8
Definition

(1) For the purpose of this Act, an embryo already means the human egg cell, fertilised and capable of developing, from the time of fusion of the nuclei, and further, each totipotent cell removed from an embryo that is assumed to be able to divide and to develop into an individual under the appropriate conditions for that.

(2) In the first twenty four hours after nuclear fusion, the fertilised human egg cell is held to capable of development except when it is established before expiry of this time period that it will not develop beyond the one cell stage.

(3) Germ line cells, for the purpose of this Act, are all cells that lead of the egg and sperm cells to the resultant human being and, further, the egg cell from capture or penetration of the sperm cell until the ending of fertilisation by fusion of the nuclei.

Section 9
Medical proviso

Only a physician may carry out
1. artificial fertilisation,
2. transfer of a human embryo into an women,
3. preservation of a human embryo or human egg cell which has already been penetrated by, or has artificially captured, a human sperm cell.

Section 10
Voluntary participation

No one is obliged to carry out the measures described in section 9 above or to take part in them.

Section 11
Offences against the medical proviso

(1) Anyone who, without being a physician,
1. carries out an artificial fertilisation contrary to section 9 number 1 or
2. transfers a human embryo into a woman contrary to section 9 number 2,

will be punished with up to one year's imprisonment or a fine.

(2) In the case of section 9 number 1, a woman who has carried out on her an artificial insemination, and the man whose sperm is used for artificial insemination will not be punished.

Section 12
Administrative fines

(1) An administrative offence shall be deemed to have been committed by a person who, without being a physician, in violation of section 9 number 3, preserves a human embryo or a human egg cell as described therein.

(2) The committing of an administrative offence may be punished with a fine not exceeding five thousand deutsche marks.

Section 13
Entry into force

The present Act shall enter into force on 1st January 1991.

21. Basic Law of the Federal Republic of Germany (excerpts) (Grundgesetz der Bundesrepublik Deutschland)

(Promulgated by the Parliamentary Council on 23 May 1949, as Amended by the Unification Treaty of 31 August 1990 and Federal Statute of 23 September 1990)

Preamble

Conscious of their responsibility before God and Men, Animated by the resolve to serve world peace as an equal partner in a united Europe, the German people have adopted, by virtue of their constituent power, this Basic Law.

The Germans in the Länder of Baden-Württemberg, Bavaria, Berlin, Brandenburg, Bremen, Hamburg, Hesse, Lower Saxony, Mecklenburg-Western Pomerania, North-Rhine-Westphalia, Rhineland-Palatinate, Saarland, Saxony, Saxony-Anhalt, Schleswig-Holstein, and Thuringia have achieved the unity and freedom of Germany in free self-determination. This Basic Law is thus valid for the entire German People.

Basic Rights

Article 1
Protection of human dignity

(1) The dignity of man is inviolable. To respect and protect it is the duty of all state authority.

(2) The German people therefore acknowledge inviolable and inalienable human rights as the basis of every community, of peace and of justice in the world.

(3) The following basic rights bind the legislature, the executive and the judiciary as directly enforceable law.

Article 2
Rights of liberty

(1) Everyone has the right to the free development of his personality insofar as he does not violate the rights of others or offend against the constitutional order or the moral code.

(2) Everyone has the right to life and to inviolability of his person. The freedom of the individual is inviolable. These rights may only be encroached upon pursuant to a law.

Article 3
Equality before the law

(1) All persons are equal before the law.

(2) Men and women have equal rights.

(3) No one may be prejudiced or favored because of his sex, his parentage, his race, his language, his homeland and origin, his faith or his religious or political opinions.

Article 4
Freedom of faith, of conscience and of creed

(1) Freedom of faith and of conscience, and freedom of creed religious or ideological, are inviolable.

(2) The undisturbed practice of religion is guaranteed.

(3) No one may be compelled against his conscience to render war service as an armed combatant. Details will be regulated by a Federal law.

Article 5
Freedom of expression

(1) Everyone has the right freely to express and to disseminate his opinion by speech, writing and pictures and freely to inform himself from generally accessible sources. Freedom of the press and freedom of reporting by radio and motion pictures are guaranteed. There shall be no censorship.

(2) These rights are limited by the provisions of the general laws, the provisions of law for the protection of youth and by the right to inviolability of personal honor.

(3) Art and science, research and teaching are free. Freedom of teaching does not absolve from loyalty to the constitution.

Article 6
Rights of the Family

(1) Marriage and family enjoy the special protection of the state.

(2) Care and upbringing of children are the natural right of the parents and a duty primarily incumbent on them. The state watches over the performance of this duty.

(3) Separation of children from the family against the will of the persons entitled to bring them up may take place only pursuant to a law, if those so entitled fail in their duty or if the children are otherwise threatened with neglect.

(4) Every mother is entitled to the protection and care of the community.

(5) Legitimate children shall be provided by legislation with the same opportunities for their physical and spiritual development and their position in society as are enjoyed by legitimate children.